Wood and Wood Products

THE MERRILL SERIES
IN CAREER PROGRAMS

Publications in the
Career Programs Series

Adult Education in Agriculture
Ralph E. Bender, et al.

Career Behavior of Special Groups
Campbell/Picou

Career Guidance: A Handbook of Methods
Campbell/Walz/Miller/Kriger

Organization and Administration of Distributive Education
Crawford/Meyer

Home Economics Evaluation
Aleene Cross

Elementary School Careers Education
Frank Cross

Agricultural Education: Approaches to Learning and Teaching
Drawbaugh/Hull

Foundations of Vocational Education
Rupert N. Evans

Career Development in the Elementary School
Robert L. Gibson

Principles of Post-Secondary Vocational Education
Angelo Gillie

Career Education: Perspective and Promise
Goldhammer/Taylor

Developing Careers in the Elementary School
Gysbers/Miller/Moore

Teaching Related Subjects in Trade and Industrial and Technical Education
Milton E. Larson

Principles and Techniques of Vocational Guidance
H. H. London

Planning Facilities for Occupational Education Programs
Richard F. Meckley

Curriculum Development for Trade and Industrial and Technical Education
Gordon G. McMahon

Family Crises
Neuhaus/Neuhaus

Teaching Shop and Laboratory Methods
Albert J. Pautler

Vocational Education and Guidance—A System for the Seventies
James A. Rhodes

Career Guidance: An Individual Developmental Approach
K. Norman Severinsen

Introduction to Trade, Industrial and Technical Education
Strong/Schaefer

Leadership in Administration of Vocational and Technical Education
Wenrich/Wenrich

Wood and Wood Products

Albert G. Spencer
Eastern Kentucky University

Jack A. Luy
Eastern Kentucky University

CHARLES E. MERRILL PUBLISHING COMPANY
A Bell & Howell Company
Columbus, Ohio 43216

Published by
CHARLES E. MERRILL PUBLISHING COMPANY
A Bell & Howell Company
Columbus, Ohio 43216

Library of Congress Catalog Card Number: 74–75406

International Standard Book Number: 0–675–08798–8

2 3 4 5 6 7 8 9—81 80 79 78 77 76 75

The photos of wood samples used in Figures 3–1, 3–2, 3–3, 3–4,
3–5, and in the Macroscopic Key for Selected North American
Woods in chapter 3 are from E. S. Harrar, *Hough's Encyclopedia
of American Woods,* Part I, Vols. I–XIII (New York: Robert
Speller & Sons, 1957–71). Used by permission of the publisher.

Printed in the United States of America

Foreword

To those whose instructional efforts involve the study of wood as a material or the variety of processes through which wood is transformed into an object of utility or beauty, *Wood and Wood Products* will be an invaluable resource. This book draws upon the practical experience the two authors have gained as teachers at the secondary and collegiate levels. As teachers, the authors are exposed to a wide variety of publications which focus upon the processes inherent in producing objects of wood. However, most textbooks in the field have very limited information about wood in its various forms ranging from lumber to insulation board.

In developing *Wood and Wood Products,* the authors involved themselves in a combination of formal and informal study of the broad field of forestry, including the specialities of wood anatomy, wood processes, wood products, and wood technology.

In part one the authors present the source of the material and explain the growth, structure and composition of wood. To aid the woodworker they provide a meaningful way to translate the anatomy of wood into a logical system to be used for identification purposes. They go beyond the traditional classification system to identify wood and to explain its properties in meaningful ways which allow the woodworker to select the material most appropriate for a given set of conditions.

In part two the authors describe the wood industry and provide the reader with an up-to-date word and picture story of the transformation of the tree into lumber, plywood, wood composition board, modified wood, wood building products, secondary wood products, and other forest products. The range of wood products described and the depth of explanation is unparalleled in textbook form. This kind of information has previously been secured by individual instructors from manufacturers and suppliers of wood products, professionals in the discipline of forestry and wood technology, as well as trade associations such as the Southern Pine Association.

Part three of the publication provides the woodworker with both the theory and practical considerations for using adhesives, preservatives, and finishing materials with wood and wood-related products.

Recognizing that this publication will be used to improve production processes and the resulting wood products, the authors seek to present scientific and technical information about wood and wood-related materials in a meaningful context. In brief they provide the reader with many of the "whys" that underlie the "what" and "how" that has been the forte of the student and teacher for decades. Through a combination of meaningful illustrations and charts, scientific knowledge has been transformed into a readable style which provides the technical knowledge essential to the practitioner.

Wilbur R. Miller
Columbia, Missouri

Preface

Throughout recorded history wood has proven to be one of man's most valuable natural resources. It has always been a readily available material and is adaptable for use in a wide variety of applications. Even in the rapidly changing technological world of today, wood and wood products continue to serve mankind in thousands of ways. Of all our natural resources, wood is the only one which is capable of replenishing itself in a relatively short time span—a condition which enhances the position of wood as one of our most cherished materials.

All of those who deal with wood—from the amateur to the professional and from the student to the scholar—share the need for a more intimate knowledge of this material and the many ways in which it can serve mankind. Although untold thousands of publications have been written about wood, they are prone to focus on rather specific aspects of the material or its uses. As these publications also tend to fall at two extremes—the very general or the highly technical—this book has been written to provide a "meeting ground" for the two. It has further been planned to provide a comprehensive view of wood —one which ranges from the nature and properties of the material itself, to the products and industries which utilize it directly, and finally to certain materials and processes employed in conjunction with it.

Such an approach should increase the value of this book, not only to the student in industrial education, technology, or forestry, but to craftsmen, hobbyists, and consumers as well.

Contents

PART TWO—WOOD PRODUCTS

Part One

Wood Technology

Chapter One

Forests,
Trees, and
Wood

If forests, trees, and wood were suddenly not available, American life would have to change greatly. Think for a moment how dependent our way of life actually is upon forests and forest products. Without lumber, how many Americans would enjoy the privacy and comfort of an individual family dwelling? Without lumber and veneer, how well would the houses be furnished? Without our forests, what would happen to the millions of hours of recreation that are now spent hunting, hiking, and sightseeing? Wood enters into other leisure-time activities in the form of boats, sports equipment, and toys, and what a loss it would be to the great orchestras of our time to be without their wood instruments. If wood were suddenly no longer available, the first sign Americans would receive might be the absence of the morning newspaper, one of the most noticeable of the hundreds of paper products we use every day.

Without forests and wood, not only would our cultural and social life suffer, the economy of the nation would be altered considerably. From the forest ranger to the logger, the sawyer, the factory worker, the wood craftsman, and the furniture salesman, the forests and forest industries provide jobs directly or indirectly to millions of Americans. Many of the products flowing into the hands of the consumer cannot be duplicated satisfactorily by any other material, and those which can be duplicated often lack the intrinsic qualities of wood.

Why is wood such an important material? Part of the answer lies in the structure and composition of wood, which are responsible for the properties that make wood so useful. The honeycomb pattern of the cellular structure gives wood one of the most favorable strength-weight ratios of any common material, and also makes it easier to cut, shape, and fabricate. The extractive materials deposited in the heart-

FIG. 1–1. *Forests like this supply our nation's demand for wood products. (Courtesy of California Redwood Association.)*

wood of many woods add durability as well as attractive colors and even pleasant odors.

While in certain instances detracting from its usefulness, the great variability of wood is actually one of the main reasons for its wide utilization. Not only are there hundreds of species possessing differing properties, but even within a species there are never two boards exactly alike. The refreshing variation in color and grain patterns of different woods make it an ideal medium for artists, craftsmen, and designers, in whose work appearance is of paramount importance.

Another reason wood is such an important material is that it has always been readily available. The fact that this is still true today is due to the greatest advantage that wood has—it is a renewable resource. With proper management and utilization, our forests can provide this country with wood indefinitely. Perhaps more than any other reason, this will assure that wood will always hold an important position in the life of America and Americans.

Botanical Classification of Trees

From a wood utilization standpoint, a tree may be defined as a perennial plant reaching a height of at least twenty feet and producing a trunk of sufficient diameter to be of value in the production of wood products (Harlow, 1968). There are of course many other woody

FIG. 1–2. *Attractive and durable homes of wood are among our most important forest products. (Courtesy of California Redwood Association.)*

perennial plants such as bushes, vines, and shrubs, but they are of little importance as sources of wood for commercial purposes.

Trees, being plants, fall into the botanical classification system of taxonomic groups—divisions, classes, orders, families, genera, and species. Hardwoods are included in the class Angiospermae, also called angiosperms, while softwoods fall in the Gymnospermae class, called gymnosperms. The gymnosperms are divided into seven orders, one of which is Coniferales (conifers), and includes all commercially useful softwoods. The angiosperms are further classified into the two sub-classes of Monocotyledonae and Dicotyledonae. Hardwoods of commercial importance belong to the Dicotyledonae sub-class.

Trees (as well as other plants) are referred to most precisely by scientific names, which are composed of their genus and species; black walnut, for example, is *Juglans nigra* L. However, the common name (black walnut) is sufficient for most practical purposes. The initial following the scientific name denotes the scientist who named the plant, in this case, Linnaeus, a Swedish botanist.

Forests of the United States

When explorers first touched the shores of what is now the United States, they entered the edge of forests totaling an estimated 822 million acres (Allen, 1960), almost one half of the total land area of this country (not including Hawaii and Alaska). The diversity and quality of trees in these forests made them possibly the most valuable ever discovered.

Over three hundred years of use and abuse have reduced the forests to about one-third of the land area of the United States. The total acreage is now 754 million acres (U.S. Forest Service, 1972), but that

FIG. 1–3. *The unsurpassed beauty and variety of wood is utilized to the fullest extent in fine furniture. (Courtesy of Fine Hardwoods-American Walnut Association.)*

includes Hawaii and Alaska, which were not part of the estimated original forest land. Of this 754 million acres, two-thirds (499.7 million acres) is what is called "commercial" forests, defined as land suitable and available for growing timber crops. Noncommercial forests include marginal, scrubby stands not suitable for production, national and state parks and preserves, and other areas restricted to non-production uses.

The total forest area is fairly evenly divided between the eastern and western halves of the country, but nearly three-fourths of the commercial forest area is in the East. This is due in large part to the vast acreages in national parks and other federally owned forests in the western states.

Slightly over half of the commercial forest area is softwoods. The western half of the nation has just a few more acres of softwoods than the eastern half, but the East has almost all of the hardwoods. Although the area of forest land occupied by hardwoods and softwoods is about the same, three times as many board feet of softwoods were cut in 1970.

The forests of the United States fall into six natural forest areas— the Northern, Southern, Central Hardwood, Tropical, Western (Rocky Mountain), and West Coast Forests. (See fig. 1–4.)

The Northern Forest, with its balsam fir, northern white-cedar, eastern white pine, and other fine softwoods and hardwoods, supplied the early settlers with abundant high quality wood. This area led the nation in lumber production until the turn of this century, when the lead shifted to the South. Despite the fact that the Northern Forest was extensively logged for over two hundred years with little or no attempt at conservation or management, it was not completely decimated, and much of it is now under scientific management. The 1970 Forest Service survey (1972) indicated that the volume of sawtimber in both the North and South increased substantially from 1962 to 1970.

By far the most important species in the Southern Forest are the "southern pines"—longleaf, shortleaf, slash, and loblolly. Hardwoods such as tupelo, ash, cottonwood, and elm are also found in certain areas and are valuable where available.

WEST COAST FOREST. Conifers: Douglas fir, coast redwood, western hemlock, western red cedar, Sitka spruce, sugar pine, lodgepole pine, incense cedar, Port Orford cedar, and white fir. Broadleaved trees: Red alder and bigleaf maple. Produces almost one third of U.S. lumber, about one fifth of U.S. pulpwood, 75 percent of U.S. softwood plywood. Commercial forest area: 31,000,000 acres.

WESTERN FOREST. Conifers: Ponderosa pine, Idaho white pine, sugar pine, Douglas fir, Engelmann spruce, western larch, white fir, incense cedar, lodge pole pine, and western red cedar. Broadleaved trees: Aspen. Produces almost one third of U.S. lumber. Commercial forest area: 98,000,000 acres.

NORTHERN FOREST. Conifers: Eastern white pine, red, black, and white spruce, red or Norway pine, jack pine, balsam fir, white cedar, tamarack, and eastern hemlock. Broadleaved trees: Aspen, beech, northern red oak, white oak, yellow birch, paper birch, black birch, black walnut, sugar maple, black gum, white ash, black cherry, and basswood. Produces about one tenth of U.S. lumber, almost one fifth of U.S. pulpwood. Commercial forest area: 115,000,000 acres.

CENTRAL HARDWOOD FOREST. Conifers: Shortleaf pine, Virginia pine, eastern white pine and red cedar. Broadleaved trees: Beech, red maple, northern red oak, white oak, hickory, elm, white ash, black walnut, sycamore, cottonwood, tulip or yellow poplar, black gum, and sweet or red gum. Produces about one twentieth of U.S. lumber, almost one tenth of U.S. pulpwood. Commercial forest area: 135,000,000 acres.

TROPICAL FOREST. Leading species are all broadleaved trees: Mahogany, mangrove, and bay tree. Commercial forest area: none.

SOUTHERN FOREST. Conifers: Loblolly pine, shortleaf pine, longleaf pine, slash pine, and bald cypress. Broadleaved trees: Red gum, black gum or tupelo, northern red oak, white oak, swamp red oak, water oak, live oak, pin oak, willow, yellow poplar, cottonwood, white ash, hickory, and pecan. Produces about one third of U.S. lumber, more than three fifths of U.S. pulpwood and about one fourth of U.S. softwood plywood. Commercial forest area: 124,000,000 acres.

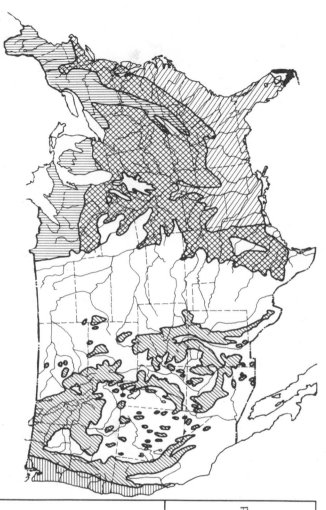

ALASKA

COAST FOREST. Conifers: Western hemlock, Sitka spruce, western red cedar, and Alaska yellow cedar. Produces pulpwood and lumber. Commercial forest area: 6,000,000 acres.

INTERIOR FOREST. Conifers: White and black spruce. Broad-leaved trees: White birch, aspen, and other poplars. Forest area: 105,000,000 acres.

HAWAII

WET FOREST. Leading species are all broadleaved trees: Ohia, koa, tree fern, kukui, mamani, eucalyptus, and tropical ash. Used for furniture, souvenirs, lumber. Production negligible. Commercial forest area: 1,000,000 acres.

DRY FOREST. Leading species: Algaroba, koa haole, wiliwili, and monkeypod. Non-commercial. Used for fence posts and fuel-wood.

FIG. 1–4. *Forest areas of the United States. (Courtesy of American Forest Institute.)*

The Southern Forest led the country in lumber production from about 1900 to 1920, when the West took over as the most productive region. However, the South continued to produce a great deal of lumber, and as many abandoned cotton fields reverted to forest, thousands of acres of trees suitable for pulping soon became available. The Southern Forest is now the nation's leading producer of pulpwood and, in addition, controlled management of more and more of the forest area is beginning to show results in sawlog and veneer-size trees. Since the early 1960s southern pine plywood has "come of age" and by 1972 there were over fifty plywood mills in the area, and more being planned.

The Central Hardwood Forest is the second largest in total land area, exceeded only by the Western Forest. The Central Hardwood region supplies the great bulk of all the hardwoods used in the United States. Producers of furniture and cabinetry, flooring, veneer, sports equipment, and many other manufacturers of hardwood products have located in the Central Hardwood zone.

The most extensive species-type of forest in the United States is the oak-hickory of the Central Hardwood region. Other species of importance in this area include beech, elm, black walnut, yellow-poplar, American sycamore, black cherry, black and green ashes, and cottonwood. The only softwoods found to any extent in the area are shortleaf, pitch, and Virginia pines, and eastern redcedar.

The Tropical Forest of southern Florida and Texas is more nearly subtropical, and is composed mainly of mangrove and palms. The total area covered is less than 400,000 acres, and neither of the predominant species has much commercial value.

The Western Forest (Rocky Mountain) is distributed over the largest land area of any of the forests, being scattered through thirteen of the westernmost states. The most important commercial species from this forest are ponderosa pine, western white pine, Douglas fir, lodgepole pine, and Engelmann spruce. Other species of importance include western larch, western hemlock, and western redcedar.

Compared to the West Coast and Southern Forests, the Western Forest rates quite low in productivity. Inaccessibility of some areas in the mountains accounts for part of this, as well as restrictions placed on cutting in some of the federally-owned tracts.

The West Coast Forest is the smallest of the natural forests, but it has led in lumber production since 1920. It has been in production for a shorter period than any of the other forests, however, and considerable areas are still in old-growth trees. Douglas fir is the most important species, often reaching a diameter of fifteen feet at breast height in this area (as do western redcedar and sitka spruce). Also included in the West Coast Forest are the famous giant sequoias and the magnificent and valuable redwoods. Hardwoods of some importance in this area include red alder, bigleaf maple, cottonwood, and Pacific madrone.

Resources

Allen, Shirley Walter, and Grant William Sharp. *An Introduction to American Forestry.* New York: McGraw-Hill Book Company, 1960.

Forest Service, U.S. Department of Agriculture. *Timber Trends in the United States.* Washington, D. C.: Government Printing Office, 1965.

Harlow, William M., and Ellwood S. Harrar. *Textbook of Dendrology.* New York: McGraw-Hill, 1968.

Sternitzke, Herbert S., and Joe F. Christopher. "Southern Timber Supply Trends and Outlook." *Forest Products Journal* 22 (July 1972): 13–16.

Tsoumis, George. *Wood as Raw Material.* New York: Pergamon Press, 1968.

U. S. Forest Resource Inventory Statistics, Preliminary data. Washington, D. C.: U. S. Forest Service, 1972.

Chapter Two

Growth, Structure, and Composition of Wood

An understanding of the properties of wood is prerequisite to intelligent utilization of the material. However, it is futile to attempt a study of wood properties without first gaining some knowledge of the growth, structure, and composition of the material, because these factors determine the properties of wood.

A tree grows in three directions: trunk and limbs grow upward, roots grow downward, and all grow laterally (or in diameter). As with all living things, trees are made up of cells, and growth occurs by means of cell division. Vertical growth, which takes place at the tips of branches, is of little concern here, because the bulk of the wood in the tree trunk is formed by lateral growth. Growth in diameter, also called *secondary growth,* takes place in a very narrow zone between the wood of the tree trunk and the bark. This area, called *cambium,* is only a few cells thick, but it produces all the different types of cells in both the wood and the bark. The cambium proper consists of a layer only one cell thick, but as the cells divide and mature, there is a region on each side of the cambium which contains living cells in various stages of development.

When a wood cell is mature, it is technically dead, for it contains no nucleus or protoplasm. Thus, even the wood of a living tree is made up mainly of dead cells, although certain kinds of cells in the sapwood remain alive longer than others.

During a normal growing season, the cambium produces millions of cells, and a layer of new wood is formed. Since the cambium is a sheath surrounding the tree trunk, the layer of wood produced each year is in the same form, and when the tree is only a year or two old,

Growth of a Tree

11

the layer of wood is roughly a cone as high as the tree (fig. 2–1). During each successive growing season, another cone-shaped layer of wood is added around the ones underneath. Thus, in order to find the age of a tree by the time-honored method of counting growth rings, one must cut the tree very near the ground or the first year or two is missed.

During each growing season, a layer of bark is also added, but it is added to the *inside* of the bark. It would seem, then, that since a tree enlarges in diameter each year, the outer layers of bark must be stretched to accommodate the increased circumference. What actually happens is that the outer layers of bark become dry and brittle and, instead of stretching, they crack and scale and are gradually sloughed off. This accounts for the scaly, fissured appearance of most bark.

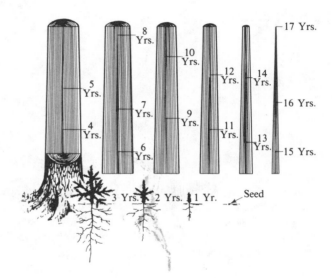

FIG. 2–1. *Tree growth. [Reprinted from A. J. Panshin and Carl de Zeeuw, Textbook of Wood Technology, 3rd ed., Vol. I (New York: McGraw-Hill, 1970), by permission of the publisher.]*

Structure of Wood

The structure of wood may be best explained by proceeding from larger elements to smaller ones, but some basic ideas involving the smaller elements must be presented first. The fundamental concept necessary for understanding wood structure is that wood is made up of hollow cells cemented together in a honeycomb fashion (see fig. 2–2). Also, while there are several shapes, the majority of cells are long and tubular with pointed ends, and are oriented vertically in the tree.

FIG. 2–2. *Basic wood structure.*

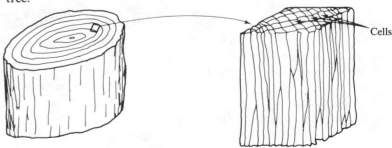

In any discussion of wood structure, it is necessary to specify the direction from which the wood is being viewed. This is usually accomplished by labelling three principal surfaces, or planes of reference, as shown in figure 2–3.

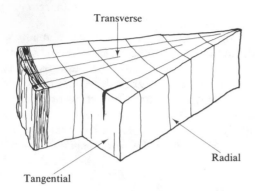

FIG. 2–3. *Planes of reference.*

The *transverse* or cross-sectional surface is used most frequently because the arrangement of cells is easily observed there. This is the surface one sees when looking at the end of a log or a board. The *tangential* (tangent to growth rings) surface is the plane observed in slab-sawn lumber, while the *radial* surface is presented in quarter-sawn lumber.

Gross Features of Wood

Gross features are those attributes of wood which are most visible and easily recognizable. The features are easily discerned on a complete cross section of a tree trunk (see fig. 2–4).

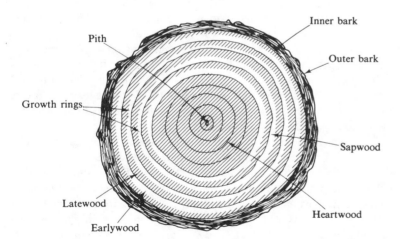

FIG. 2–4. *Gross features of wood.*

From the outside to center, a tree is made up of *bark, wood,* and *pith.* The bark is a layer of corky material ranging from a fraction of an inch in thickness to as much as a foot or more, depending on the age and species of tree. The *inner bark,* nearest the cambium, is alive and provides a complete, protective sheath around the tree. Sieve tubes in the inner bark conduct food materials from the leaves of the tree downward. The *outer bark* is the non-living portion of the bark, and it gradually becomes dry and brittle. Without the protection of the bark, trees would be attacked by many insects and stricken with a variety of diseases more easily.

The *pith* is a small area at the center of the trunk which ranges in size from very small and barely visible, as in oak, to quite conspicuous, as in elder. In most commercial woods, it is not large enough to reduce the value of lumber.

The *wood* of the tree trunk is the most commercially valuable part, and the remainder of this chapter is devoted to its structure. In most trees, wood is divided into two easily recognizable areas, heartwood and sapwood. *Sapwood* is the light-colored layer of wood nearest the bark. Though made up of mature cells, most of which are dead, the sapwood is active in the life processes of the tree, namely conduction and storage of food materials (sap). For this reason sapwood is called the living portion of the wood. The *heartwood* is the normally darker-colored wood in the center of the trunk. It is made up of cells which have ceased to function in the life processes of the tree. Each year a portion of the sapwood changes to heartwood when some sapwood cells undergo several chemical and physiological changes. The most obvious of these is the deposition of chemical materials which cause the color in heartwood. The materials formed are tannins, resins, and other compounds which not only produce color changes, but also make heartwood more durable in most respects than sapwood. The difference in color between heartwood and sapwood is not a characteristic of all trees, but even in those which exhibit no visible separation, heartwood can be identified by chemical staining techniques.

Contrary to popular belief, heartwood is not stronger (although it is more durable) than sapwood of the same species. At the time of cutting, differences in moisture content between heartwood and sapwood often do exist, and, as already mentioned, the formation of chemical deposits in heartwood makes it more resistant to decay, insects, and other agencies of wood deterioration.

Another feature that is normally prominent on a cross-sectional surface is the *growth rings*. These are the concentric layers of wood added each season to the diameter of the trunk. They are often referred to as annual rings, but during abnormal growing seasons, more than one or less than a complete ring may be formed, so the term growth rings is more accurate.

The rings are usually quite distinct because in temperate climates, the wood formed during the early part of the growing season is different from the wood formed later. The wood formed in the spring when growth is more rapid is called *earlywood* or *springwood,* and is characterized by cells which are larger and thin-walled, making a rather porous layer of wood. Slower growth later in the growing season produces *latewood* or *summerwood,* which has smaller, thick-walled cells, forming relatively more dense wood.

The transition from springwood to summerwood may be gradual or abrupt, but the pattern in a given species is usually fairly consistent, making this a useful feature for identification purposes. In tropical climates, the growing season is more uniform, and earlywood and latewood are often not distinguishable. However, for reasons not well understood, the growth rings themselves are usually distinct, even in tropical wood.

Macroscopic Features of Wood

Macroscopic features of wood are those features visible under a hand lens, at a magnification no greater than 10X. At this level, differences in structure between hardwoods and softwoods become apparent, and features must be discussed in relation to these classifications.

On the transverse surface of most hardwoods, fine lines can be seen radiating from the center of the tree outward. These are wood *rays,* made up of cells oriented horizontally in the tree instead of vertically, as the majority of the cells are. The horizontal orientation of ray cells facilitates the lateral conduction of food materials in the tree. Rays are literally thin ribbons of wood ranging from only one cell thick (uniseriate) in many softwoods to many cells thick (multiseriate) in oaks. Many of the thicker rays of hardwoods are visible to the naked eye, while the uniseriate rays of softwoods are usually not visible, even with a hand lens. The rays of softwoods are fairly uniform in size, especially within a species, while the rays of hardwoods vary greatly in thickness, even within a species.

The appearance of rays on the three surfaces of wood is quite different. On the transverse plane, they appear as long lines, some originating at the center of the tree (*medullary rays*) and some farther out, but all continue to the bark (see fig. 2–5). In this view we see the *edge* of the ribbon-like ray. Rays on the tangential surface are short vertical lines. This is the *end* of the ray. If a true radial cut were made, the rays would appear there as continuous horizontal bands (the *side* of the ray). In practice, however, a cut does not follow one ray exactly, but rather passes through the rays at a slight angle, giving the familiar ray "fleck" pattern.

Examination of the transverse surface of a hardwood with a hand lens reveals many small openings resembling the ends of tubes. These are *pores* (or more technically, *vessels*), and they are quite literally small tubes running vertically in the tree trunk. Their main function is the conduction of sap through the tree. Vessels are a characteristic of hardwoods, and are not found in softwoods.

The size of vessels ranges from very large, as in oak, to quite small, as in hard maple. The large pores can be seen with the naked eye, and even the smaller ones can usually be distinguished with a hand lens. In some woods there is considerable variation in the size of vessels within growth rings.

Different arrangements of pores are characteristic of different species, a fact which is very useful in the identification of wood. In woods such as the oaks, hickories, and elms, the pores in the springwood are quite large and conspicuous, while those in the summerwood are much smaller. These are called *ring porous* woods, because the band of large springwood pores is delineated sharply from the summerwood, and the growth rings are quite distinct (see fig. 2–6). Other woods, such as poplar, cottonwood, and maple, have pores which are more uniform in size and are distributed evenly throughout the growth ring. These are called *diffuse porous* woods. Many woods are not typical of either arrangement, however, and they are referred to as either *semi-ring porous* or *semi-diffuse porous* woods. Examples of these are beech and black walnut.

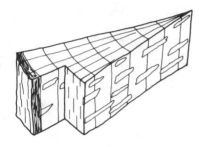

FIG. 2–5. *Wood rays.*

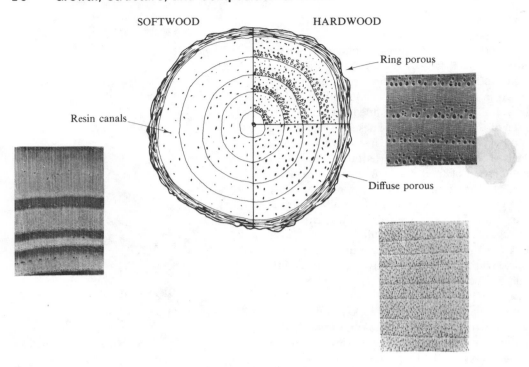

FIG. 2–6. *Pores and resin canals.*

A final macroscopic feature, *resin canals,* is primarily a characteristic of softwoods, although some may be found in certain hardwoods. Those in hardwoods are called *gum canals,* but they are present in very few commercially important woods. Resin canals in softwoods appear on the transverse surface as whitish or brownish dots when viewed with a hand lens. They extend both vertically and horizontally in the tree, forming a network. The canal itself is simply an opening surrounded by special cells called *epitheliel cells,* which secrete the resin.

Cellular Structure

Wood is made up mainly of four types of cells; fibers, tracheids, parenchyma, and vessel members. There are other types, but most are variations of these four.

Fibers. Fibers are the cells which constitute the bulk of hardwood tissue, often as much as 50 percent of the wood volume. They are very long and thin, averaging about 1 or 2 mm in length, but only a fraction of that in diameter (see fig. 2–7). Fibers function mainly as strengthening or support members, although some take part in conduction of food.

Vessel segments. Another type of cell found only in hardwoods is vessel members or vessel segments. As their name implies, they are cells which make up the sap-conducting vessels, or pores. Since a vessel is basically á tube, the vessel segments are of the same configuration (see fig. 2–7). They are usually shorter than fibers, but considerably greater in diameter.

Tracheids. Tracheids are the principal conducting cells found in softwoods. Shaped much like hardwood fibers, tracheids are generally longer, averaging from 3 to 4 mm in length. These cells constitute as much as 90 percent of the bulk of softwoods, and may be oriented either vertically (*axial tracheids*) or horizontally (*ray tracheids*). Tracheids are occasionally found in hardwoods, but are quite different from those of softwoods.

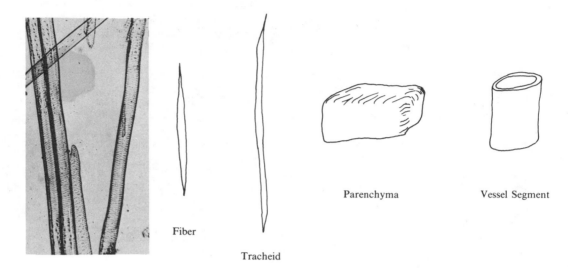

Fiber

Tracheid

Parenchyma

Vessel Segment

Parenchyma. A type of cell common to both hardwoods and softwoods is parenchyma, which is principally a storage cell. Parenchyma cells are brick-like in shape and are usually full of living material (in sapwood) or non-living deposits (in heartwood). These are the only mature wood cells which are technically alive (in sapwood only).

Much of the parenchyma in wood is located in rays (*radial parenchyma*), but it is also found interspersed in various manners with vertical cells (*axial parenchyma*). Parenchyma tissue (a group of parenchyma cells) appears as whitish areas in hardwoods, and the arrangement and location of this tissue is a valuable aid in wood identification. Chapter 3 deals with this in more detail.

FIG. 2–7. *Schematic of approximate shape of different types of wood cells. Photo at left shows softwood tracheids at a high magnification. (Photo courtesy of U.S. Forest Products Laboratory Forest Service, U.S. Department of Agriculture.)*

Individual cell structure. The components of a cell in wood are, as shown in figure 2–8, the lumen, the cell wall, and the middle lamella. The *lumen* is the hollow portion of the cell, although it may contain water or chemical deposits. In some woods, such as white oak, the lumen of vessel segments is completely filled with *tyloses,* a material produced by parenchyma cells surrounding the vessel.

The *cell wall* may be quite thick or very thin, depending on the type of cell. Springwood cells tend to have large lumina and thin walls, whereas summerwood cells have smaller lumina and thick walls. Cell walls are composed of tiny strands called microfibrils, which are so small that an electron microscope is needed to detect them.

The microfibrils are oriented in a roughly longitudinal direction in the cell, but in different layers of the cell wall they deviate at various angles from the cell axis. Because the microfibrils are oriented at slight angles, wood shrinks slightly in the longitudinal direction. If the microfibrils were parallel and aligned longitudinally in the cell, there would be no longitudinal shrinkage.

The walls of many cells are perforated with small openings called *pits.* Pits allow passage of liquid materials through the cell wall, and are found in great numbers in tracheids, which in the absence of

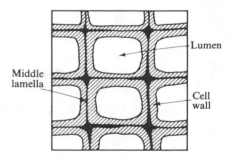

Middle lamella

Lumen

Cell wall

FIG. 2–8. *Cell structure.*

vessels in softwood must perform in the conduction of liquids. Some pits are found in other types of cells in both hardwoods and softwoods, but not in such great numbers.

Pits usually are found in pairs, one in each of two adjacent cell walls. The illustration in figure 2–9 is a schematic showing the types and location of pits, and an enlargement of a pit cross section. Pits may be either *simple* or *bordered,* as shown.

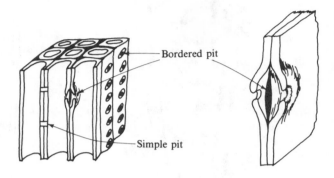

FIG. 2–9. *Types of pits.*

Hardwoods and Softwoods

No elementary study of wood structure should be completed without reviewing the structural differences between hardwoods and softwoods. These are, very briefly:

1. Cells in softwoods are arranged in radial rows, while those in hardwoods are more randomly grouped.

2. The structure of softwoods is much more homogenous than that of hardwoods.

3. Hardwoods contain rays of widely varying thicknesses and widths, whereas softwood rays are smaller and more nearly uniform in size.

4. Vessels are a characteristic of hardwoods only.

5. Resin canals are primarily a feature of softwoods.

6. Fibers are exclusively hardwood cells.

7. Tracheids are primarily softwood cells.

Chemical Composition of Wood

The microfibrils of cell walls are the smallest units of wood structure visible under any type of microscope presently in use. Further breakdown in structural units brings us to the molecular level, where two components make up the great bulk of wood substance. *Cellulose,* a long-chain polymeric compound, constitutes the cell wall material. Each microfibril is literally a bundle of long strand-like cellulose molecules. The middle lamella and the tiny spaces at the "corners" of cells are mainly *lignin,* commonly referred to as the cementing substance that binds cells together. The dividing line between the cell wall and the middle lamella is not a sharp one, because lignin infiltrates the outer portions of the cell wall to some extent. The chemical composition of lignin is complex, and it is difficult to separate from cellulose, factors which have prevented it from being completely analyzed with present equipment.

Other chemical materials in wood, known collectively as *extractives,* are not actually part of the wood substance, but are responsible for several properties of wood. Extractive materials are deposited in the cell lumen and the cell wall, and include substances such as gums, fats, waxes, and resins. The color, odor, and taste of woods which have such characteristics are due to the presence of extractives. Many woods such as redwood and black locust are very durable and more resistant to decay and insects because of these materials.

The structure of wood does not lend itself to testing and experimentation in a classroom situation as well as some other areas of wood technology. However, there is one activity which, if carried out, will provide much insight into the structure of wood. Any number of illustrations, schematics, and even pictures can be used to illustrate wood structure, but to people who have seen wood only in the form of lumber or furniture, it is difficult to relate that solid substance to the very porous honeycomb structure made evident by magnification. Instructions for this activity may be found in the appendix, page 233.

Investigating Wood Structure

Resources

Harlow, William M. *Inside Wood, Masterpiece of Nature.* Washington, D.C.: The American Forestry Association, 1970.

Kollmann, Franz F. P., and Wilfred A. Côté, Jr. *Principles of Wood Science and Technology.* Vol. I, *Solid Wood.* New York: Springer-Verlag, 1968.

Panshin, A. J., and Carl de Zeeuw. *Textbook of Wood Technology.* Vol. I. New York: McGraw-Hill Book Company, 1970.

Tsoumis, George. *Wood As Raw Material.* New York: Pergamon Press, 1968.

Chapter Three

Identification of Wood

Wood identification can be quite an exact science to a wood technologist or more nearly an art to many wood craftsmen. All methods of identification are based on the appearance of wood. Since the various structural features appear at different levels of magnification, the process of identification can be based on gross features, macroscopic features, or microscopic features, depending on the training of the individual and on the degree of accuracy required. *Microscopic identification* is based on the most consistent factors, and is very accurate if carried out by an experienced wood technologist or scientist. *Gross features identification* (naked eye method) can also be quite accurate when practiced by someone with a great deal of experience with wood, but even then it is usually less accurate than microscopic methods. In general, identification based on macroscopic features of wood (*macro identification*), falls between the above two in accuracy, but it has several advantages over them.

While each of the methods mentioned is useful in certain instances, macro identification is more appropriate as a practical, yet reasonably accurate means of identification. The advantages of this method will become apparent in the following discussion, and the greater part of this chapter will be devoted to macro identification.

Identification of wood with no magnification is the most commonly practiced method because it is quick, convenient, and requires no equipment other than good eyesight. By this method, identification is usually made by observing the tangential surface of a piece of wood (since that surface appears in plain-sawn lumber) and evaluating such characteristics as color, grain pattern, and figure, which either singly

Identification with Unaided Eye

or together are distinctive of a particular species. In order to recognize a particular kind of wood, it is necessary not only to have seen that kind of wood before, but also to have observed it closely enough to distinguish and remember its distinctive characteristics.

While visual characteristics are the main basis of gross features identification, other properties such as weight, hardness, odor, and even taste can be utilized. In many cases one of these factors could be the only difference detectable by the gross features method. Sassafras, for instance, is easily distinguished from chestnut and other similar woods by its characteristic odor.

Microscopic Identification

The process of identifying wood with the aid of a microscope is not extremely complicated, but it does require a thorough understanding of the minute structure of wood. The use of a light microscope allows comparison of cellular characteristics such as pits and spiral thickenings of the cell walls.

This method is not often needed for hardwoods, because hardwoods have many diverse characteristics visible with the aid of a hand lens. Softwoods, on the other hand, are more homogenous at the macroscopic level, and microscopic methods must often be employed in their identification.

Microscopic identification, while the most accurate, has the disadvantages of requiring considerable knowledge of wood structure and the use of somewhat specialized, non-portable equipment. Utilization of this method is most frequent in laboratory situations.

Macro Identification

Macro identification of wood is accomplished by observing the transverse surface of a wood sample through a hand lens (about 10X) and checking the observed features with written statements in a wood identification key. The only equipment needed is a sharp knife or razor blade, a 10X hand lens, and an identification key. Although not as accurate (especially for softwoods) as microscopic identification, the macroscopic method requires neither complicated equipment nor as much understanding of the minute features of wood. On the other hand, a greater degree of accuracy can be acquired in less time than would be possible for naked eye identification.

The essential element in macro identification is the *key,* which is a series of pairs of opposite statements which describe features of groups of species. Each statement leads to another pair of statements, which lead to other statements, and so on until a final statement is reached which identifies the sample being considered. The use of the key will be described in more detail later in this chapter.

Important Structural Features of Hardwoods

Before identification of wood is attempted by the macroscopic method, the structural features used in keys should be thoroughly understood. A brief discussion of the most important of these is presented below, along with illustrations where appropriate.

Pores. Pores are useful for identification purposes because they vary in both size and arrangement. The ring-porous and diffuse-porous patterns were covered in chapter 2 and need no further explanation. In addition, pores are arranged in wavy concentric lines in some woods, such as elm, shown in figure 3–1a. Pores in flame-shaped patches occur in only a few woods, and are thus a helpful feature for identification purposes (see fig. 3–1b).

FIG. 3–1. *Size and arrangement of pores.*

(a) American elm

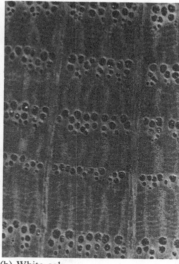

(b) White oak

Parenchyma tissue. Parenchyma tissue is a group of parenchyma cells. The benefit of such tissue in wood identification lies in the fact that in hardwoods it appears as light-colored spots, patches, or lines, the particular pattern being distinctive to certain species. Parenchyma tissue is very sparse in softwoods, and (when visible) appears as dark spots.

If the parenchyma tissue surrounds or partially surrounds the pores, as in figure 3–2a, it is called *paratracheal* parenchyma. Parenchyma tissue which is not associated with the pores is called *metatracheal* parenchyma and often appears as short broken lines at right angles to the rays, as in hickory (see fig. 3–2b). *Terminal* parenchyma appears as a continuous, whitish line between growth rings (see fig. 3–2c).

FIG. 3–2. *Types of parenchyma: (a) paratracheal, (b) metatracheal, (c) terminal.*

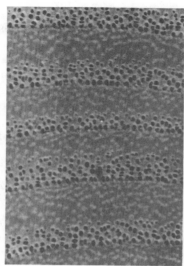

(a) White ash

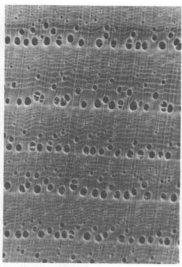

(b) Shellbark hickory

(c) Yellow poplar

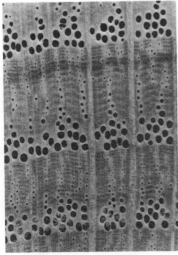

(a) Red oak

(b) Sycamore

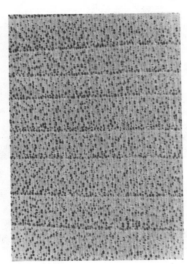

(c) Yellow poplar

(d) Cottonwood

FIG. 3–3. *Sizes of rays.*

Rays. The size, spacing, and appearance of rays are distinguishing features of many hardwoods. Oaks have larger rays than any common hardwood, so much larger, in fact, that they are in a class by themselves (see fig. 3–3a). In a key they are described simply as "oak-type rays." Other hardwoods, such as sycamore (see fig. 3–3b), have rays described as "large," or "broad." Still others, such as poplar, have small rays, visible only with a hand lens (see fig. 3–3c). A few hardwoods have rays so small that they are practically invisible even with a lens (see fig. 3–3d).

The spacing of rays is also of value in some cases, because certain woods have rays closely spaced while in others the rays are more widely spaced.

Tyloses. The pores of some woods are partially or wholly blocked with a crystalline material called tyloses. This substance is formed when cells adjacent to the vessels expand and force their contents (usually protoplasm) through pits in the vessel wall. Authorities do not agree as to the exact cause of this activity, but the presence of tyloses can be useful in identifying certain woods. White oak (see fig. 3–1b) is an example of wood with pores completely occluded with tyloses.

Important Structural Features of Softwoods

Resin canals. Softwoods classified as "resinous" possess resin canals, which appear as small dots or openings on the transverse surface, and as dark streaks on other surfaces. The size, number, and arrangement of resin canals varies among the different species, so these are useful features for identification. An example of a softwood with resin canals which would be described in a key as "many large resin canals" is shown in figure 3–4a. Such an arrangement is characteristic of the pines. "Small, widely scattered resin canals" are illustrated by the sample of spruce (see fig. 3–4b). The distinctive arrangement of resin canals in tangential rows in Douglas fir (see fig. 3–4c) makes them valuable for the identification of that species.

(a) Loblolly pine   (b) Sitka spruce   (c) Douglas fir

Transition. The nature of the transition from springwood to summerwood within a growth ring can be helpful in separating some species. If the change from the thin-walled cells of the springwood to the thick-walled cells of summerwood is sharp and distinct, there is *abrupt transition* from springwood to summerwood (fig. 3–5a). On the other hand, if the change in cell size is gradual, and the line is indistinct, there is a *gradual transition* from springwood to summerwood (fig. 3–5b).

Texture. Texture is the character of wood caused by the relative size and arrangement of cells within a growth ring. *Fine, medium,* and *coarse* textures are produced by cells of small, medium, and large diameters, respectively. Different textures result when the cells within one growth ring are either fairly uniform in size (*even texture*) or exhibit some degree of variation in size (*uneven texture*). In softwoods, abrupt transition between springwood and summerwood causes uneven texture, while gradual transition results in an even texture.

FIG. 3–4. *Relative size and spacing of resin canals.*

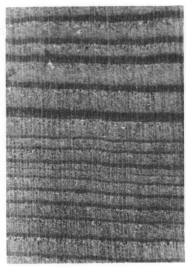

(a) Western larch

(b) Fraser fir

FIG. 3–5. *Abrupt and gradual transition.*

Parenchyma. Parenchyma in softwoods is very scarce, visible only in redwood, baldcypress, and certain cedars. For this reason, however, its presence is a good feature for identification. Softwood parenchyma usually appears as darker spots, rather than the whitish areas found in hardwoods.

Color, odor, and density. Although it is not a structural feature, practically all keys make reference to the color of wood. It is a difficult attribute to describe, but the presence of color can be very helpful in identifying some species. Lack of color, on the other hand, is of less value, for it may simply mean that the sample is all sapwood.

Many softwoods have distinctive odors, which are also difficult to describe, but once they have been experienced are easily recognizable thereafter. Since odors are produced by volatile substances in the wood, the strongest aroma is given off by freshly-cut wood. Wetting the wood sometimes increases the strength of the odor of dry wood.

The density of wood is most often referred to in keys indirectly, as statements about weight and hardness. These attributes can be judged quickly and easily by simply lifting the sample and scratching it with the thumbnail. However, the observer must have some experience with wood for the weight and hardness to be of value, as both are relative terms. A certain wood is soft, for example, only when compared to harder woods. An untrained observer may think that yellow poplar is a hard wood, but when compared to oak or hickory, it is quite soft. Such wood is often described in keys as "moderately hard" or "moderately soft."

Procedure for Macro Identification

Tools and equipment. The equipment needed for macro identification of wood is very simple and inexpensive, a *sharp* jackknife or razor blade, a 10X hand lens, and the macroscopic key. A source of light may be needed in a dimly-lit room, because the sample must be well illuminated. Small high-intensity desk lamps work well for this purpose. If the sample is being observed outdoors, normal daylight or direct sunlight is sufficient.

Selecting and preparing the sample. The ideal sample of wood to be used for identification purposes would be a clear, straight-grained sample containing both heartwood and sapwood. Wood too near the center of the tree is called *juvenile* wood and often exhibits characteristics different from mature wood in outer growth rings, and should be avoided. Heartwood is generally of more value for identification purposes because its color and odor are more distinct than that of sapwood. Decay and defects such as knots, burls, and irregular grain patterns produce atypical features and confuse the identification process.

To prepare the sample for observation, make a *smooth* cut on the transverse surface with a jackknife. The cut need not be large, but it should expose the complete width of one growth ring. It is very important that the cut surface be smooth, otherwise small features, especially in softer woods, will be obscured. To insure that the surface is smooth, a *slicing* cut should be made (see fig. 3–6).

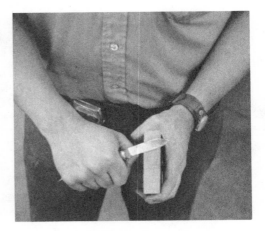

FIG. 3–6. *Making a slicing cut.*

Using the hand lens. The sample should be held so that good light falls directly on the smooth-cut portion. Hold the hand lens close to the eye (about an inch or less), and move the sample until it is in focus. Most beginners want to move the lens instead of the sample, but if the lens is very far from the eye, extraneous light enters between the eye and the lens and reduces the clarity of the image.

Using the macroscopic key. The macroscopic key on the following pages is made up of five parts—a basic key and four sections. The basic key (p. 29) is simply a chart containing the first two decisions which must be made in the identification process. The whole key could be arranged in this fashion, but as the alternatives multiply, such a chart would become too cumbersome to use easily.

The key is simply a series of paired statements about certain features of wood. A sample to be identified is observed, then compared against the first pair of statements in the key. In this case, the first pair is contained in the basic key, and involves a decision as to whether the sample is a hardwood or a softwood. If the sample is a hardwood, the next pair of statements help classify it as either ring-porous or diffuse-porous. If the sample is a softwood, the decision must be made to classify it as resinous or non-resinous. All of these decisions are contained in the basic key.

FIG. 3–7. *Proper use of hand lens.*

From the basic key, the observer is directed to proceed to one of four sections in the body of the key. If the sample were a ring-porous hardwood, the first set of statements in that section would be as follows:

1. Rays very wide, easily visible to naked eye, appear as dark lines as much as an inch high on tangential surface and broad flecks on radial surface. Oak-type rays   **2**
1. Rays smaller, not oak-type   **3**

If the first statement describes the sample being observed, the observer is directed to the pair of statements preceded by the number two. On the other hand, if the second statement applies, pair number three is the next set of statements to be considered. This process is continued until the sample is identified.

One principle a beginner must learn about a key is that practically all the statements are *relative.* When features are described as being large or small, numerous or sparse, they are being compared to the same features of other woods in that section of the key. Thus, the resin canals of pine are "numerous" only when compared to those of spruce and other softwoods in that section, and the pores of cottonwood are "small" compared to those of walnut but relatively large compared to those of buckeye.

The best way to overcome this initial difficulty is to "run through" the key several samples of known species, noting the key description of features at each decision level. Until the observer has a clear idea of the appearance of rays, pores, resin canals, and other features, as described by the key, he will be continually frustrated by that instrument.

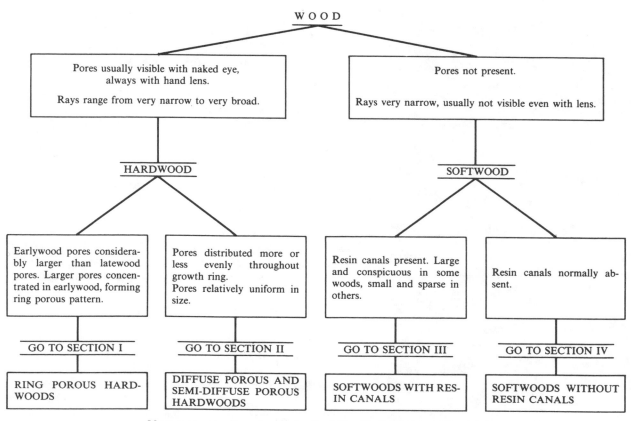

WOOD

| Pores usually visible with naked eye, always with hand lens. Rays range from very narrow to very broad. | Pores not present. Rays very narrow, usually not visible even with lens. |

HARDWOOD   SOFTWOOD

| Earlywood pores considerably larger than latewood pores. Larger pores concentrated in earlywood, forming ring porous pattern. | Pores distributed more or less evenly throughout growth ring. Pores relatively uniform in size. | Resin canals present. Large and conspicuous in some woods, small and sparse in others. | Resin canals normally absent. |

| GO TO SECTION I | GO TO SECTION II | GO TO SECTION III | GO TO SECTION IV |

| RING POROUS HARDWOODS | DIFFUSE POROUS AND SEMI-DIFFUSE POROUS HARDWOODS | SOFTWOODS WITH RESIN CANALS | SOFTWOODS WITHOUT RESIN CANALS |

Macroscopic Key for Selected North American Woods.

**Section I
Ring Porous Hardwoods**

1. Rays very wide, easily visible to naked eye, appear as dark lines as much as an inch high on tangential surface and broad flecks on radial surface. Oak-type rays   2
1. Rays smaller, not oak-type   3

2. Latewood pores very small, difficult to distinguish with hand lens. Earlywood pores of heartwood occluded with tyloses. Rays on tangential surface often exceeding an inch in height. Heartwood light brown.
   WHITE OAK GROUP—*Quercus* spp.
2. Latewood pores sparse, but plainly visible with lens. Very little or no tyloses present. Rays on tangential surface seldom as much as an inch in height. Heartwood reddish brown.
   RED OAK GROUP—*Quercus* spp.

3. Pores in latewood numerous. Usually appear in groups as light-colored bands or patches   4
3. Pores in latewood relatively sparse, usually appear as single openings or in groups of only two or three   12

4. Latewood pores arranged in wavy tangential bands   5
4. Latewood pores arranged mostly in clusters   7

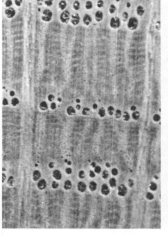

White oak   Red oak

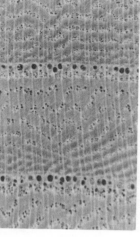

American elm

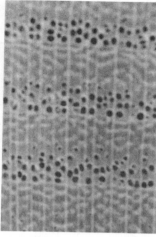

Hackberry

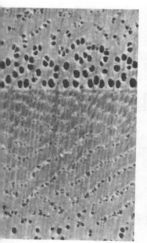

Slippery elm

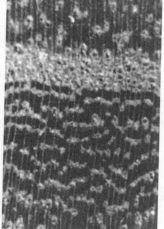

Osage orange

5. Earlywood pores in a single row. Heartwood light brown, frequently with reddish tint.
AMERICAN ELM—*Ulmus americana* L.

5. Earlywood pores in more than one row   **6**

6. Rays visible to naked eye. Heartwood gray or yellowish gray.
HACKBERRY—*Celtis occidentalis* L.

6. Rays not distinct to naked eye. Heartwood dark brown or reddish brown.
SLIPPERY ELM (RED ELM) —*Ulmus rubra* Muhl.

7. Tyloses abundant, pores completely occluded   **8**

7. Tyloses sparse or absent. Pores mostly or completely open **10**

8. Outline of earlywood pores indistinct   **9**

8. Outline of earlywood pores distinct. Rays visible to naked eye. Conspicuous fleck on radial surface. Heartwood orange-yellow or yellow-brown, becoming reddish chocolate brown upon exposure.
RED MULBERRY—*Morus rubra* L.

9. Latewood pores small, outlines indistinct with lens. Heartwood bright yellow when fresh, turning dark orange-brown upon exposure. Coloring matter easily soluble in water.
OSAGE ORANGE—*Maclura-pomifera* (Raf.) Schneid.

9. Latewood pores large, mostly distinct with lens. Heartwood greenish yellow or golden brown. Coloring matter not readily soluble in water.
BLACK LOCUST—*Robina pseudoacacia* L.

10. Rays visible to naked eye   **11**

10. Rays not visible to naked eye. Latewood pores in radial flame-like patches of light tissue.
AMERICAN CHESTNUT—*Castanea dentata* (Marsh) Borleh.

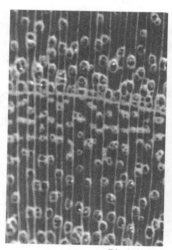

Black locust

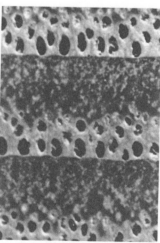

American chestnut

11. Rays distinct to naked eye. Latewood pores in outer portion of growth ring in groups surrounded by parenchyma, appearing as short, light-colored tangential lines. Heartwood reddish brown.
HONEYLOCUST—*Gleditsia triacanthos* L.

11. Rays visible, but not distinct to naked eye. Parenchyma in rings around latewood pores, which appear as white spots. Fresh wood with aromatic odor.
SASSAFRAS—*Sassafras albidum* (Nutt) Nees.

12. Earlywood pores closely spaced   **13**
12. Earlywood pores irregularly spaced. Transition from earlywood to latewood gradual   **15**

13. Rays not visible without lens. Transition from earlywood to latewood abrupt   **14**
13. Rays visible without lens. Transition from earlywood to latewood gradual. Heartwood reddish brown.
KENTUCKY COFFEETREE—*Gymnocladus dioicus* (L.) K. Koch.

14. Latewood pores surrounded by conspicuous parenchyma, sometimes grouped into bands near end of growth ring. Heartwood light grayish brown.
WHITE ASH—*Fraxinus americana* L.
GREEN ASH—*Fraxinus pennsylvanica* Marsh.

14. Parenchyma surrounding latewood pores not as conspicuous, seldom united into bands. Heartwood darker grayish brown.
BLACK ASH—*Fraxinus Nigra* Marsh.

15. Fine tangential bands of parenchyma visible in latewood with hand lens, creating a lace-like pattern. Tyloses present but not abundant.
HICKORY—*Carya* spp.

15. Tangential bands of parenchyma very difficult to distinguish with lens. Tyloses absent. Ripple marks often conspicuous on tangential surface.
PERSIMMON—*Diospyros virginiana* L.

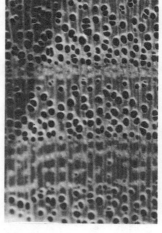

Honeylocust

Sassafras

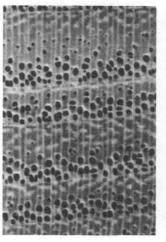

Kentucky coffeetree

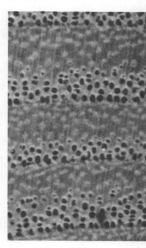

White ash

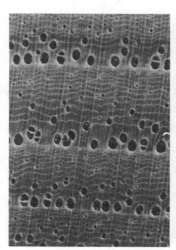

Shellbark hickory

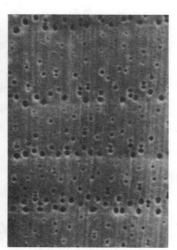

Persimmon

Section II
Diffuse Porous and Semi-Diffuse
Porous Hardwoods

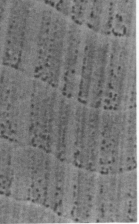

American hornbeam   American beech

1. Pores more or less uniform in size and distributed fairly uniformly throughout growth ring. Typically diffuse porous   **7**
1. Pores more numerous and/or larger in earlywood. Semi-diffuse porous   **2**

2. Rays not distinct without lens   **4**
2. Rays distinct without lens   **3**

3. Many broad rays. Pores relatively sparse. Growth rings wavy. Heartwood yellowish-white, often not distinguishable from sapwood.
    AMERICAN HORNBEAM—*Carpinus caroliniana* Walt.
3. Broad rays relatively few. Pores small and numerous. Heartwood brown to reddish brown.
    AMERICAN BEECH—*Fagus grandifolia* Ehrh.

4. Pores large, easily distinguishable to naked eye   **5**
4. Pores difficult or impossible to distinguish without lens   **6**

5. Wood moderately hard and heavy, heartwood rich chocolate brown.
    BLACK WALNUT—*Juglans nigra* L.
5. Wood soft and light. Heartwood pale grayish-brown.
    BUTTERNUT—*Juglans cinerea* L.

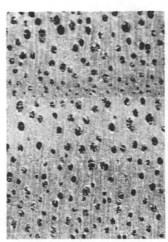

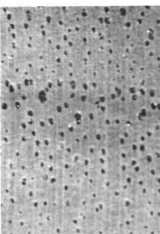

Black walnut   Butternut

6. Wood hard and heavy, heartwood light brown, sometimes with reddish tinge.
    EASTERN HOPHORNBEAM—*Ostrya Virginiana* (Mill.) K. Koch.
6. Wood soft and light, heartwood light brown, often with gray or purplish streaks.
    BLACK WILLOW—*Salix nigra* Marsh.

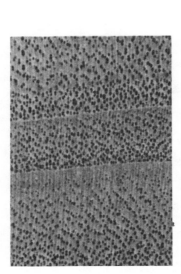

Black willow

7. Rays difficult or impossible to distinguish with naked eye   **8**
7. Rays distinct to naked eye   **14**

8. Rays not visible or difficult to distinguish with lens   **9**
8. Rays distinct with lens   **10**

9. Pores very small, difficult to distinguish with lens. Wood soft and light. Heartwood pale yellowish-white, sometimes with reddish or brownish streaks.
    OHIO BUCKEYE—*Aesculus glabra* Willd.
    YELLOW BUCKEYE—*Aesculus octandra* Marsh.

9. Pores small but easily distinguished under lens. Wood soft and light. Heartwood creamy white, sapwood not clearly defined.
    ASPEN—*Populus* spp.
    COTTONWOOD—*Populus* spp.

10. Pores numerous, crowded, but very small, difficult to distinguish with lens   **11**

10. Pores relatively sparse, larger, easily seen under lens. Wider than rays. Wood hard and heavy, heartwood brown to reddish brown.
    BIRCH—*Betula* spp.

Ohio buckeye

11. Growth rings terminate in a distinct light line (terminal parenchyma)   **12**

11. Growth rings terminate in a faint brown or light line   **13**

12. Wood soft and light. Heartwood very pale brown.
    BASSWOOD—*Tilia* spp.

12. Wood moderately soft. Heartwood generally yellowish, but often streaked with purple, green, blue, and black.
    YELLOW POPLAR—*Liridendron tulipifera* L.

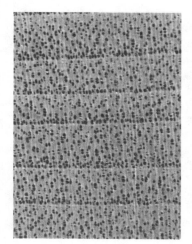

Black cottonwood

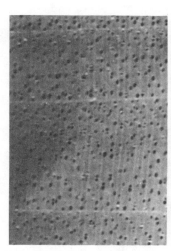

Yellow birch

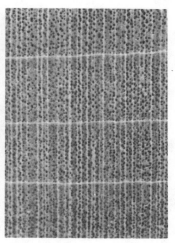

Yellow poplar

13. Heartwood greenish or brownish gray.
    TUPELO—*Nyssa* Spp.

13. Color of heartwood variable, from light to dark reddish brown, often with darker streaks.
    SWEETGUM—*Liquidambar styraciflua* L.

14. Boundaries of growth rings distinct, marked by a thin light line   **16**

14. Boundaries of growth rings not distinct   **15**

Black tupelo

American holly   Flowering dogwood

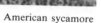

Red alder   American sycamore

15.   Heartwood ivory-white. Rays relatively wide, forming pronounced white lines on transverse surface. Pores very tiny, barely distinguishable with lens, arranged in radial strings.
AMERICAN HOLLY—*Ilex opaca* Ait.

15.   Heartwood dark brown. Rays not as wide and less pronounced. Pores very small, but not in radial strings.
FLOWERING DOGWOOD—*Cornus florida* L.

16.   Broad rays present, many times as wide as largest pore   **17**
16.   Broad rays absent   **18**

17.   Broad rays few, irregularly spaced, sometimes far apart, often inconspicuous without lens. Narrow rays closely spaced. Heartwood light brown with reddish tinge.
RED ALDER—*Alnus rubra* Bong.

17.   Broad rays numerous, more closely and regularly spaced. Few narrow rays present. Heartwood light to dark brown or reddish brown. Wood moderately hard and heavy.
AMERICAN SYCAMORE—*Platanus occidentalis* L.

18.   Pores very small, difficult to distinguish with lens. Wood moderately hard and heavy, heartwood yellow, greenish yellow to brown or greenish black.
SOUTHERN MAGNOLIA—*Magnolia grandiflora* L.

18.   Pores small, but easily visible under lens   **19**

19.   Heartwood deep brownish red after exposure; lighter, almost pink, when freshly cut. Wood moderately hard and heavy.
BLACK CHERRY—*Prunus serotina* Ehrh.

19.   Heartwood pale brown with very slight reddish or grayish cast   **20**

20.   Rays uniform in width. Few or no narrow rays visible between larger rays.
SOFT MAPLE—*Acer saccharinum* L.

20.   Rays not uniform in width. Very fine rays barely visible between larger rays.
HARD MAPLE—*Acer saccharum* Marsh.

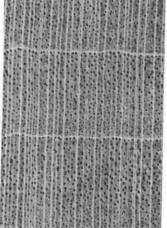

Black cherry   Hard maple

1. Resin canals large, numerous, visible without lens   **2**
1. Resin canals small, sparse, difficult or impossible to distinguish without lens   **6**

2. Transition from earlywood to latewood definitely abrupt   **3**
2. Transition from earlywood to latewood gradual to fairly abrupt   **4**

3. Latewood very prominent, dense, sometimes wider than earlywood. Wood hard and heavy.
   SOUTHERN PINES
       LONGLEAF PINE—*Pinus plaustris* Mill.
       SHORTLEAF PINE—*Pinus echinata* Mill.
       LOBLOLLY PINE—*Pinus taeda* L.
       SLASH PINE—*Pinus eliottil* Engelm. etc.
       PITCH PINE—*Pinus rigida* Mill.
3. Latewood somewhat less prominent, seldom if ever as wide as earlywood. Wood moderately soft and light.
   RED PINE—*Pinus resinosa* Ait.

4. Transition from earlywood to latewood fairly abrupt. Split tangential surface sometimes dimpled.
   JACK PINE—*Pinus banksiana* Lamb.
   LODGEPOLE PINE—*Pinus contorta* Dougl.
   PONDEROSA PINE—*Pinus ponderosa* Laws.
4. Transition from earlywood to latewood gradual   **5**

5. Resin canals appear as small openings on transverse surface; as dark streaks on radial and tangential surfaces. Wood relatively coarse-textured. Exudes sugary substance when fresh-cut.
   SUGAR PINE—*Pinus lambertiana* Dougl.
5. Resin canals appear as small whitish spots on transverse surface. Wood fine-textured.
   EASTERN WHITE PINE—*Pinus strobus* L.
   WESTERN WHITE PINE—*Pinus Monticola* Dougl.

**Section III
Softwoods with Resin Canals**

Loblolly pine   Red pine

Lodgepole pine

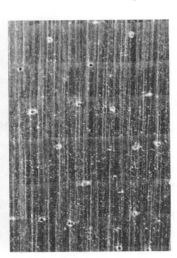

Sugar pine   Western white pine

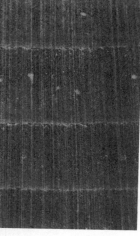

Sitka spruce   Engelmann spruce

6. Bands of latewood distinct, but transition from earlywood to latewood rather gradual   **7**

6. Bands of latewood quite prominent, transition abrupt   **8**

7. Heartwood pale brown, often with purplish tinge. Split tangential surface often dimpled.
SITKA SPRUCE—*Picea sitchensis* (Bong) Carr.

7. Heartwood not distinct from sapwood. Wood almost white to light yellowish brown. Split tangential surface not dimpled.
ENGELMANN SPRUCE—*Picea engelmannii* Parry.

8. Characteristic odor evident on freshly cut surfaces. Resin canals often in tangential lines. Wood with reddish tone.
DOUGLAS FIR—*Pseudosuga taxifolia* (Poir) Britton.

8. Wood without characteristic odor. Resin canals in groups of 2–5, but not in lines. Wood tending to brownish rather than reddish tone.
WESTERN LARCH—*Larix occidentalis* Nutt.
TAMARACK—*Larix laricina* (DuRoy) K. Koch.

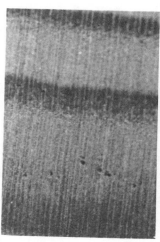

Douglas fir   Western larch

Section IV
Softwoods without Resin Canals

1. Distinctive odor present, easily detected when fresh cut is made   **2**

1. No noticeable odor present   **9**

2. Heartwood color fairly dark, various shades of brown   **3**

2. Heartwood color rather light, yellowish white to pale brown **5**

3. Fine-textured wood, tracheids not visible with lens. Wood quite firm, smooth cut easy to obtain. Heartwood reddish to purplish brown.
EASTERN RED CEDAR—*Juniperus virginiana* L.

3. Medium- or coarse-textured wood, tracheids sometimes visible with lens on smooth cut. Wood soft, smooth cut difficult to obtain. Heartwood dull brown often with reddish tinge   **4**

Eastern red cedar

4. Wood with distinct spicy taste if small shaving is placed on tongue. Odor characteristic of most pencils.
INCENSE-CEDAR—*Libocedrus decurrens* Torr.

4. Wood without distinct taste. Odor faint, sweetish.
WESTERN REDCEDAR—*Thuja plicata* Donn.

5. Transition gradual   **6**

5. Transition rather abrupt. Darker bands of summerwood prominent. Wood variable in color from light yellowish brown to dark brown or blackish. Wood with oily or greasy surface and unpleasant odor, especially darker-colored wood.
BALDCYPRESS—*Taxodium distichum* (L.) Rich.

6. Parenchyma present in all growth rings. Appears as dark tangential lines, often visible to naked eye.
ATLANTIC WHITE-CEDAR—*Chamaecyparis thyoides* (L.) B.S.P.

6. Parenchyma not visible   **7**

7. Wood very soft and light, smooth cut difficult to obtain. Heartwood dull medium to light brown. Sapwood nearly white. Distinctive odor.
NORTHERN WHITE-CEDAR—*Thyja occidentalis* L.

7. Wood moderately soft to moderately hard. Smooth cut obtained more easily. Heartwood light in color, often not distinct from sapwood   **8**

Western redcedar

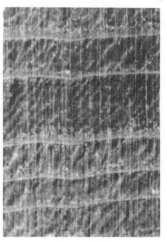

Northern white cedar

California torreya

8. Wood yellow in color. Odor distinctive and somewhat unpleasant.
CALIFORNIA TORREYA—*Torreya Californica* Torr.

8. Wood yellowish brown in color. Odor distinctive, ginger-like.
PORT-ORFORD CEDAR—*Chamaecyparis lawsoniana* (A. Murr.) Parl.

9. Heartwood dark reddish brown or dull medium brown   **10**

9. Heartwood light yellowish brown   **11**

10. Wood coarse-textured, individual tracheids visible under lens. Fairly soft and light to moderately hard. Heartwood dark reddish brown.
REDWOOD—*Sequoia sempervirens* (D. Don) Endl.

10. Wood fine-textured, individual tracheids not visible with lens. Wood dense, fairly heavy. Heartwood orange or pinkish red when fresh but changes to medium brown upon exposure.
PACIFIC YEW—*Taxus brevifolia* Nutt.

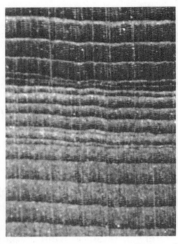 

Redwood   Pacific yew

11. Wood whitish to pale brown. Earlywood whitish, latewood darker, orange-brown.
TRUE FIR—*Abies* spp.

11. Wood light brown with reddish tint, latewood having an almost purplish tone.
HEMLOCK—*Tsuga* spp.

Fraser fir   Hemlock

Resources

Coleman, Donald G. *Woodworking Factbook.* New York: Robert Speller & Sons, 1966.

Harrar, E. S. *Hough's Encyclopedia of American Woods.* New York: Robert Speller & Sons, 1957.

Panshin, A. J., and Carl DeZeeuw. *Textbook of Wood Technology,* Vol. I. New York: McGraw-Hill Book Company, 1970.

Tsoumis, George. *Wood As Raw Material.* New York: Pergamon Press, 1968.

Chapter Four

Properties of Wood

The utilization of wood as a raw material or in a finished product depends to a great extent on the physical properties of the material. The fact that wood is very strong, yet light in weight, makes it an ideal building material. The attractive colors and grain patterns of wood, as well as its ease of cutting and fabrication, are responsible for its unsurpassed beauty and wide use in fine furniture.

The properties of wood are determined largely by the structure and composition of the material. The size, number, and distribution of cells, the amount of cell wall substance, its chemical composition, all contribute to the different properties of wood. Since the structure and composition of different species and even individual trees of the same species vary widely, there is a similar variability in the properties of different woods.

Wood-Moisture Relations

The relationship between wood and moisture has more significance for the utilization of wood than any other single property of the material, because practically all its other physical properties are affected by the amount of moisture wood contains at any given time. The nature of this relationship is usually expressed by referring to wood as a *hygroscopic* material, which means that it absorbs moisture readily, in both liquid and vapor form. The honeycomb structure of wood allows it to absorb large amounts of water, as much as two or three times the weight of the wood substance itself.

Moisture content. The amount of moisture contained in wood is called moisture content, and is expressed as a percent of the oven-dry weight

Physical Properties

of the wood. Moisture content may be determined by the use of meters designed for that purpose, but the most accurate method is the *oven-dry* process. To measure the moisture content of a sample of wood by this process, the sample is first weighed in the green or partially-dry state, and the weight is recorded. Next, the sample is dried in an oven at a temperature of 212° F. until a constant, oven-dry weight is reached. The moisture content is then calculated by subtracting the oven-dry weight from the original weight of the sample and dividing by the oven-dry weight. The formula is:

$$\text{M.C. (\%)} = \frac{\text{Wet weight} - \text{Oven-dry weight}}{\text{Oven-dry weight}} \times 100$$

In shortened form, the formula becomes:

$$\text{M.C. (\%)} = \frac{W W - O D}{O D} \times 100$$

It should be observed that the original weight of the sample minus the oven-dry weight yields the weight of the water which the wood contained. Dividing this by the oven-dry weight of the sample and multiplying by 100 indicates the percent of the oven-dry weight which the water represents.

The oven-dry weight is used as a basis for calculating moisture content because it is a more nearly constant property than the original weight, which varies with the amount of moisture present.

Electrical moisture meters are available which measure moisture content of wood quickly and conveniently. There are two principal types of moisture meters: one makes use of the effect of moisture content on the electrical resistance of wood, and one measures the power loss when high frequency current passes through wood. The former is called a *resistance meter* and the latter a *power loss meter*. The limitations of these devices are that they are most accurate in a moisture content range from about 0 to 25 percent, they must be calibrated for each species of wood and for different temperatures, and they are overly sensitive to abnormal conditions.

Location of moisture in wood. Water exists in two locations in wood, in the cell wall and in the cell lumen, the hollow portion of the cell. Water in the cell lumen is in liquid form and is called *free water.* Water in the cell wall material is called *bound water,* because it is held there by hydrogen bonds between water molecules and the cell wall material.

When wood absorbs water, it is first taken up into the cell wall. As more water enters the spaces in the cell wall structure, the framework of the structure becomes strained until the point is reached where no more liquid can enter the cell wall. This point is called the *fiber saturation point* (fsp), and water entering wood above this point is contained in the cell lumina as free water. The fiber saturation point for most woods native to the United States is around 25 to 30 percent.

Equilibrium moisture content. Wood absorbs moisture in the form of vapor from the air until a steady moisture-content condition, called equilibrium moisture content, is reached. Equilibrium moisture content varies with the temperature and relative humidity of the air; for example, when the relative humidity is high, equilibrium moisture content rises, and when relative humidity is low, equilibrium moisture content decreases. As might be expected, equilibrium moisture content values have been determined for wide ranges of temperature and relative humidity. A table of such values is included in the *Wood Handbook* (U. S. Forest Service).

Under normal conditions, wood in outdoor uses maintains an equilibrium moisture content of 12-15 percent over much of the United States. Indoors, equilibrium moisture content may fall as low as 4-8 percent, the lower figure being reached during the winter when wood is subjected to dry, heated air.

Moisture movement in wood. Since wood gains and loses moisture very readily, it follows that considerable movement of moisture occurs in the wood itself. Several forces act on water in wood to cause it to move through different passageways in the wood.

Capillary action causes free water to flow through cell cavities and small openings in the cell wall, similar to the movement of liquid in a wick. Water vapor moves through cell cavities, pits, pit membranes, and other passageways when differences in relative humidity occur in the wood, following the principle of diffusion (a fluid tends to move from an area of higher concentration of the fluid to an area of lower concentration). Differences in moisture content in different areas of a piece of wood cause bound water to move through small openings in the cell wall by diffusion.

The movement of moisture in wood is a relatively slow process compared to the temperature and humidity changes in the air. Moisture near the surface of wood is thus lost and gained more easily than that toward the center of the piece. The result is that, in normal circumstances, the outer layers of wood may vary considerably in moisture content while that of the bulk of the piece fluctuates very little.

Moisture does not move at the same rate in all directions in wood. Due to the tubular structure of cells and their orientation in the longitudinal direction, moisture travels from twelve to fifteen times as fast along the grain as it does across it. Ordinarily, however, most of the water evaporates from the sides of a board because of the comparatively small area of end grain exposed.

Shrinkage and Expansion of Wood

One of the main disadvantages of wood, from an engineering standpoint, is that it is dimensionally unstable. Other structural materials such as metal and concrete expand and contract with temperature changes, but wood is affected very little by temperature. Instead, wood is quite sensitive to changes in moisture content.

When moisture enters a dry piece of wood, it is taken up first by the cell walls as bound water. The water molecules enter minute spaces between the microfibrils of the walls and cause expansion of the microfibrillar net. The expansion of the cell walls is of course cumulative, so that the entire piece of wood expands as the cell walls expand. This expansion continues with the addition of more water until the fiber saturation point is reached. The addition of free water in the cell cavities causes no further expansion. Similarly, when free water is removed from cell cavities, no shrinkage occurs until the fiber saturation point is reached. Reduction in moisture content below the fiber saturation point is accompanied by a somewhat proportional shrinkage of the wood.

Shrinkage of a piece of wood is expressed as a percent of the size of the piece when green, or wet. If "wet" wood is defined as that containing moisture over the fiber saturation point and "dry" wood as that having moisture content below fsp, then the formula for calculating shrinkage when wood is dried to a certain level of moisture content is:

$$\text{Shrinkage } (\%) = \frac{\text{Wet dimension} - \text{Dry dimension}}{\text{Wet dimension}} \times 100$$

This formula provides a shrinkage value for only one dimension at a time, and since wood is generally used in three-dimensional form, two other similar calculations are needed to give a complete description of the shrinkage of the piece. This is especially necessary because wood is *anisotropic,* which means that the dimensional changes are unequal along the three principal dimensions. Shrinkage along the grain, or longitudinal shrinkage, is very slight, ranging from 0.1 to 0.3 percent when dried to oven dry conditions. For practical purposes, this shrinkage is negligible and is not a consideration in most applications of wood.

Tangential and radial shrinkage, however, constitute changes which must be considered whenever wood is used in intact forms such as boards and veneer. Radial shrinkage, when wood is dried to 6 percent moisture content, ranges from about 2 to 4 percent for softwoods and from 2 to 6 percent for hardwoods. Under the same conditions, tangential shrinkage is roughly twice as great as radial shrinkage (fig. 4–1).

Shrinkage is of considerable importance to sawmill operators, who are constantly confronted with shrinkage-related problems. Consider the following situation: A sawmill receives an order for a quantity of 2" × 6" white oak boards, kiln dried. In order to provide boards measuring 2" × 6" after kiln drying, the sawmill operator must saw them oversize to allow for the shrinkage. Assuming that the boards are to be slab-sawn, they would have to be about an eighth of an inch thicker and nearly one half inch wider when green.

FIG. 4–1. *Characteristic shrinkage and the resulting distortion caused by the direction of the growth rings. (Courtesy of U.S. Forest Service.)*

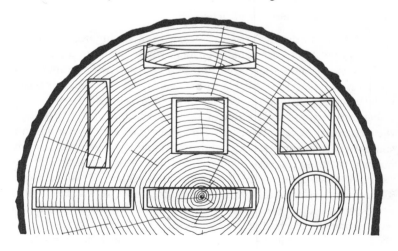

Density and Specific Gravity

Specific gravity is usually defined as the ratio of the weight of a substance to the weight of an equal volume of water. Specific gravity is expressed as a pure number, which means that no units such as inches, feet, or pounds, are attached to the number. *Density,* on the other hand, is not a pure number, and in this country it is defined as the weight per unit volume of a substance. It is most often expressed in pounds per cubic foot.

Density and specific gravity involve the weight and volume of wood, both of which vary with changes in moisture content of the wood. Because of this, the calculation of values of these properties is more complicated than for other materials. One method of calculating specific gravity for wood is as follows:

$$\text{Sp. gr.} = \frac{\text{Oven dry weight of wood}}{\text{Wt. of displaced volume of water}}$$

In this case the oven dry weight of wood is specified in the numerator and will be relatively constant within the same species of wood. The "weight of displaced volume of water" can vary, however, because no constant moisture content (and hence no constant volume) for the wood is specified in the denominator. This means that different values for the specific gravity for the same kind of wood will be obtained at different moisture content levels.

To avoid variation in the value of specific gravity with changes in moisture content, another method of calculating specific gravity was developed and is the most useful and commonly accepted procedure. Called *basic specific gravity,* it is calculated as follows:

$$\text{Basic sp. gr.} = \frac{\text{Oven dry weight of wood}}{\text{Wt. of water displaced by green wood}}$$

Notice that the oven dry weight is still used in the numerator, but in the denominator, the volume of the piece of wood in question was taken when green. Since the moisture content of green wood is always above the fiber saturation point, the volume of green wood is relatively constant.

Density of wood is usually calculated on the basis of weight and volume at the same moisture content. The calculation is very simple, as follows:

$$\text{Density} = \frac{\text{Weight of wood (at } x\% \text{ m.c.)}}{\text{Volume of wood (at } x\% \text{ m.c.)}}$$

The moisture content of the wood must be specified when the density is reported, as different values result at different levels of moisture content. In practice, density is not used as often as basic specific gravity, which is less variable.

The specific gravities of most commercial woods in this country range from .35 to .81, although the extreme ranges are .21 for corkwood and 1.04 for black ironwood. Specific gravities over 1.00 mean that the wood is heavier than water and will not float.

Thermal Properties of Wood

Three points regarding the reaction of wood to heat will be considered here: insulating properties, conductivity, and expansion. Thermal conductivity and thermal insulating values are reciprocals, which means that a material with high thermal conductivity will have low insulating values, and vice versa. Wood transmits heat very slowly, so its thermal conductivity is quite low, while its insulating value is high. The low rate of heat transmission of wood explains why wood feels "warm" to the touch, and accounts, in part, for its value in furniture making.

Thermal expansion of wood is very small in comparison to other structural materials, and for practical purposes is negligible. Normally, the changes in wood due to temperature variation are hidden by the much larger changes caused by fluctuation in moisture content.

Electrical Properties of Wood

The reactions of wood to alternating and direct current are similar but the two situations are usually discussed separately, because the terminology applied in each case is different.

The two properties of wood related to direct current are *resistivity* and *conductivity,* and both of these vary with changes in moisture content of the wood. Dry wood is a good insulator, which means its resistivity is high. As the moisture content increases toward the fiber saturation point, however, resistance decreases, and at the fiber saturation point or above, wood has little more resistance than water. In other words, dry wood is a good insulator, but wet wood is a good conductor of direct current.

The resistivity of wood is affected by temperature as well as moisture content. For reasons not quite understood at present, electrical resistance decreases with increasing temperature. Also, woods of high density present more resistance to direct current than woods of lower density.

Resistance-type moisture meters utilize the electrical resistance of wood to direct current, but so many factors influence resistivity that such meters must be calibrated and corrected for each situation, and their use and accuracy is consequently limited.

The measure of the resistance of wood to the passage of alternating current is called its dielectric constant. As in the case of direct current resistivity, the dielectric constant increases with addition of moisture up to the fiber saturation point (resistance decreases as the dielectric constant increases).

The dielectric constant is also used in measuring moisture content by means of a power-loss moisture meter. This type of meter is only slightly more widely applicable than the resistance type.

One useful reaction of wood to alternating current is its tendency to heat during the passage of high-frequency alternating current. This principle is utilized in the radio-frequency heating of the glue line to greatly accelerate the setting time for glue joints, and in a super-fast method of drying wood under radio-frequency current.

Mechanical Properties

The mechanical properties of wood are those properties which have to do with the strength of the material; its reaction to forces applied to it. In practice, a force is simply a load of a certain weight. For instance, a wood post holding up part of a floor that weighs 4000 pounds may be withstanding a force of 1000 pounds.

Strength of Materials

A common misconception is the idea that "strength" is a single property of a material. This is not correct, because any material has several strength properties; tensile, compressive, and bending strengths, for example. Thus, it is seldom correct to make a statement such as "wood A is stronger than wood B." One strength property of wood A may be better, but another one may not be good as that of wood B. To complicate things further, the anisotropic nature of wood, which causes unequal shrinkage, also is responsible for non-uniform strength properties in different directions. Wood is many times as strong when a force is exerted parallel to the grain as it is when a force is acting across the grain.

A force applied to a material causes an internal resistance in the material. This resistance to an external force is called *stress*. Stress is often confused with the applied force, because as long as the material is stationary the stress is equal to the applied force. Thus, if someone says that a beam is under 5000 pounds of stress, he usually means that a force of 5000 pounds is being applied to it.

In order to make stress expressions comparable and more convenient to use, they are usually written as *unit stresses*. Unit stress is simply the stress per unit of cross sectional area, and is usually expressed in pounds per square inch (psi). The unit stress for a piece of wood one inch square under a load of 100 pounds would be 100 pounds per square inch. If the piece were one inch by two inches in cross section, however, the unit stress would be 50 pounds per square inch, as shown in figure 4–2.

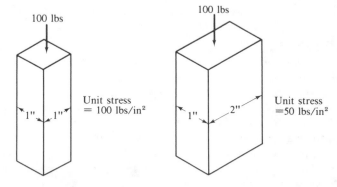

FIG. 4–2. *Unit stress*

A material may be subjected to three "basic stresses," depending upon the manner in which the force is applied. A *tensile* stress is produced by a force which tends to lengthen the piece of material on which it is acting. It may be thought of as a stretching force. A *compressive* stress, on the other hand, tends to shorten the piece. The third type, a *shear* stress, is caused by forces which tend to make one part of the material slide in relation to the material immediately adjacent to it (see fig. 4–3).

In addition to the three basic stresses, another factor of prime importance in wood utilization is *bending* stress, which is a combina-

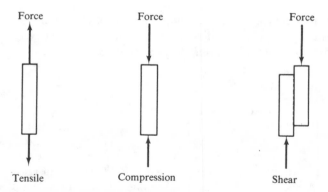

FIG. 4–3. *Basic stresses.*

tion of all three of the basic stresses. A beam supported at both ends and loaded in the middle tends to bend downward (fig. 4–4). When this happens, the lower half of the beam stretches, which is a tensile stress, and the upper half shortens, under a compressive stress. Near the middle of the beam is an area called the neutral axis, where neither stress is acting.

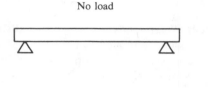

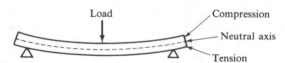

FIG. 4–4. *Bending stress.*

The ability of a material to withstand or resist an applied force is the strength of that material. Thus, for each type of force, or stress, a material has a specific strength property. Tensile strength is the ability to resist stretching, compressive strength is the ability to resist compression, and so on. Furthermore, a material which has high tensile strength does not necessarily have high compressive strength, and vice versa.

When a force is applied to an object, it is deformed to some extent. The deformation may be so small that it cannot be observed without accurate measuring devices, or it may be enough to noticeably or even drastically alter the shape of the piece. In any case, the deformation of a material under a load is referred to correctly as *strain.* Strain is measured in inches, but it is most often expressed as *unit strain,* or in inches per inch.

As an example, consider a beam 1 inch in cross section and 20 inches long, undergoing a tensile stress of 1000 pounds. If the piece measured exactly 20 inches long under no load, and 20.1 inches under a load of 1000 pounds, the total strain is .1 inch. The unit strain, however, is the total strain divided by the total length of the piece, which would be .1 in/20 in or .005 in/in, read as ".005 inch per inch."

In view of the fact that a force (or stress) applied to wood causes some deformation (strain) of the piece, it is easily concluded that there is a relationship between stress and strain. The nature of the relationship varies according to the magnitude of both factors, and the concepts related to this are best illustrated by what is called a "stress-strain diagram," shown in figure 4–5.

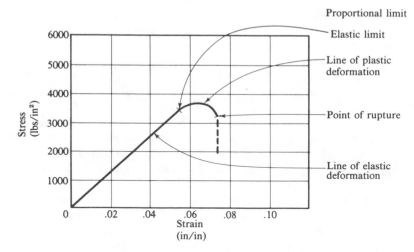

FIG. 4–5. *Relationship of stress and strain.*

When a small force is applied to a material, only a small deformation results, and when the force is removed, the material regains its original shape. This is known as elastic behavior, or elastic deformation, and the ability of a material to regain its original shape after a load has been applied is its *elasticity.* Increasing the load on a particular piece of material will eventually result in so much deformation that when the force is removed the piece will not regain its original shape. In this case, the material has been permanently deformed, which is to say that *plastic* deformation has taken place.

As long as a piece regains its original shape after a load is released, it is within the *elastic limit* of the material, and the stress applied is proportional to the strain. In other words, an increase of stress causes a proportional increase in strain, and in the case illustrated in figure 4–5, an increase of 1000 lbs/in² in stress results in a .015 in/in increase in strain, or deformation. For this reason the point at which stress is no longer proportional to strain, and at which the curve ceases to be a straight line, is called the *proportional limit.* Technically, there may be some difference between the elastic limit and the proportional limit, but for practical purposes they may be considered identical. Beyond the proportional limit, a small increase in force will result in relatively larger increases in strain, because the piece under load is being bent, pulled, or compressed rapidly. Finally, of course, the piece will break, and the stress-strain curve is no longer meaningful.

The relationship between stress and strain is most often described by the *modulus of elasticity,* which is defined as the stress divided by the strain, or

$$\text{Modulus of Elasticity} = \frac{\text{Stress (lbs/in}^2)}{\text{Strain (in/in)}}$$

The modulus of elasticity for bending is an indication of the stiffness of the beam, a high modulus being indicative of a stiff material. This is easily deduced from the formula, for in order to obtain a high modulus, the numerator (stress) would have to be a large number, and the denominator a relatively smaller one. Or, in other words, a large force would be required to bend the beam a small amount, which of course defines a stiff material.

The modulus of elasticity for tensile, compressive, and other strength properties can be interpreted similarly. That is, a high modulus indicates a material which is strong in resisting that type of force. A high modulus for tensile strength means the material resists stretching, and for compressive strength it means high resistance to compression, and so on for other strength properties.

Another property of wood related to strength is *toughness,* which can be defined as the ability of wood to resist shock. An impact bending test is normally used to test for toughness. To be described as tough, a wood sample must be able to bend a relatively large amount before breaking. Ash and hickory are noted for this property. A wood which will bend very little before breaking exhibits *brashness,* which is the opposite of toughness. Redwood is an example of a somewhat brash wood.

Unlike the other strength properties of wood which increase as moisture content decreases, toughness has either the opposite or no relationship to moisture content. In general, wood is more flexible at higher moisture contents, and hence often exhibits greater toughness. As it dries (below the fiber saturation point), the lesser flexibility contributes to increased brashness.

Factors Affecting the Strength of Wood

It is quite generally known that some wood is stronger than other wood. Few people, for instance, doubt that oak is stronger than pine in most respects. The differences in strength among different species of wood are due mostly to differences in specific gravity. As a group, therefore, hardwoods are stronger than softwoods, because they are more dense. Individually, however, there are a few very light hardwoods which are not as strong as many of the heavier softwoods.

Structure and specific gravity. There is a direct relationship between specific gravity and strength of wood. As specific gravity increases, strength likewise increases, because a higher specific gravity indicates that more cell wall substance is present, which is usually a result of thicker-walled cells.

In addition to the thickness of cell walls, the size, number, and arrangement of the different types of cells in wood cause some variations in strength properties. A relatively large number of summerwood cells, as compared to springwood, for instance, means that the wood is more dense, and hence stronger.

Moisture content. In the green condition, wood contains considerable moisture, much of which is in the cell walls. Saturated or partially saturated cells are in a swollen state, because water molecules are absorbed between the microfibrils, creating large spaces in the cell wall filled with water. Thus, green wood has a somewhat spongy nature. When seasoned, however, wood loses most of the water molecules separating the cell wall structure, and the microfibrils draw closer together, forming a stiffer and generally stronger material.

Decay and defects. Decay acts on either the cellulose or lignin components of wood, leaving it very weak and crumbly. Incipient decay, though hardly noticeable, may weaken wood to a considerable extent.

In the latter stages, the wood may be consumed to the point that it will not support its own weight, and crumbles when touched.

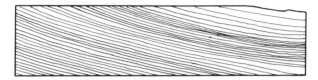

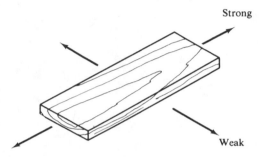

FIG. 4–6. *Examples of cross grain (top) and straight grain (bottom).*

Grain direction. Grain direction in a board affects most strength properties. In general, a straight-grained board is stronger than one with cross grain, spiral grain, or other irregular patterns such as that resulting from knots, burls, and crotches.

Anisotropic nature of wood. One of the greatest limitations of wood as an engineering material is its *anisotropic* nature, which means that it is not equally strong in all directions. Because of the orientation of the wood fibers, a board is much stronger along the grain than across the grain (fig. 4–7). In compression, for example, wood is about four to twelve times as strong parallel to the grain as perpendicular to the grain. The cross-layered structure of plywood, which more nearly equalizes strength properties in different directions, is the most successful effort to date to overcome these inequalities.

FIG. 4–7. *Anisotropic nature of wood.*

Investigating the Properties of Wood

The properties of wood provide one of the most fruitful areas in wood technology for study and experimentation. The experiments and tests appearing in the appendix, pages 234–39, have proven to be both interesting and valuable, but they may be modified in different ways if necessary. It is always possible, for example, to broaden an experiment by using several different kinds of wood and making comparisons between species.

Due to the great variability of wood, even within a species, it should not be expected that two tests on two pieces of wood of the same species will yield identical results. On the other hand, more accurate results can always be obtained by replicating the test a number of times and averaging the results of the individual tests.

Resources

Coleman, Donald G. *Woodworking Factbook.* New York: Robert Speller & Sons, 1966.

Côté, Wilfred A., Jr., and Franz F. P. Kollman. *Principles of Wood Science and Technology,* Vol. I. New York: Springer-Verlag, 1968.

Panshin, A. J., and Carl DeZeeuw. *Textbook of Wood Technology,* Vol. I. New York: McGraw-Hill Book Company, 1970.

U.S. Forest Service, Forest Products Laboratory. *Wood Handbook,* Agriculture Handbook No. 72. Washington, D.C.: Government Printing Office, 1955.

Wood Deterioration and Degradation

Because it is an organic material, wood is subject to several forces of degradation, including decay, insects, weathering, mechanical wear, and fire. In some instances, wood can be rendered virtually useless by one or more of these agencies, while in less severe cases, the wood is only damaged enough to degrade it from a high-quality to a lower-quality product. However, it should be noted that deterioration occurs only under conditions favorable for a particular type of deteriorating force. If wood is kept dry and/or treated with suitable preservatives, it will last indefinitely.

Decay in wood is caused by *fungi,* a group of what is called "lower" plants. They contain no chlorophyll and hence do not produce their own food but grow within or upon other materials. That decay was caused by fungi was not known until 1874, when proof was presented by Robert Hartig, a German pathologist.

   Wood is subject to decay as trees, logs, and manufactured products. This text will deal mostly with the effect of fungi upon wood products in storage and service.

Fungi

Types of Fungi

Although there are literally dozens of separate species of fungi which attack or inhabit wood, they are classified for practical purposes into groups according to the appearance of the wood affected or their physical and chemical action on wood. On this basis, the three major groups of fungi are those which cause *decay,* including brown rot, white rot, and soft rot, *wood-staining fungi,* and *surface molds.*

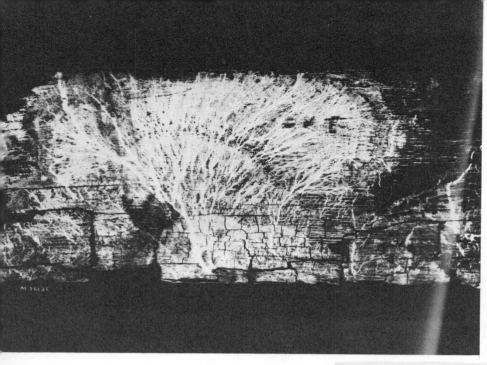

FIG. 5–1. *Characteristic appearance of wood during advanced stages of brown rot. Notice fan-shaped area covered by strands of hyphae (mycelium). (Courtesy of U.S. Forest Products Laboratory, Forest Service, U.S. Department of Agriculture.)*

Decay. Fungi which cause decay are called wood-destroying fungi because the structural elements of wood are consumed, eventually to such an extent that the wood is rendered unfit for any useful purpose. The *brown rot* fungi are so called because they attack primarily the cellulosic portion of the cell, leaving a brownish residue composed mostly of lignin. In these later stages, wood attacked by brown rot acquires a characteristic checkered pattern on the surface when dried (see fig. 5–1) and becomes brittle and crumbly. The *white rot* fungi utilize both the lignin and cellulose materials and leave the wood rather spongy. White rot can often be identified by the presence of dark-colored *zone lines* separating decayed wood and sound wood. *Soft rot fungi* attack the surface of wood, usually under very wet conditions such as in wooden water containers.

Most wood-destroying fungi are limited in the number of species of wood subject to their attack. As a general rule, white rots prefer hardwoods, and brown rots are found more frequently in softwoods, although there are exceptions in both cases. The activities of some fungi are restricted to a certain group of wood species, while others seem to attack one species only. Soft rot fungi are the most species-tolerant and will attack most common woods.

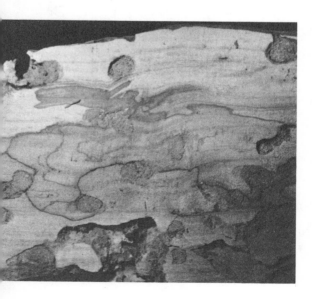

FIG. 5–2. *Dark zone lines are characteristic of white rot fungi attack. Note also evidence of grub damage.*

Wood-staining fungi. Fungi which stain wood do not consume the cell wall materials, but exist instead on the contents of the cell. For this reason, they tend to attack mainly sapwood, which contains more food materials than the non-living heartwood. The most common and most damaging of the wood staining fungi is the *blue stain* so prevalent in softwoods.

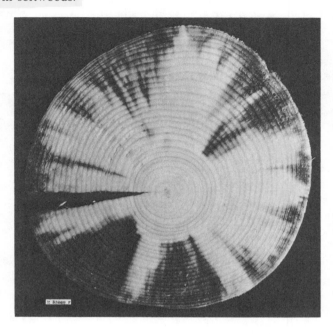

FIG. 5–3. *A log infected with blue-stain fungi. Note how deep into the log the stain has penetrated. (Courtesy of U.S. Forest Products Laboratory, Forest Service, U.S. Department of Agriculture.)*

Lumber is especially susceptible soon after sawing, or when stacked under damp conditions. Since the fungi does not attack the cellular structure of wood, strength properties in general are not affected appreciably, although toughness seems to be lessened somewhat more than other strength properties. The greatest damage caused by blue stain is the degradation of lumber's appearance, because the fungi penetrate completely through the board. The unsightly stain, while not affecting construction grades of lumber significantly, greatly reduces the value of wood intended for natural finish purposes.

Molds. The fungi that form molds on wood are similar to mold found on other materials in damp places. They tend to limit their activities to the surface, although some penetration occurs on hardwoods. Molds are easily recognized by the fluffy growth produced on the surface of wood, very much like that present on moldy food.

While mold-producing fungi themselves do little damage to wood (the mold can be scraped off easily), their presence should be a danger signal. The conditions necessary for molds to grow are likewise favorable for the development of wood-staining fungi and decay.

Growth and Spread of Fungi

In order for fungi to live and grow, four conditions must exist: (1) a suitable temperature, (2) a supply of moisture, (3) sufficient air, and (4) food material (wood). Denying the fungi one or more of these conditions can greatly inhibit or prevent development of decay.

The temperatures favorable for fungi growth vary with different species, but for most types, the *optimum* lies between 75° and 90° F. The range around the optimum within which fungi can function also varies with species. Some may operate over a wide range, while others can tolerate only a fairly narrow range. Cold temperatures prevent the growth of fungi, but do not kill it. They simply lie dormant and may not perish for several years, and will begin to grow again whenever a suitable temperature is reached. High temperatures, on the other hand, destroy the fungi existing in the wood. The temperatures reached in kiln drying of lumber are sufficient to kill all types of fungi, in effect "sterilizing" the wood. This does not, however, prevent future attacks if conditions are favorable.

Moisture sufficient for the development of most fungi must exceed the fiber saturation point, which is 25 to 30 percent moisture content for most native woods. No fungi is known to attack U.S. woods containing less than 20 percent moisture. The most effective and economical means of preventing the development of fungi is to keep the wood dry, which is one reason lumber is seasoned before being further processed.

Fungi consume oxygen and give off carbon dioxide, but the amount of air required is quite small. However, completely saturated wood is unsuitable for fungi development, a fact that is used at mills where logs are stored in ponds. Wood that is completely submerged or buried over four feet underground contains too little air to support fungi. River boats over one hundred years old have been recovered from the mud at the bottom of rivers with their woodwork intact and sound. Likewise, pilings driven deep into the ground last indefinitely because only the surface layers of earth contain enough air to allow fungi growth.

Fungi inhabit or attack wood because it provides food material, in the form of either cell contents or the cell wall itself. All wood cannot be attacked with equal ease, however, for it is well known that some woods have more "natural resistance" to decay and other fungi. The decay resistance of several native species has been evaluated by the U.S. Forest Products Laboratory and the wood classified accordingly (see table 5–1).

FIG. 5–4. *Fruiting bodies produced by decay fungi (sporophores). (Courtesy of U.S. Forest Products Laboratory, Forest Service, U.S. Department of Agriculture.)*

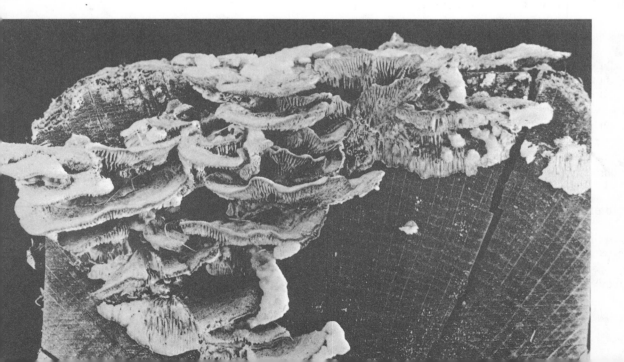

TABLE 5-1

Comparative Decay Resistance of the Heartwood of Some Common Native Species

Resistant or Very Resistant	Moderately Resistant	Slightly or Nonresistant
Baldcypress (old growth)[1]	Baldcypress (young growth)[1]	Alder
Catalpa	Douglas-fir	Ashes
Cedars	Honeylocust[2]	Aspens
Cherry, black	Larch, western	Basswood
Chestnut	Oak, swamp chestnut	Beech
Cypress, Arizona	Pine, eastern white[1]	Birches
Junipers	Pine, longleaf[1]	Buckeye[2]
Locust, black[3]	Pine, slash[1]	Butternut
Mulberry, red[3]	Tamarack	Cottonwood
Oak, bur		Elms
Oak, chestnut		Hackberry
Oak, Gambel		Hemlocks
Oak, Oregon white		Hickories
Oak, post		Magnolia
Oak, white		Maples
Osage-orange[3]		Oak (red and black species)[2]
Redwood		Pines (most other species)[2]
Sassafras		Poplar
Walnut, black		Spruces
Yew, Pacific[3]		Sweetgum[2]
		Sycamore
		Willows
		Yellow-poplar

SOURCE: U.S. Forest Service, Forest Products Laboratory, *Research Note FPL-0153,* 1967.

[1] The southern and eastern pines and baldcypress are now largely second-growth, with a large proportion of sapwood. Consequently, it is no longer practicable to obtain substantial quantities of heartwood lumber in these species for general building purposes.

[2] These species, or certain species within the groups shown, are indicated to have higher decay resistance than most of the other woods in their respective categories.

[3] These woods have exceptionally high decay resistance.

The higher natural decay resistance of some woods is due primarily to the presence of extractive materials in the heartwood. These materials include oils, tannins, and phenols which are toxic to fungi in greater or lesser degree. Extractives are deposited when heartwood is formed, hence sapwood, being free of such materials, has little or no resistance.

Decay resistance seems to be unrelated to the density of wood. Some very heavy woods, such as osage-orange, are very decay-resistant, but others of almost equal weight, such as red oak, have very little resistance. Similarly, some light woods such as redwood have high decay resistance, whereas hemlock and spruce are practically nonresistant.

In latter stages of development, fungi produce fruiting bodies called *sporophores,* which in turn produce microscopic *spores,* equivalent to the seeds of higher plants. Spores are so light that they are carried about freely by the wind, and are present in the air everywhere except in areas deliberately sterilized. When a spore comes to rest on a piece of wood under favorable conditions of temperature and moisture, it begins to multiply and grow, developing tiny strands called *hyphae* which extend into the wood. These strands, collectively called *mycelium,* pass through cell walls with ease, by means of pit openings or *bore holes* which they create as they go. Each hypha of the developing fungus secretes enzymes which break down the cell wall materials into simpler substances suitable for assimilation by the fungus. When decay is far advanced and the greater part of the wood has been consumed, fruiting bodies will again be produced to release thousands upon thousands of spores. The fruiting bodies take many forms characteristic of the individual types of fungus. Some are similar to mushrooms, others are semicircular in shape (see fig. 5–4), while some resemble the growth of lichens.

Effect of Decay on Wood

The property of wood affected most by decay is strength. All strength properties are affected as decay progresses, but toughness seems to be affected first. An increase in brashness is often the first evidence of incipient decay, although other signs soon become apparent.

Due to the fact that part of the wood is consumed by the fungi, several noticeable changes take place. First, the wood becomes less dense and softer, often described as "punky." Also the bore holes and cavities carved out by the fungi make the wood more porous and thus able to absorb more water than normal. When decayed wood is dried, it is softer and lighter and thus ignites easier and burns faster than sound wood.

Probably the most obvious effect of decay on wood is the color change produced. Depending on the type of decay, the wood is either bleached lighter or left somewhat darker than normal. Furthermore, the color is not uniform, but tends to blotch the surface of the wood. Blotches are sometimes defined by the zone lines mentioned earlier.

Insects

Insects cause extensive damage to both wood in living trees and wood in service. Literally hundreds of kinds of insects attack wood for various reasons and by many methods.

Damage caused by insects in standing trees or green logs and lumber is usually described by the nature of the excavation rather than the type of insects doing the damage. *Pin holes* are those 1/4 inch or less in diameter, while those larger than 1/4 inch are called *grub holes*. Both of these are caused by several types of insects, although pin holes are mainly the result of the activities of a group of insects called *ambrosia* beetles.

More detailed discussion of damage to trees or logs is beyond the scope of this text. Primary emphasis is placed on insects which attack wood in service, the most important of which are the termites, powder-post beetles, and carpenter ants.

FIG. 5–5. *The long wings of the termite (A) and the narrow waist of the flying ant (B) are distinguishing features of these insects. (Courtesy of U.S. Forest Products Laboratory, Forest Service, U.S. Department of Agriculture.)*

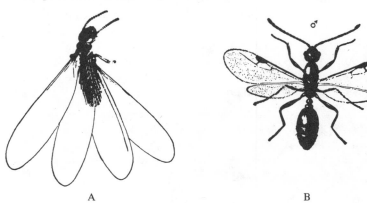

A   B

FIG. 5–6. *The mud tunnel along the masonry column has allowed termites to enter the wood structure of this building. (Courtesy of U.S. Forest Service, Southern Forest Experiment Station.)*

Termites

Termites are small, ant-like insects varying in size from less than 1/4 inch in length to 1/2 inch. They were once confined mainly to forested areas, but with the clearing of forests for farmlands and the increasing numbers of wood buildings, termites became more and more of a menace to wood in service. Millions of dollars worth of damage is caused each year by these pests.

Termites are most familiar to the general public in the form mistakenly called "flying ants." They are actually *winged reproductives,* only one of the castes in the three-level termite society. In addition to the reproductives, most termite colonies also contain *soldiers* and *workers,* both of which are wingless. The soldiers try to keep the colony secure in their excavated home and guard against attack by enemies such as ants. Workers are the ones that perform the most essential work of the colony, namely that of excavating the wood and reducing it to fragments, providing food for themselves as well as the other castes.

Subterranean termites. Termites in the United States are usually divided into three types, *subterranean, damp-wood,* and *dry-wood.* Of these, the subterranean termites are by far the most damaging.

Subterranean termites operate over most of the United States. They are earth-dwelling, and always enter wood from their burrow in the ground. If wood is not in contact with the ground, they will construct a mud and wood fiber tunnel from the earth along a masonry wall or other support, often for a distance of several feet to reach the wood (fig. 5–6). These tunnels are often the most visible evidence of the presence of this type of termites. Upon entering the wood, they carve out galleries along the grain, preferring sapwood to heartwood and springwood to summerwood. However, as soon as the more favorable portions are mostly consumed, the heartwood and summerwood are attacked as well.

Once a piece of wood has been inhabited, subterranean termites do not leave it. They live completely shut off from the outside, and may consume practically the entire interior of the piece without breaking the surface. For this reason, a wood member may look completely sound from the outside, but be riddled inside, being nothing but a shell.

After termites are well established in their habitat, the winged reproductives swarm each spring. Such swarming is a sure indicator of a well-developed colony which has probably caused considerable damage already.

Damp-wood and dry-wood termites. Dry-wood termites are so called because they can attack wood having as little as 10 or 12 percent moisture content. They enter wood directly from the air, usually gaining access at a small check, knot hole or other natural opening. The colonies are smaller than those of subterranean termites, but the damage wrought in a given piece of wood or structure can be just as serious. The total loss due to their action is much less than that caused by subterranean termites, simply because they operate in only a narrow strip along the southern coasts of the United States.

. Compared to other types, damp-wood termites cause very little loss. Their activities are limited to wood either in contact with moist soil, or in other very damp conditions.

Control of Termites

In the past, *termite shields* were often used in house construction, but their effectiveness is limited and they have been largely replaced by other methods. The shield consists of a continuous metal strip covering the top of masonry foundation walls with edges extending to form two-inch to four-inch flanges on each side of the wall. In order to enter the wood framing above the metal shield, termites are forced to build their tubes out over the flange where they are easily detected.

The method most frequently practiced today is that of *soil treatment*. When the house is under construction, the soil under and around the foundation is treated with poisonous chemicals to prevent termite colonies from establishing themselves near the building.

Another effective way to prevent termite attack is to use preserved wood for the lower framing of the house. Wood that has been pressure-treated with pentachlorophenol or another good preservative is impervious to attack, and will remain so for many years. Brushing or spraying of preservative is not effective because too little penetration is achieved by these methods.

FIG. 5–7. *Termite damage on a piece of wood which had been in contact with the ground for less than a year.*

Powder-Post Beetle

A great deal of damage is done to wood by a group of insects called collectively powder-post beetles. Their name derives from their habit of reducing wood to a fine powder-like dust as they burrow through a board or other piece of wood.

One of the most widespread types of powder-post beetles is the *Lyctus* beetle. Although their activities are confined to hardwoods with pores large enough to receive the eggs, they operate over most of the United States. Woods commonly attacked by Lyctus beetles include oak, hickory, walnut, cherry, ash, and pecan.

As soon as the eggs deposited in the pores hatch, the larvae of the Lyctus beetle begin tunneling into the wood, packing the hole behind with the fine wood residue. The larvae, which look like small white worms, are responsible for all the excavating of the wood. They continue their destruction of the wood (sometimes for as long as a year) until they change into pupae, which in turn become adult beetles. The adult, a black beetle about 1/4 inch long, emerges from the wood, leaving a small hole from which the powdery residue falls when the wood is moved or shaken. Small piles of dust on or under a wood member are obvious indicators of powder-post beetles at work.

The adults often lay eggs in the same piece from which they emerged, thus multiplying greatly the number of larvae infesting a given piece of wood. The Lyctus larvae seek starch for food, most of which exists in wood in the parenchyma cells of the sapwood. For this reason, heartwood is rarely attacked by these beetles.

Lyctus beetles prefer dry wood, often infesting kiln-dried lumber, flooring, and furniture. Very dry wood, less than 6 or 7 percent moisture content, or wood wetter than 40 percent moisture content, is not suitable for their development.

Carpenter Ant

Although not as prevalent as termites and powder-post beetles, carpenter ants can, over a period of time, do considerable damage to wood. These brown or black ants prefer logs, stumps, or standing trees, but often attack posts and other wood in service. Carpenter ants usually enter wood from the ground, then excavate tunnels, both above and below the ground line, attacking the softer springwood first. The appearance of carpenter ant damage resembles that of termites, but they excavate wood for shelter only, not for food.

Marine Borers

Extensive damage is caused each year in wood wholly or partially submerged in salt water by several species of small marine animals called collectively, *marine borers.* Three genera of marine borers, *Teredo, Bankia,* and *Martesia,* belong to the *Molluscan* group which includes other mollusks such as clams and snails. Three other genera, *Limnoria, Sphaeroma,* and *Chelura,* fall into the *Crustacean* classification.

Teredo and *Bankia* are commonly called *shipworms* because of their wormlike appearance. These borers are the most damaging of the marine borers, and under favorable conditions can render an

FIG. 5–8. *A white oak pole heavily infested by powder-post beetles. Note that only the sapwood has been attacked.*

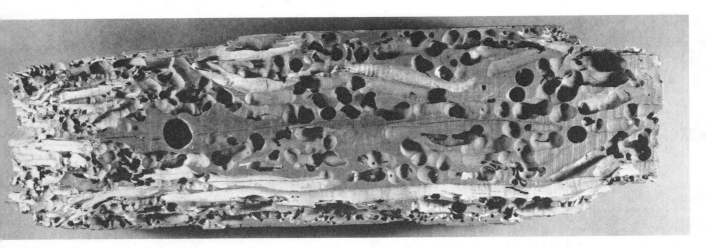

FIG. 5-9. *Damage to marine pilings caused by the marine borer, Teredo. (Courtesy of U.S. Forest Products Laboratory, Forest Service, U.S. Department of Agriculture.)*

eighteen-inch piling useless in a few months. Shipworm larvae enter wood from the water when they are still very small. As soon as they are attached to wood they begin burrowing into it, soon imprisoning themselves as their bodies enlarge. The posterior end of the shipworm remains at the entrance hole, where two tube-like siphons are extended into the water. The shipworm takes water in through one siphon and expels water and waste from the other.

Shipworms excavate wood for both food and shelter, although part of their sustenance is derived from the contents of the sea water. The burrow is carried toward the center of the log for a short distance,

FIG. 5-10. *Example of damage caused by the crustacean Limnoria. (Courtesy of Koppers Company, Inc.)*

then it follows an irregular path along the grain. The burrow is enlarged as the shipworm grows, usually to a diameter of 1/8 to 1/4 inch and a few inches long. However, under favorable conditions, shipworms have grown to an inch in diameter and a length of four feet.

Martesia borers resemble their relatives the clams in appearance, but their habit of attacking wood places them in the marine borer category as well. Their method of attack is similar to that of ship-worms, and they can wreak considerable destruction of wood under favorable conditions. *Martesia* are confined mainly to the coasts of the Gulf of Mexico and Hawaii.

Limnoria are the most destructive of the crustacean borers, and they are active in all the coastal waters of the United States. They are only 1/8 to 1/4 inch long, and their burrows do not penetrate deeply into the wood. They attack wood in such great numbers, however, that the surface layers are completely riddled and wear away under the action of waves and currents. *Limnoria* prefer to attack wood between the high- and low-tide levels, a practice which produces a characteristic hour-glass shape in infested poles.

Weathering of Wood

Unprotected wood exposed to the weather is affected in several ways by the forces of nature. Light, especially ultraviolet rays, very quickly causes noticeable color changes. Some wood turns darker at first, then fades to lighter shades. All wood, however, eventually weathers to a light gray. The gray layer is only a few thousandths of an inch thick, and immediately under it is found a brown layer. It is believed that the brown layer is at least partially due to the action of light on the lignin and extractive components of wood.

The action of wind, dust, and rain abrade and leach the broken-down lignin from the surface of the wood, leaving a mat of fibers. Constant changes in atmospheric conditions produce corresponding changes in the moisture content of exposed wood, especially the surface layer. The repeated shrinking and swelling accompanying moisture content changes loosens the fibers and eventually produce surface checks which in time extend deeply in the wood. Loosened fibers are gradually worn away by wind and rain, but this is a very slow process, and it is many years before an appreciable amount of the wood is disintegrated. Wood is often destroyed more quickly by "weathering" because the action of the elements is supplemented by the attack of soft-rot fungi.

Resources

Duncan, Catherine G. *Wood-Attacking Capacities and Physiology of Soft-rot Fungi.* Madison, Wisconsin: U.S. Forest Service, Forest Products Laboratory, 1960.

Duncan, Catherine G., and Frances F. Lomard. *Fungi Associated with Principal Decays in Wood Products in the United States.* U. S. Forest Service Research Paper WO-4. Washington, D.C.: Government Printing Office, 1965.

Hunt, George M., and George A. Garrett. *Wood Preservation.* New York: McGraw-Hill Book Company, 1967.

Panshin, A. J., and Carl DeZeeuw. *Textbook of Wood Technology,* Vol. I. New York: McGraw-Hill Book Company, 1970.

"Powder-Post Beetles in Buildings." U.S. Department of Agriculture, Leaflet No. 358. Washington, D.C., 1959.

Termite Control. Small Homes Council—Building Research Council Circular F 2-5. Champaign, Illinois: University of Illinois, 1963.

Tsoumis, George. *Wood as Raw Material.* New York: Pergamon Press, Inc. 1968.

Part Two

Wood Products

Chapter Six

The Wood Industry

Industry can be defined as the system by which raw materials are secured, converted to intermediate and finished products, and distributed to the consumer. The wood industry, therefore, is the enterprises in this system which are devoted to the securing, processing, and distribution of wood and wood products. In the broadest sense, this would include forestry and forest management, logging, sawmills, planing mills, veneer and plywood plants, wood composition board plants, paper mills, wooden container manufacturers, furniture plants, building construction, building materials wholesalers and retailers, and furniture stores. Such a wide range of enterprises and the diverse technology employed by them cannot be covered in a text of this scope. Instead, main emphasis will be placed on the intermediate and finished wood products—the processes used in their manufacture, their properties, and their main applications. The technology of the raw material, wood, has already been covered in some depth in the previous five chapters. Brief attention will be given to the means by which the raw material for the wood industry is provided, namely, the management of forests, and the harvesting of trees.

The purpose of this chapter is to provide an overview of the wood products industry, to give some insight into its nature and characteristics, and finally, to explore some of the present trends in the industry.

Composition of the Industry

If the idea regarding an industry as a system for changing raw material into products is pursued, the system can be analyzed as illustrated by the chart in figure 6–2. To oversimplify, this chart involves essentially three things—materials, processes, and products. A material, when processed, yields a product. This product can in turn become

FIG. 6–1. *Logs are the raw materials for the wood products industry. (Courtesy of Southern Forest Products Association.)*

the material which is further processed to yield another product, and so on. Such an analysis applied to the wood industry produces a chart with products grouped at two or three levels, according to the degree of manufacture.

Forests, when properly managed, furnish trees suitable for commercial uses. These trees are harvested to produce the element from which the great majority of wood products are derived—logs. Logs are processed in many ways to yield an array of *primary* or *intermediate* products. Most of these products are subsequently processed further to yield an even wider range of *secondary* products, some of which continue to yet another stage of manufacture, while some are sold to the consumer as finished products.

This analysis is not intended to be comprehensive, but rather illustrative, depicting the most important activities in which wood is the main, if not the only, object. It should be understood that wood as a raw material or as one of the many products shown enters into the manufacture of many other products in combination with other materials. Obviously, these activities are not included in the chart. Likewise, all products made of wood are not represented. If every specialized item such as pencils, toothpicks, and matches were included, the analysis would be unnecessarily complicated.

The Nature and Characteristics of the Industry

The enterprises that compose the wood products industry are many in number and varied in character. The industry as a whole is made up of a great many small firms, several medium-sized industries, but

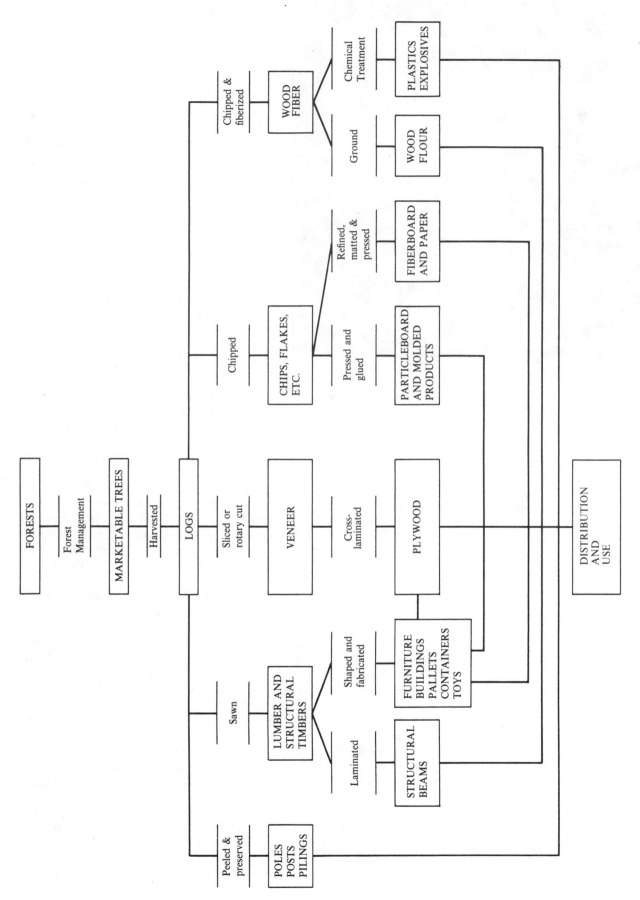

FIG. 6–2. *Composition of the wood industry.*

FIG. 6–3. *This piece of furniture is an example of a secondary product nearing the end of the manufacturing process. (Courtesy of Thomasville Furniture Industries, Inc.)*

hardly any that could be termed very large or "giant" corporations. Although the U.S. Department of Commerce Publication "Industry Profiles" (Bureau of Domestic Commerce, 1971) ranked several wood products industries among the one hundred largest industries in 1969, each industry was composed of many small or middle-sized companies rather than a few large corporations. The extent of the fragmentation in the wood industry is illustrated by a comparison between it and the automobile industry. According to the same publication mentioned above, in 1969 the automobile industry employed about three hundred thousand *more* workers than the wood products industry, but the wood products industry was composed of *fourteen times as many* establishments as the automobile industry. The average number of employees per factory in the automobile industry was 316, but only 15 in the wood products industry.

As might be expected in an industry made up mainly of small segments, the technology being applied in the wood products industry is somewhat behind that of other industries, and while a fairly high degree of mechanization is common, automation is not widespread. This is not due entirely to the size of the firms, however, but also to the nature of the activities. The manufacture of furniture, for instance, does not lend itself to a high degree of automation. The production of certain components could doubtlessly be automated, but the final assembly and finishing operations are much more difficult to mechanize.

Despite the smallness of individual enterprises, the wood products industry as a whole ranks as one of the largest manufacturing industry groups in terms of the number of workers employed. The "lumber and wood products" group as classified by the *Standard Industrial Classification Manual* (Office of Management and Budget, 1972) falls in the lower half of the twenty-one manufacturing industry groups, but this classification includes neither wood furniture and fixtures nor paper and paper products. When these are considered, the wood industry group becomes the fifth largest manufacturing industry in the United

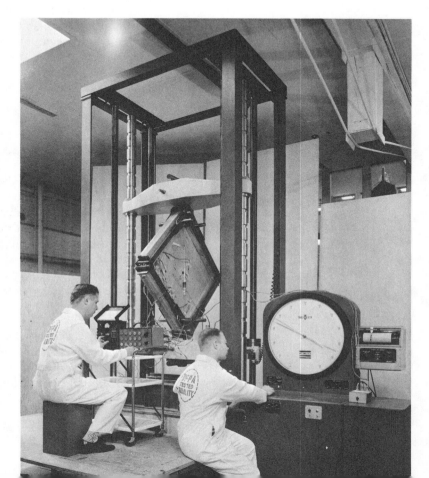

States. In 1969 these industries employed almost a million and a half workers. Add to this the tens of thousands employed in forest management, harvesting, construction, and the transporting and marketing of wood, and the importance of wood and the industry fostered by it becomes very apparent.

Within the industry, the largest user of wood is construction, which consumes about three-fourths of all lumber and plywood produced in the United States, as well as large quantities of other wood products such as building board, particleboard, and other panel products. The paper and paper products industry is next in size, consuming 34 percent of the total roundwood production in 1970. Other manufacturing industries including furniture, pallet and wooden containers, and other fabricated products use over 4.6 billion board feet of lumber annually (*U.S. Forest Resource Inventory Statistics,* 1972). Of these the furniture industry is the largest single consumer of lumber.

The Future of the Wood Industry

The small size and independent nature of wood product industries have been major handicaps in the technological race to develop new products and processes. Larger corporations in other fields have budgeted huge sums of money and employed specialized staff for research and development for many years. The results of these efforts have been a proliferation of new consumer and industrial products, as well as a tremendously improved technology in processing and fabricating techniques. Smaller firms in the wood products industry could not afford costly research and development programs, and by the late 1950s, wood products were encountering increasingly severe competition from plastics, metals, and related materials. Under this pressure, the larger wood products industries were forced to invest in research

FIG. 6–4. *Research activities are becoming increasingly important to the wood industry. (Courtesy of American Plywood Association.)*

and development, while smaller ones sought to better utilize the technology already available as well as the results of the research undertaken by larger companies, the U.S. Forest Products Laboratory, and other agencies.

During the sixties, great strides were made by the wood products industry in the development and promotion of new products and processes, despite the nature of the industry and the declining quality of raw materials. While the industry as a whole is still handicapped to some extent by the size and backwardness of many individual enterprises, more and more corporations are emerging which are of sufficient size to support ongoing research programs.

The progress made during the sixties and early seventies indicates that the wood products industry is well on its way to satisfying the demands of a more discriminating consumer and countering the inroads made by competitive materials. A brief look at some of the most promising developments in the industry should provide some perspective of the future of wood and the wood products industry.

Wood products research has already yielded many dividends for the industry and should continue to do so in the future. In general, the future will see wood being used in more and more forms other than its natural state. The beauty of natural wood color and grain pattern will insure its continued use in that form for many purposes, but in view of the declining quality of veneer- and sawlog-size trees, it seems likely that more and more wood will be utilized for products which are less wasteful of the resource. This does not mean that the use of wood in the form of lumber will fall drastically overnight, but that products such as plywood, particleboard, hardboard, and others not even discovered yet will gradually take over for many applications.

Per capita consumption of lumber in the United States began leveling off in the forties, and declined steadily throughout the following two decades. Consumption of veneer and plywood on the other hand, has increased quite sharply and continuously since 1940. While the total amount of lumber consumed has increased, its share of the market has declined, reflecting the gains made by plywood and other products.

Another factor in the decline in the use of wood in its natural state is the present and probable future need for "engineered" wood products. In order to qualify as such a material, wood must be broken down into small units such as chips, flakes, or fibers and then reassembled in larger pieces. This allows considerable control of the properties of the product, a condition essential for many engineering purposes.

Emphasis on pollution control and the conservation of resources has already prompted much research in the wood industry, and the results are just beginning to be used. One result has been the increased use of residues by the wood composition board and paper industries. As much as 90 to 95 percent of all particleboard produced in this country is now made of wood residues from sawmills, planing mills, plywood plants, and other wood users. Some sawmills are now using a chipper in combination with the headsaw to produce valuable chips instead of sawdust and slabs. The logs are cut into square cants by passing them across the chipper, immediately reducing the wood that would normally become slabs to relatively high-quality chips. The square cant is then sawed into boards as usual. The amount of sawdust, a relatively poor quality residue, is further reduced by the use of a thinner high-tension band headsaw.

Utilization of the tremendous volumes of bark produced by sawmills each year is under intensive study, and it is expected that new products composed partly or wholly of bark will soon be available. Bark is now used for agricultural and decorative mulches, and to a limited extent in the manufacture of wood composition board, but these uses consume a relatively small percentage of the total bark residue available.

A great number of new and different wood products have been developed, and more are being marketed each year. Many of these products are composites, wood combined with some other material, such as plastic, metal, or paper. Plastic-impregnated wood is now being used for flooring and speciality products, and great quantities of plastic are being used in furniture in the form of moldings, plastic laminates, and vinyl films. New adhesives have made possible the bonding of wood and other materials. A thin sheet of metal adds considerable strength and stiffness to a sheet of plywood or composition board. Low-quality or unattractive woods are being overlaid with vinyl films or resin-impregnated paper to produce a very uniform surface better suited for painting, grain printing, or other finishing processes.

The wood products industry will continue to face a challenge as it seeks to maintain or improve its position in this country. The social, economic, and technical limitations affecting any industry's development will be an ever-present obstacle, but with some foresight and the kind of energetic development that has characterized the industry in recent years, wood products should retain their popularity and importance to both industry and consumers.

Resources

Bureau of Domestic Commerce, U.S. Department of Commerce. *Industry Profiles 1958–1969.* Washington, D.C.: Government Printing Office, 1971.

Fleischer, H. O. "The Impact of Utilization Research on the Complete Use of the Forest." *Wood Science and Technology* 5 (1971): 247–54.

————. "Systems Research Sharpens Woodworking Technology," *Woodworking Furniture Digest* 63 (1971): 32.

Hair, Dwight, and L. E. Lassen. "Potential Gains in Wood Supplies through Improved Technology." *Journal of Forestry* 68 (1970): 404–7.

Marra, George C. "The Future of Wood as an Engineered Material." *Forest Products Journal* 22 (1972): 43–51.

Office of Management and Budget, Statistical Policy Division. *Standard Industrial Classification Manual.* Washington, D.C.: Government Printing Office, 1972.

U.S. Forest Resource Inventory Statistics, Preliminary Data. Washington, D.C.: U.S. Forest Service, 1972.

Chapter Seven

Growing and Harvesting Timber

Any manufacturing industry is dependent upon raw materials which can be processed and converted into useful products. In the case of the wood products industry, the raw material is wood, and the source of supply is the forest. As has been stated before, wood is a renewable resource, because forests will reproduce themselves, as they have been doing for centuries. The natural process of reproduction, however, is very slow and does not always produce the best kind or quality of trees. In order to insure that high-quality wood is available in the quantities demanded by our society, forests must be carefully managed, and the harvests must be controlled. This is the job of forestry.

When this country was first settled, and for many years thereafter, the forests seemed limitless. At first they were obstacles to progress, and there were more reasons to remove them than to leave them growing. The land was needed for agriculture, clearings were needed for buildings, and the forests offered protection for Indians and dangerous animals. Some wood was used for buildings, ships, and fuel, but untold quantities were simply burned to get rid of it. As the colonies were established and the population of the new land increased, greater and greater demands were made for timber, and soon the settlers, axes in hand, were pushing the frontier westward.

The philosophy of the early loggers was simple—when the supply of trees in one area was depleted, move on. Logging was regarded in

The Development of Forestry in the United States

FIG. 7–1. *This redwood forest is typical of the virgin forests encountered by the early settlers of this country. (Courtesy of California Redwood Association.)*

much the same light as mining, and it was not expected that an area once logged would ever bear another crop of trees, at least not in their lifetime, and they were not concerned about the future generations. With this idea prevailing, the great forest areas of the United States were successively logged (perhaps "mined" would be a better term) out. The Northeastern forest went first, then the Northern, or lake states area, then the South, and finally, in the first half of the nineteenth century, the Western forest began to fall to the lumberman's saw.

As this last forest frontier was reached, however, it gradually became apparent that if such exploitation continued unchecked, America would eventually be without a native supply of wood. Forestry in this country was practically nonexistent at that time, however, and an awareness of the problem did little to solve it because hardly anyone knew what to do. Finally, by the 1900s, public concern for the forests became so great that it demanded that something be done. One response by the government to this pressure was to establish several national forests where proper forestry could be practiced. Also, forestry had been practiced in Europe for many years by this time, and

FIG. 7–2. *An impressive stand of second-growth southern pine. (Courtesy of U.S. Forest Service, Southern Forest Experiment Station.)*

the techniques used there were gradually being promoted and accepted in this country. Still another factor which helped cause a change of attitude toward forests was that second-growth stands of timber were reaching merchantable size by 1920, especially those in the South which had sprung up in cottonfields abandoned following the Civil War. Here was proof that, even without management, successive crops of trees could be grown on the same land. Since it was even more obvious now that the virgin forests of the West would not long supply the demands of a burgeoning population, the promise of forestry to shorten the natural reproduction period of a forest as well as to upgrade the quality of trees became more acceptable, even to lumbermen.

What, then, is forestry, and what does it do? Without getting into the multiplicity of elements involved in the practice of forestry, it may be defined in principle as the management of forests to insure maximum benefit to mankind. While the continuous production of timber products is generally the main objective, secondary benefits such as recreation, wildlife protection, and watershed maintenance are almost always involved. In the practice of forestry, trees are regarded as a crop, much like any agricultural effort. Obviously, an important difference when growing trees is the length of time between "planting" and harvesting. Trees seldom reach a useful size before thirty years of age, and most require from fifty to one hundred years. Another problem encountered by foresters is the multiple use of forests. Which should receive priority: production of lumber and other timber products, protection of wildlife, preserving scenic natural beauty, or any of several other possibilities? Fortunately, all of these uses are not mutually exclusive, and timber production can often be carried on while a watershed is maintained, cover is provided for wildlife, and opportunities for recreation are also made available. On the other hand, certain situations arise where two or more possible uses conflict, and a choice must be made. An example of such a choice is the establishment of national parks and other areas where forests are to be left forever in their natural state. Although these forests are not producing tangible benefits to man, they are invaluable examples of our natural heritage. The beauty, serenity, and solitude found among the ancient giants of a virgin forest are prizes sought by more and more people in this frenetic society. It would be disastrous to our economy if too much of our forest land were restricted in this way, but there is a very definite need for some forests of this type.

With our haphazard methods of the past, forests were logged once for the maximum yield at the time, then abandoned for long periods (fifty to seventy-five years) until a second-growth stand of timber had become merchantable. It has been demonstrated that through proper management, forests can be *continuously* productive, without long lapses between harvests. This allows a forest products enterprise to remain in one location near a forest rather than move from place to place as the timber supply is exhausted. Continuous productivity is probably the greatest incentive forestry may offer most forest owners, and it is very likely the best hope we have of maintaining our supply of wood.

Silvicultural Practices

The cultivation of timber as a crop is necessary to assure continuous production of timber products and continuous reproduction of the forest. A branch of forestry called *silviculture* deals with all the factors which affect the growth of trees, especially the methods of cutting which promote, rather than hinder, the rapid reproduction of the forest. Several distinct cutting methods used in managed forests are discussed below, but it should be understood that they are often used in combination and it is not always obvious to the untrained observer which method is being employed.

Two general types of cuttings are made in managed forests: cutting to improve the stand, and cutting for harvest. *Intermediate cuttings,* made before the main harvest to improve the stand, are made for several reasons. When a young stand of timber becomes too crowded, *thinning* may be necessary to provide enough growing space for the remaining trees. Trees removed in thinning may be large enough to be sold for pulpwood or posts. In a forest with an overabundance of large bushy-topped trees, *liberation* cuttings are made to allow the younger trees room to grow properly. This cutting sometimes provides marketable logs. Cuttings which are made to remove diseased or damaged trees are called *sanitation* or *salvage* cuttings, respectively.

Four types of harvest cuttings are commonly employed in silviculture, each having advantages in different situations. The *clear-cutting* method is used when all the trees in a stand are the same age and have reached merchantable size, or when reforestation is planned following the harvest. Clear-cutting is almost always followed by reseeding or planting of new stock, since all timber is removed. If reseeding is to be done by natural means, relatively small patches or strips are clearcut so that the adjacent remaining trees can reseed the cutover areas (see fig. 7–3). On the other hand, if artificial reseeding or planting is to be done, larger areas can be clear-cut.

Clear-cutting has several advantages, not the least of which is that the method makes logging easier and more economical, especially if the operation is highly mechanized, as many are now. Large harvesting equipment can be used only to a limited extent if it is necessary to take only certain trees while leaving others to grow. Other advantages of the method are (1) growing stock which is not being harvested is not damaged, (2) new seedlings on the cutover area are not in competition with older trees for light, water, and food, and (3) wildlife increases because during the early years of reforestation, the clear-cut areas provide food plants for deer and other animals which would not inhabit the old forest.

Some of the disadvantages of the clear-cutting system are (1) natural reproduction is not always successful, and costly artificial planting is necessary to re-establish the forest, (2) the large quantities of limbs, tops, and other debris (called *slash*) left increases the fire hazard, (3) sudden removal of tree cover from the ground causes several prob-

FIG. 7–3. *Clear-cut areas in a second-growth western forest. (Courtesy of Weyerhauser Company.)*

FIG. 7–4. *Use of shelterwood cutting in a Michigan hemlock-hardwood stand. (Courtesy of U.S. Forest Service.)*

lems, including erosion, and (4) the clear-cut area is very unsightly, often ruining for a few years the scenic beauty of the forest land.

Clear-cutting has been severely criticized by conservationists and others concerned about our forests, and in many instances the criticism seems warranted, because the system has caused irreparable damage in some areas of the country. In most cases, however, damage results when the system is not used in appropriate places, or when it is used improperly. Failure to begin reforestation immediately upon completion of the cut, for example, will allow the area to erode, especially on steeper slopes.

A modification of the clear-cutting method is the *seed-tree* system, whereby about one-tenth of the trees on a given plot are left to reseed the area. The trees left are picked for their seed-bearing capability, wind resistance, and general strength. This method is useful only with species which bear large quantities of seeds, and can thrive in full sunlight.

Another type of cutting called the *shelterwood* system is often used when the seedlings of the species need partial shade and shelter in their early development. When this system is used, total removal of all merchantable trees requires several cuttings, with enough time between cuttings for reproduction to become established. The first cutting removes a relatively small percentage of the timber. When a good crop of seeds has been released and seedlings are established, a heavier cutting is made, but enough timber is left to provide additional seeds and continued shelter for the cutover areas. Final removal cutting of the original timber may not be completed until ten or twenty years after the first cutting.

The *selection* system of cutting is less traumatic to the life of the forest and less damaging to its appearance than any of the other systems. Selection cutting is an appropriate method to use on a forest containing trees of all ages, such as farm woodlots. As the name indicates, trees are selected to be cut on the basis of their size, age, and their benefit or detriment to the remaining timber. When the system is applied to an existing forest, the first cuttings may be sort of a "clean-up" operation, removing mainly diseased and damaged trees. Subsequent cuttings may also remove such trees, but their main purpose would be the harvest of profitable timber. Harvest cuttings may be scheduled at periodic intervals of five to ten years, and if only the older trees are removed each time, the younger trees remaining grow faster. Properly carried out, the selection system allows a forest to be continuously productive and profitable to the owner for an indefinite length of time.

FIG. 7–5. *Nurseries such as this provide millions of seedlings each year to renew our forests. (Courtesy of Weyerhauser Company.)*

As has been mentioned, the main purpose of forestry is the continuous production of timber products, so in one sense, harvesting is the focus of these efforts. A tree is of little use to a wood products manufacturer

Harvesting Trees

FIG. 7–6. *One logger's chain saw bites out the backcut while the other hammers a wedge to relieve pressure on the saw. (Courtesy of Weyerhauser Company.)*

FIG. 7–7. *A multipurpose machine, shown here shearing a tree off near ground level. Trees up to eighteen inches in diameter are snipped in this manner. (Courtesy of Weyerhauser Company.)*

until it is cut down, trimmed of branches, and reduced to sizes suitable for sawing, slicing, or chipping. Harvesting timber, or logging, thus becomes the initial step in the processing of the raw material wood into wood products.

The techniques and methods of timber harvesting are many and varied, and could easily be the subject for an entire book. The basic activities of harvesting are generally the same, however, no matter what means are employed to complete the task. The basic operations are (1) felling the trees, (2) trimming, (3) bucking, (4) skidding, (5) bunching or piling, and (6) transporting.

Cutting the tree down, or *felling,* is the first of the logging operations. In former years, the ax and crosscut saw were the primary tools used for felling trees, but the power chain saw has completely replaced the handsaw, and to some extent the ax as well. Once a tree is down, the next two operations follow each other closely as the branches and top are *trimmed* from the tree and the trunk is *bucked* or sawed into the desired lengths. Once again, the power saw has to a great extent replaced the hand tools formerly used for this purpose.

Moving logs from the cutting site to an intermediate storage yard or pickup point is called *skidding.* This was originally done mostly by horses and oxen, but first steam and then gasoline and diesel tractors replaced the slower animals. Logs are moved by either direct tractor skidding or by cable skidding. In the first case, a tractor, often

FIG. 7–8. *Tree snipped and trimmed (top) is then bucked and loaded by the same machine (bottom). (Photos courtesy of International Paper Company, Southern Kraft Division.)*

with a bulldozer blade mounted in front, simply drags the logs from where the tree was cut to the yard. Cable skidding, on the other hand, makes use of a stationary engine and winch plus a long cable which is attached to the logs. Whenever all the logs within reach of the cable have been brought in, the apparatus is moved to another location and the process is repeated. *Bunching* and *piling* are intermediate steps in the movement of logs from the forest. Logs are bunched, or gathered into small stacks, to make a load for the tractors doing the skidding. Piling is the collection and arrangement of the logs at the loading point. Modern mechanical equipment has greatly speeded up this laborious phase of the logging operation.

The final step in the timber harvest is the transportation of logs from the forest to the mill. Transportation by water, including driving, rafting, and other means was at one time the method most widely used, and is still employed in parts of Canada. Land transportation, by railroad first, then by truck, has replaced water transportation. The adaptability and mobility of trucks make them the most popular means of log transportation in most parts of the United States.

Harvesting timber is not a single operation, but rather a complicated process involving many men, machines, and a variety of individual operations. It is interesting to note, however, that modern methods of harvesting emphasize the consolidation and integration of the activities as much as possible. The extensive mechanization of logging has expedited this consolidation. Whenever feasible, mechanical equipment is used for two or more operations rather than a single function; for instance, the tractor in figure 7–7 is used not only for cutting but also for skidding. In pulpwood operations, single machines are now performing the functions of cutting, trimming, topping, bucking, and loading (see fig. 7–8). With such devices, the harvesting of timber approaches the efficiency of other agricultural harvests.

Resources

Allen, Shirley Walter, and Grant William Sharpe. *An Introduction to American Forestry.* New York: McGraw-Hill Book Company, 1960.

Anderson, David A., and William A. Smith. *Forests and Forestry.* Danville, Illinois: The Interstate Printers and Publishers, Inc., 1970.

Wackerman, A. E., W. D. Hagenstein, and A. S. Michel. *Harvesting Timber Crops.* New York: McGraw-Hill Book Company, 1966.

Chapter Eight

Lumber

Of the many types of wood products available today, lumber is by far the most familiar. In fact, the very word "wood" is synonymous with lumber in most peoples' minds, and no wonder, because more wood is made into lumber than into any other product. In recent years, plywood and other panel products have made inroads into the lumber market, but the versatility of lumber guarantees it a very large share of the market for many years to come.

The three main activities associated with lumber production are sawing, grading, and seasoning. Each of these is covered in some detail in this chapter.

Sawing Lumber

Lumber may be sawn from a log by either of two methods, flat sawing (also called plain sawing) and quarter sawing (also called radial sawing). Flat sawn lumber is produced by making cuts tangent to the growth rings, while quarter sawn lumber is cut across the growth rings. Figure 8–1 illustrates both plain and quarter sawing techniques and the appearance of the lumber in each case. The grain pattern of the flat sawn lumber is probably more familiar, because most lumber is sawn in this manner. Notice that when a board is cut tangent to the growth rings, a cross section is made of the rays, which then appear (if large enough to be visible) as short vertical lines. The cut for quarter sawing, on the other hand, is more nearly parallel to the rays, which causes them to appear as characteristic "flecks."

Flat sawn lumber can often be cut from a log faster than quartered lumber, and an attractive grain pattern is produced, but the orientation of the growth rings causes it to be susceptible to warping as well as considerable shrinking across the width of the board. Quarter sawn

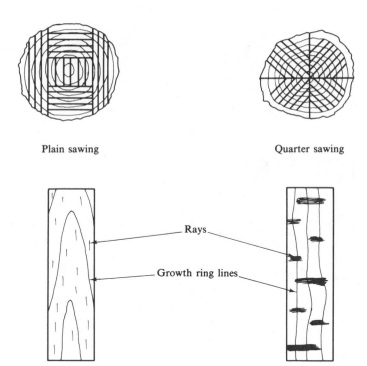

FIG. 8–1. *Methods of sawing lumber.*

lumber is somewhat more difficult to saw, and lower yield is obtained from a log, but it has less tendency to warp. Also, quarter sawing produces a distinctive grain pattern in woods with large rays.

The process of converting logs into lumber involves a considerable layout of facilities and equipment, most of which are included in a sawmill. Sawmills vary greatly in size and complexity, from small units equipped with little more than an engine and a saw, to huge operations utilizing hundreds of thousands of dollars worth of equipment. The schematic in figure 8–2 illustrates a fully-equipped, medium-size sawmill. Smaller mills would not include everything shown, while larger ones might have considerably more equipment. The main parts of the sawmill are discussed individually below.

Log Storage

Logs arriving at the sawmill from the forest must be stored until they can be sawn into lumber. Those arriving by water are usually stored in a pond or simply held in place on the river or bay by a log boom, a "chain" of logs fastened together surrounding loose logs. Water storage facilitates sorting of the logs and greatly reduces damage due to end-checking and insect attacks. Only lighter woods, mainly softwoods, are usually stored in water, and even those become saturated and sink after an extended period of time. Logs transported to the mill by land may be stored in water or simply piled in a yard. Open-air storage is often the simplest method, but in certain areas, the logs must be sprayed with insecticides and fugicides to prevent attacks by insects and decay. Also, it is necessary to coat the ends of the logs to prevent too-rapid water loss and resultant end-checking.

Barking

From the storage area, logs are delivered to the mill proper by some type of conveyor arrangement or cable lift. The first operation on the logs is usually the removal of bark, which is done for two reasons.

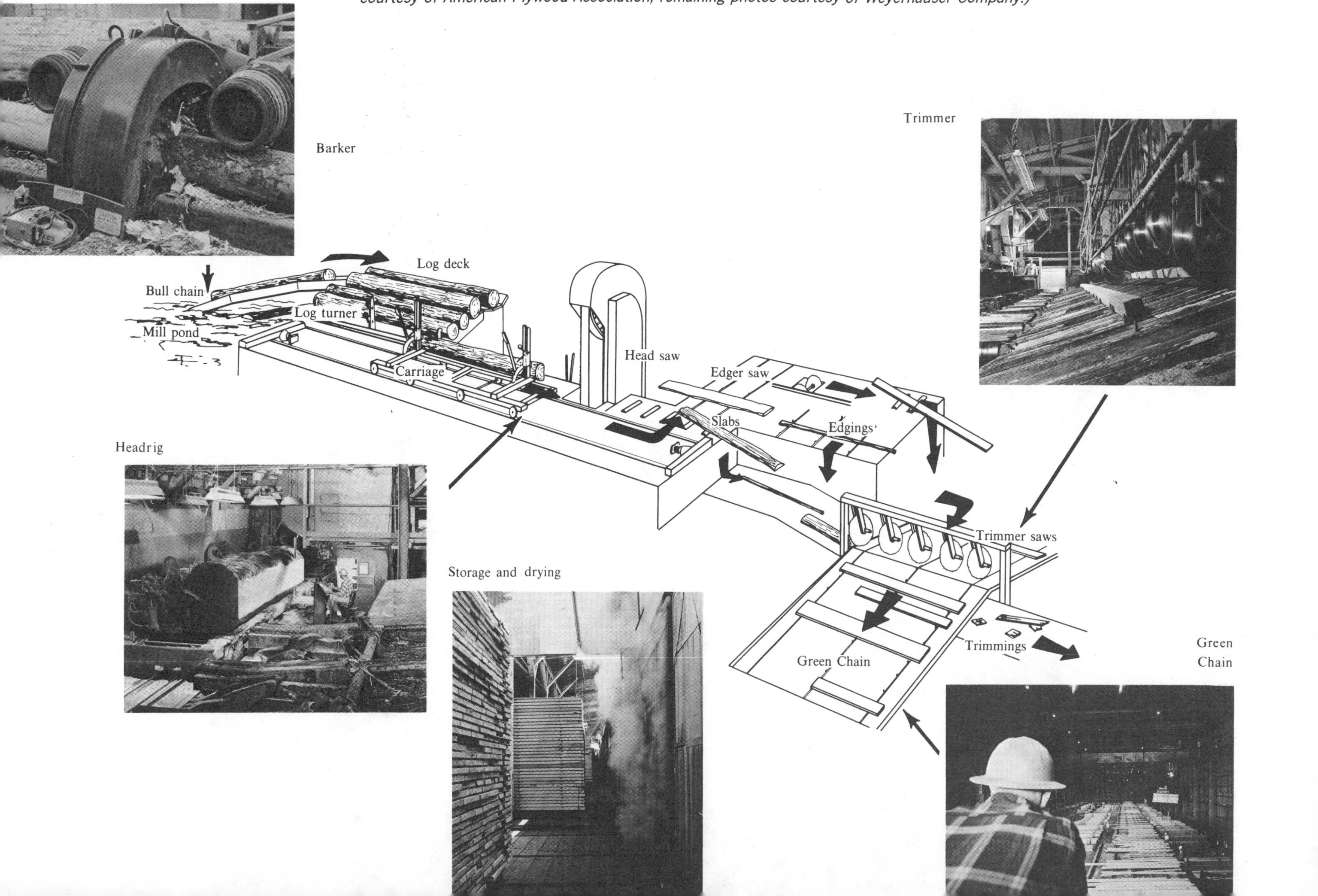

FIG. 8-2. Lumber manufacture at a typical sawmill. (Drawing courtesy of American Forest Institute, barker photo courtesy of American Plywood Association, remaining photos courtesy of Weyerhauser Company.)

Barker

Trimmer

Green Chain

Trimmer saws

Trimmings

Edgings

Green Chain

Edger saw

Slabs

Head saw

Storage and drying

Log deck

Carriage

Log turner

Headrig

Bull chain

Mill pond

First, the bark usually collects dirt and abrasive grit which increases the wear on saw blades. Second, the emphasis on bark utilization in recent years has made it more profitable to separate the bark from the wood. All mills, however, do not remove the bark before sawing, especially if large logs are being sawn.

There are three basic types of barkers in use, each employing a different means of removing bark. One type literally beats the bark from the logs with swinging hammers or chains as the logs pass through the machine. Other machines remove the bark by a peeling or shaving action. This type often removes a small amount of the wood at high points under the bark. A third kind of barker removes bark by means of very high-pressure jets of water which blast the bark loose.

FIG. 8–3. *Hydraulic barker, using pressures up to 1500 pounds, removes bark from logs. (Courtesy of Weyerhauser Company.)*

Log Breakdown

Logs from the barker are placed on the *log deck* from whence they are loaded one at a time on the *carriage*. The function of the carriage is to hold the log and carry it past the headsaw which cuts it into boards. The carriage travels on tracks past the headsaw and has devices not only for holding, but also for positioning the log so that one board of the correct thickness is cut from the log each time it passes the headsaw.

The heart of the sawmill is the *headsaw,* of which there are three general types: circular saws, band saws, and gang saws. The circular saw preceded the band saw in the development of sawmills, and it is still widely used in smaller operations. The main disadvantages of the circular headsaw are the limited size of logs which can be sawn and the considerable waste due to the wide kerf made by the saw teeth. Both of these problems are reduced by the band headsaw, and for this reason it is used by most large modern sawmills.

Gang saws are employed by many sawmills because they can reduce a log to lumber much faster than a single blade headsaw. While a single headsaw removes only one board at each pass of the carriage, the gang saw cuts the whole log into boards at one pass. *Circular gang saws* are similar to regular circular headsaws, except that several saw blades are mounted on one shaft and spaced the proper distance apart for the size of lumber being sawn. The spacing between blades can be varied from one inch to two inches, or to whatever thickness is desired. *Sash gang saws* consist of a large rectangular frame holding many straight removable blades in a vertical position. The whole sash moves with a reciprocating motion to saw the logs passing through it. All gang saws have one disadvantage in common: the log cannot be turned between the sawing of individual boards to allow selection of the best face and hence the highest quality lumber. Thus, a higher percentage of lower grades would be produced by a gang-saw mill.

A recent innovation in sawing logs is the use of the *chipping headrig.* Chippers have been used at sawmills for several years to produce chips for pulping and other purposes, but only to convert slabs and edgings produced by a regular headsaw. The chipping headrig, however, produces chips by converting a round log to a square cant directly, thus eliminating both slabbing and edging by normal means, and their accompanying sawdust wastage. The square cant can then be sawed into lumber by any of the common headsaws.

A chipping headrig operates as a planer with a segmented cutterhead or as an end mill (fig. 8–4). Different types of chips are produced by the different cutters, and the size of the chips can be controlled by varying the cutter and feed speeds.

FIG. 8–4. *Chipping headrig in operation. Inset shows chipper cutterhead. (Courtesy of Stetson-Ross Machine Company, Inc.)*

Boards coming off the head saw pass through two more saws, usually in quick succession. The *edger,* consisting of two circular saws, rips the edges from the boards to produce straight, parallel edges. The *trimmer,* which may be only two saws or as many as twenty, cuts the ends of the boards square, and trims them to the desired length. Defects may also be removed at the trimmer to upgrade the board.

As lumber leaves the trimmer, it is sorted according to size (thickness) and grade and sent to the dry kiln or air-drying yard for seasoning.

Classification and Grading of Lumber

Lumber is a most versatile material, adapted to a multitude of uses and applications which place different requirements of size, shape, and quality on the product. In order to meet the many different requirements satisfactorily, it has been necessary to classify lumber into groups according to those factors. The term *lumber grading* is generally used to describe this division into groups, but in actuality, the system of grouping by size and shape is a *classification* process, while *grading* is the separation of lumber of varying quality within individual groups. These smaller divisions based on quality then become *grades.* Lumber is priced, sold, and used according to the various grades assigned to the different quality groups.

Since lumber grades are so closely related to the use of the material, softwoods and hardwoods are graded by different systems. The great bulk of softwood lumber is used in fairly large pieces, while hardwood lumber is generally cut into smaller pieces before it is used. The classification and grading systems reflect this basic difference in uses of the two types.

Softwood Lumber Classification and Grading

The formation of lumber grading rules in this country has, for the most part, been left to associations of lumber manufacturers. Over the years, these associations produced a great deal of uniformity in the sizes and grades of lumber, making it possible for the consumer to secure boards of identical size and fairly uniform quality from widely separated sources. There remained, however, a considerable number of differences among the grading rules of the different associations, and these discrepancies became more acute as the applications of wood multiplied, especially for engineered structural applications. In the interest of standardizing practices in lumber grading at a national, rather than a regional, level, several efforts to formulate a national lumber standard were made over the years. The current American Softwood Lumber Standard (U.S. Department of Commerce) is a product standard (PS 20-70) issued in 1970, and it has had much influence in the standardization of grading policies. The standard specifies size, grade, and inspection guidelines, and while subscription to it is voluntary, most companies and associations find it to their benefit to pattern their grading practices after the guidelines set forth in the standard.

The softwood lumber standard classifies lumber according to use, degree of manufacture, and size, as follows:

Use Classification

1. *Yard lumber*—Lumber of those grades, sizes, and patterns which is generally intended for ordinary construction and general building purposes.

2. *Structural lumber*—Lumber that is two or more inches in nominal thickness and width for use where working stresses are required.

3. *Factory and shop lumber*—Lumber that is produced or selected primarily for remanufacturing purposes.

Manufacturing Classification

1. *Rough lumber*—Lumber which has not been dressed (surfaced) but which has been sawed, edged, and trimmed at least to the extent of showing saw marks in the wood on the four longitudinal surfaces of each piece for its overall length.

2. *Dressed (Surfaced) lumber*—Lumber that has been dressed by a planing machine (for the purpose of attaining smoothness of surface and uniformity of size) on one side (S1S), two sides (S2S), one edge (S1E), two edges (S2E), or a combination of sides and edges (S1S1E, S1S2E, S2S2E, S4S).

3. *Worked lumber*—Lumber which, in addition to being dressed, has been matched, shiplapped, or patterned.

    a. *Matched lumber*—Lumber that has been worked with a tongue on one edge of each piece and a groove on the opposite edge to provide a close tongue-and-groove joint by fitting two pieces together; when end-matched, the tongue and groove are worked in the ends also.

    b. *Shiplapped lumber*—Lumber that has been worked or rabbeted on both edges of each piece to provide a close-lapped joint by fitting two pieces together.

    c. *Patterned lumber*—Lumber that is shaped to a pattern or to a molded form, in addition to being dressed, matched, or shiplapped, or any combination of these workings.

Size Classification

1. *Nominal Size*

    a. *Boards*—Lumber less than 2 inches in nominal thickness and 2 inches or more in nominal width. Boards less than 6 inches in nominal width may be classified as strips.

    b. *Dimension*—Lumber from 2 inches to, but not including, 5 inches in nominal thickness, and 2 or more inches in nominal width. Dimension may be classified as framing, joists, planks, rafters, studs, small timber, etc.

    c. *Timbers*—Lumber 5 or more inches nominally in least dimension. Timber may be classified as beams, stringers, posts, caps, sills, girders, purlins, etc.

2. *Roughdry size*—The minimum roughdry thickness of finish, common boards, and dimensions of size 1 or more inches in nominal thickness shall not be less than 1/8 thicker than the corresponding minimum finished dry thickness, except that 20 percent of a shipment may be not less than 2/32 inch thicker than the corresponding minimum-finished dry thickness. The minimum roughdry widths of finish, common strip, boards, and dimension shall be not less than 1/8 inch wider than the corresponding minimum-finished dry width.

3. *Dressed sizes*—Dressed sizes of lumber shall equal or exceed the minimum sizes shown in Tables 1, 2, 3, 4, and 5. [Table 3 is reproduced below as table 8–1.]

TABLE 8–1

Nominal and Minimum-Dressed Sizes of Boards, Dimension, and Timbers

(The thicknesses apply to all widths and all widths to all thicknesses)

ITEM	THICKNESSES			FACE WIDTHS		
		Minimum Dressed			Minimum Dressed	
	Nominal	Dry[1] Inches	Green[1] Inches	Nominal	Dry[1] Inches	Green[1] Inches
Boards[2]	1	3/4	25/32	2	1-1/2	1-9/16
				3	2-1/2	2-9/16
				4	3-1/2	3-9/16
				5	4-1/2	4-5/8
				6	5-1/2	5-5/8
				7	6-1/2	6-5/8
	1-1/4	1	1-1/32	8	7-1/4	7-1/2
				9	8-1/4	8-1/2
	1-1/2	1-1/4	1-9/32	10	9-1/4	9-1/2
				11	10-1/4	10-1/2
				12	11-1/4	11-1/2
				14	13-1/4	13-1/2
				16	15-1/4	15-1/2
Dimension	2	1-1/2	1-9/16	2	1-1/2	1-9/16
	2-1/2	2	2-1/16	3	2-1/2	2-9/16
	3	2-1/2	2-9/16	4	3-1/2	3-9/16
	3-1/2	3	3-1/16	5	4-1/2	4-5/8
				6	5-1/2	5-5/8
				8	7-1/4	7-1/2
				10	9-1/4	9-1/2
				12	11-1/4	11-1/2
				14	13-1/4	13-1/2
				16	15-1/4	15-1/2
Dimension	4	3-1/2	3-9/16	2	1-1/2	1-9/16
	4-1/2	4	4-1/16	3	2-1/2	2-9/16
				4	3-1/2	3-9/16
				5	4-1/2	4-5/8
				6	5-1/2	5-5/8
				8	7-1/4	7-1/2
				10	9-1/4	9-1/2
				12	11-1/4	11-1/2
				14		13-1/2
				16		15-1/2
Timbers	5 & Thicker		1/2 Off	5 & Wider		1/2 Off

SOURCE: United States Department of Commerce, National Bureau of Standards, American Softwood Lumber Standard: *NBS Voluntary Product Standard PS 20–70* (Washington, D.C.: Government Printing Office, 1970).

[1] See 3.4.1 and 3.4.2 [of source] for the definitions of dry and green lumber.

[2] Boards less than the minimum thickness for 1 inch nominal but 5/8 inch or greater thickness dry (11/16 inch green) may be regarded as American Standard Lumber, but such boards shall be marked to show the size and condition of seasoning at the time of dressing. They shall also be distinguished from 1-inch boards on invoices and certificates.

It should be noted that table 8–1 contains three separate classifications of lumber, and not three divisions of the same classification. In other words, the same lumber is being described each time, but each classification uses a different attribute as a basis. For example, an ordinary 2 × 4 available at a lumber yard would be classified as "yard lumber" by the use classification, as "dressed lumber" according to the degree of manufacture, and as "dimension lumber" by the size classification.

Several changes are incorporated in PS 20-70 which have great significance for the lumber industry. For the first time, the size of lumber is related to its moisture content, and the minimum size both green (above 19 percent m.c.) and dry (below 19 percent m.c.) is specified, as shown in table 8–1. Another change is the reduction of the size of dry lumber. Before, a standard 2 × 4 was actually 1⅝" × 3⅝", whereas now it is 1½" × 3½". This change allows more lumber yield from a given log, but does not change standard spacing of framing members in construction.

In addition to these provisions, the American Lumber Standards Committee (which developed the standard) includes an autonomous National Grading Rule Committee which has published new grading rules for dimension lumber and a Board of Review composed of three members. This Board reviews the adequacy, competency, and reliability of the service performed by agencies that grade lumber under the American Lumber Standards system. These are specific grade designations to be followed nationwide, and to apply to all species. This unifies the grading of lumber to a greater extent than ever before and greatly simplifies the complex of rules promulgated by the different associations.

Under the new grading rule, dimension lumber is divided into five categories, each of which may contain several grades. Sizes as well as grades are designated, as shown below in table 8–2.

TABLE 8–2

Grades and Sizes of Dimension Lumber

Category	Grades	Sizes
Light Framing	Construction, Standard, Utility	2" to 4" thick 2" to 4" wide
Studs	Stud	2" to 4" thick 2" to 4" wide
Structural Light Framing	Select Structural No. 1 No. 2, No. 3	2" to 4" thick 2" to 4" wide
Appearance Framing	Appearance	2" to 4" thick 2" and wider
Structural Joists and Planks	Select Structural No. 1 No. 2, No. 3	2" to 4" thick 6" and wider

SOURCE: American Lumber Standards Committee, *National Grading Rule for Dimension Lumber,* 1970.

The great bulk of softwood lumber is utilized in general construction "as is," without remanufacturing other than cutting to length. The grading system for all softwood lumber except factory and shop reflects the nature of its end use in that defects are evaluated in light of their effect on the strength or utility of the entire piece. The number, size, and limitations of various defects allowed for each grade of softwood lumber are spelled out in the National Grading Rule for Dimension Lumber and grading rules published by the other authorized rule-writing agencies. Individual grades of southern pine, for instance, may be found in the rules published by the Southern Pine Inspection Bureau, while most Western lumber is graded under rules written by the Western Wood Products Association and the West Coast Lumber Inspection Bureau.

Factory and shop softwood lumber is produced for remanufacturing purposes, and it is understood that it will be cut to size, planed, and sometimes shaped when it is used. The grading system for this type of lumber is based on the number and size of clear cuttings which may be obtained from a given board.

Stress Graded Lumber

Stress grading applies only to structural lumber and consists of assigning working stress and/or modulus of elasticity values to individual boards to aid engineers, architects, and builders in utilizing the lumber to best advantage. Working stress is denoted by a figure such as 1500f, which represents the allowable bending stress the piece may be subjected to, and is essentially an indicator of the bending strength of the piece. MOE values, on the other hand, are an expression of the stiffness of the lumber, a factor often more important for floor joists than simple bending strength. MOE values appear on lumber as numbers such as 1.2, 1.4 and 1.6, the larger numbers indicating stiffer lumber.

Stress grading may be done visually as most other grading is done, or by machine, in which case the lumber is usually referred to as *machine stress rated* lumber. When lumber is rated by machine, boards are passed through an apparatus which bends the piece without breaking or damaging it. The force and deflection are measured for this bend and both MOE and working stress values are computed by the machine and stamped on the piece.

Hardwood Lumber Grading

Most hardwood lumber is sold rough to manufacturers who cut to size and surface the boards to meet their own needs. The grading system for hardwood lumber is similar to that used for factory and shop softwood lumber in that it is based on the number and size of clear cuttings which can be taken from a board. The current grading rules are promulgated by the National Hardwood Lumber Association, which has been responsible for their development and revision over the years. The standard grades of hardwood lumber are Firsts, Seconds, Selects, Number 1 Common, Number 2 Common, Sound Wormy, Number 3A Common, and Number 3B Common. Firsts and seconds are commonly combined and called FAS.

Standard lengths of hardwood lumber vary from four to sixteen feet by one-foot intervals, but the grading rules specify that not over 50 percent of a shipment can be of odd lengths. Standard thicknesses range from 3/8 inch to 6 inches, by the following increments: 3/8" – 3/4" by eighths, 1" – 2" by quarters, 2" – 6" by quarters (National Hardwood Lumber Association, 1962). These thicknesses are the dimensions of the lumber when dry but unsurfaced. Given rough thicknesses must surface to certain sizes, according to table 8–3.

TABLE 8–3

Standard Thicknesses for Surfaced Lumber

Rough		Surfaced	Rough		Surfaced
3/8	S2S to	3/16	1 1/2	S2S to	1 5/16
1/2	S2S to	5/16	1 3/4	S2S to	1 1/2
5/8	S2S to	7/16	2	S2S to	1 3/4
3/4	S2S to	9/16	2 1/2	S2S to	2 1/4
1	S2S to	13/16	3	S2S to	2 3/4
1 1/4	S2S to	1 1/16	3 1/2	S2S to	3 1/4
			4	S2S to	3 3/4

SOURCE: National Hardwood Lumber Association, *Rules for the Measurement and Inspection of Hardwood and Cypress Lumber* (Chicago: National Hardwood Lumber Association, 1971). Used by permission.

The exact requirements for each grade of hardwood lumber are stipulated in the rules which for the most part apply to all species. For any grade, the main consideration is the size and number of clear cuttings which can be obtained, a judgment which is based on observation of the worst side of the board. One exception to the "poor side" grading is Select, which must have a face equivalent to Seconds, but the back can be Number 1 Common. A brief summary of the board and cutting size requirements for the different grades is provided in table 8–4.

TABLE 8–4

Lumber Grades and Size Requirements

Grade	Min. Width of board	Min. Length of board	Maximum No. of Cuttings*	Minimum Size of Cuttings
Firsts	6″	8′	3	4″x5′ or 3″x7′
Seconds	6″	8′	4	4″x5′ or 3″x7′
Selects	4″	6′	4	4″x5′ or 3″x7′
No. 1 Common	3″	4′	5	4″x2′ or 3″x3′
No. 2 Common	3″	4′	7	3″x2′
No. 3A Common	3″	4′	No limit	3″x2′
No. 3B Common	3″	4′	No limit	1-1/2″x2′

SOURCE: National Hardwood Lumber Association, *An Introduction to the Grading and Measurement of Hardwood Lumber* (Chicago: National Hardwood Lumber Association, 1962). Used by permission.

* Maximum number of cuttings allowed in *largest* board. Smaller boards must have fewer cuttings, depending on the surface measure of each piece.

Not listed in table 8–4 is Sound Wormy, which falls between Number 2 Common and Number 3A Common. The grading rules specify that Sound Wormy shall not grade below No. 1 Common except for the wormholes and other natural defects. Sound Wormy in a better grade may be obtained by specifying "Firsts and Seconds Sound Wormy," or some other combination of grades.

Hardwood lumber grading is accomplished by visual inspection, the grader mentally estimating the placement and size of clear cuttings (fig. 8–5). Obviously, there is more than one way to cut any board, and the grader's task requires a great deal of skill, thorough knowledge of the grading rules, and considerable experience. Even with his best efforts, the optimum combination of cutting is not always evident, and his assignment of grades to boards is seldom 100 percent correct.

In an effort to overcome the difficulties of visual grading, the U.S. Forest Products Laboratory has developed a procedure for grading hardwood lumber by computer (Hallock, 1971). The system makes use of a scanning device which measures and locates the defects on each board, then sends this information to the computer. The computer calculates all possible cuttings, selects the combination which will give the highest yield of clear-face cuttings, and assigns the board to the proper grade according to grading rule specifications included in the program. The system has proved to be very accurate, and promises to be of great value to the lumber industry.

SELECTS GRADE
FAS FACE WITH NO. 1 COMMON BACK

FAS FACE

| CUTTING NO. 1 | | |
| CUTTING NO. 2 | CUTTING NO. 3 | |

NO. 1 COMMON FACE

| CUTTING NO. 1 | CUTTING No. 3 | |
| CUTTING NO. 2 | CUTTING NO. 4 | |

FIG. 8–5. *Cutting possibilities for a selects grade board. (Courtesy National Hardwood Lumber Association.)*

Lumber Seasoning

Fresh-sawn lumber is usually in a practically green condition, which means that the moisture content is very high, sometimes as much as 100 percent or more. It is neither wise nor practical to use lumber in a green condition, so it is necessary to remove most of the moisture by seasoning. The main benefits gained from drying lumber are:

1. There is a direct relationship between the moisture content and strength of wood. The lower the moisture content (below the fiber saturation point), the higher the strength. Dry lumber also possesses better screw- and nail-holding properties than wet lumber.
2. Wood containing less than 20 percent moisture is not subject to attack by wood-staining or wood-destroying fungi. Most insects likewise do not attack dry wood.
3. Wood of low moisture content is required if it is to be glued, finished, or preserved.
4. Wood shrinks when dried below the fiber saturation point, and if lumber is not dried prior to being put into service, shrinkage occurring in fabricated items or structures can be quite damaging.
5. The weight of lumber is greatly reduced by drying, because the water in green wood sometimes comprises over half its total weight. Lighter weight not only makes handling of the lumber easier, but also reduces shipping costs.

Lumber may be dried by several methods, but by far the most of it is either air or kiln dried. Both of these methods, along with variations of each, will be discussed in the remainder of this chapter. Other methods of some importance are also included.

Air Drying

Air drying of lumber is accomplished by arranging boards in layers in a stack with space between each layer to allow air circulation. Stacks are placed in an open yard and the normal movement of air carries away moisture as it evaporates from the boards.

The main advantage of air drying is that it allows the moisture content of lumber to be reduced from a very high level to 20 percent or less at a relatively low cost. Air drying is often used before kiln drying to reduce the time in the kiln. The process of air seasoning is

TABLE 8–5

Approximate Time to Air Dry Green One-inch Lumber to 20 Percent Moisture Content

SOFTWOODS		HARDWOODS	
Species	Time (days)	Species	Time (days)
Baldcypress	100–300	Alder, red	20–180
Cedar[1]	- - -	Ash:	
Douglas-fir:		Black	60–200
Coast	20–200	Green	60–200
Interior north	20–180	White	60–200
Interior south	10–100	Aspen:	
Fir[1]	- - -	Bigtooth	50–150
Hemlock:		Quaking	50–150
Eastern	90–200	Basswood, American	70–200
Western	60–200	Beech, American	70–200
Larch, western	60–120	Birch:	
Pine:		Paper	40–200
Eastern white	60–200	Sweet	70–200
Jack	40–200	Yellow	70–200
Lodgepole	15–150	Butternut	60–200
Ponderosa	15–150	Cherry, black	70–200
Red	40–200	Cottonwood:	
Southern:		Black	60–150
Loblolly	30–150	Eastern	50–150
Longleaf	30–150	Elm:	
Shortleaf	30–150	American	50–150
Slash	30–150	Rock	80–180
Sugar:		Hackberry	30–150
Light	15–90	Hickory	60–200
Sinker	45–200	Magnolia, southern	40–150
Western white	15–150	Maple:	
Redwood:		Bigleaf	60–180
Light	60–185	Red	30–120
Sinker	200–365	Silver	30–120
Spruce:		Sugar	50–200
Engelmann	20–120	Oak:	
Red	30–120	Northern red	70–200
Sitka	40–150	Northern white	80–250
White	30–120	Southern red	100–300
		Southern white	
		(chestnut)	120–320
		Pecan	120–320
		Sweetgum:	
		Heartwood	70–300
		Sapwood	60–200
		Sycamore, American	30–150
		Tanoak	180–365
		Tupelo:	
		Black	70–200
		Water	70–200
		Walnut, black	70–200
		Willow, black	30–150
		Yellow-poplar	40–150

SOURCE: U.S. Forest Service, *Air Drying of Lumber*, 1971, p. 28.

[1] These species are usually kiln dried.

rather slow, however, many species requiring from 50 to 200 days for one-inch lumber to dry to 20 percent moisture content (table 8–5). The longer period is required when most of the drying period falls in the winter months. Another disadvantage of this method is that the factors which have the most influence on the drying process, namely sun, wind, and rain, are largely beyond man's control. Thus, the drying conditions may be too severe and cause checks and splits at one point, but may be quite the opposite a few days later and allow stain and decay fungus to develop. If sufficient care is taken, the problems of air drying may be overcome, at least to a great enough extent to make it a useful and valuable seasoning method.

The three factors which have the most influence on the loss of moisture from wood are temperature, relative humidity, and air movement. Other factors such as yard layout, piling method, and thickness of the wood also affect the rate of drying and can be manipulated to some extent to take advantage of the first three.

Temperature. The effect of temperature on the drying process is simply that of speeding up evaporation of the moisture in wood. Not only does water evaporate faster at higher temperatures, but warmer air will absorb a greater amount of moisture before it is saturated. For this reason, lumber dries much faster in the summer months than in the winter. Also, lumber yards are usually located to take advantage of as much sunshine as possible to maximize the temperature.

Relative humidity. Relative humidity, as commonly used in reference to weather conditions, compares the amount of moisture in the air to the amount the air would hold at the given temperature if completely saturated. This relationship is expressed as a percentage, so a relative humidity of 50 percent means that the air contains only half as much moisture as it could hold at the given temperature. The influence of relative humidity on lumber drying is obvious: the lower the relative humidity, the easier it is for air to take on more moisture from the lumber and the faster the lumber dries.

It should be noted that temperature and relative humidity are related. If the temperature drops, but the *amount* of moisture in the air remains the same, the *relative humidity* will rise. If the temperature rises while the amount of moisture in the air remains constant, the relative humidity will drop. The most evaporation, and hence faster drying of lumber, will occur when conditions of high temperature and low humidity exist. Likewise, slower drying results when the conditions are the opposite.

To avoid areas of high humidity, lumber yards should not be built in low, damp areas or too near lakes, swamps, or other large bodies of water. High humidity not only slows drying, but also encourages the growth of fungus and attacks by insects.

Air movement. If the air in a pile of lumber were completely stagnant, the small spaces between layers of the wood (about one inch) would soon become saturated, and no further drying would occur. Air movement is an absolute necessity to carry away the evaporating water and promote the rapid drying of lumber. In this regard, a lumber yard should not be shielded from the wind, but rather arranged to take the best advantage of the prevailing winds in the area.

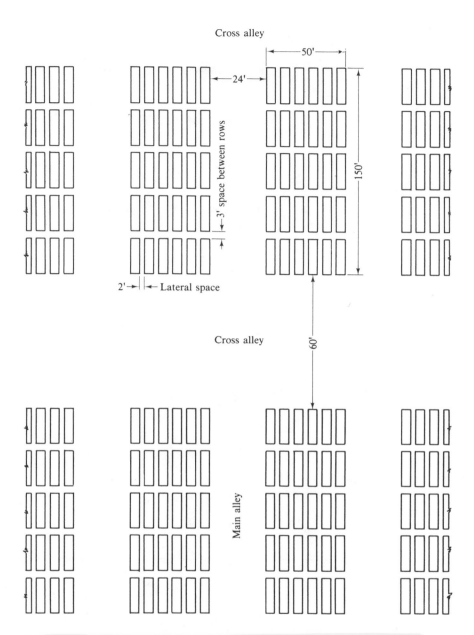

Cross alley

3' space between rows

2' Lateral space

Cross alley

Main alley

Yard layout. The manner in which a lumber yard is arranged can affect the rate of drying. A typical yard, as shown in figure 8–6, is made up of groups of lumber stacks with roadways, or alleys, running between for access with forklifts and/or trucks. The cross alleys also serve to prevent spread of fire and thus are wider than main alleys. In forklift yards, the stacks are oriented parallel to the main alleys, which in turn are oriented parallel to the prevailing winds. In yards where lumber is stacked by hand, the stacks are perpendicular to the main alleys. Orienting the piles parallel to the direction of the prevailing winds allows movement of the wind down the alleys, drawing air through the piles (Reitz, 1971).

Piling. In order to take advantage of the benefits of wind and air movement while avoiding the adverse effects of rain and snow, lumber for air drying must be carefully piled. No pile is any better than its

FIG. 8–6. *Typical forklift yard layout. (Courtesy of U.S. Forest Service.)*

foundation, which must be solid, free of mold or other fungus infection, and high enough to allow free passage of air underneath the pile.

A pile of lumber consists of many layers of boards separated by narrow pieces called stickers. A pile may be as narrow as 3½ feet or as wide as 16 feet and vary in height from 4 to 30 feet (Rietz, 1971). An average size pile would be about 8 feet wide and 12 to 15 feet high. As shown in figure 8–7, the piles are usually sloped slightly (about 1 inch per foot) to facilitate water runoff, although increased mechanization in yards has led to considerable level piling. Stickers are placed in vertical alignment and always directly over a foundation or support. A roof is placed atop the pile to protect the top layers as well as the ends from rain and direct sunlight. A modification of air drying, called *shed drying,* utilizes a single permanent roof to cover many piles of lumber.

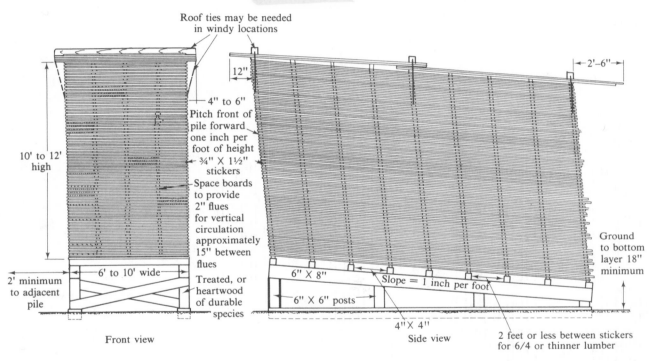

FIG. 8–7. *Lumber stacked for air drying. (Courtesy of U.S. Forest Service.)*

In each layer of lumber within the pile, the boards may be placed edge to edge or separated slightly to encourage a vertical movement of air in the pile. Sometimes one or two boards are left out near the center of each layer, creating what is called a "chimney."

Thickness. Lumber thickness is directly related to drying rate, thicker lumber requiring much longer to dry than one-inch boards. For this reason, lumber is sorted and piled according to thickness, so that all the boards in a pile will be seasoned to the same level in a given length of time.

Species. As is true with most other attributes of wood, the rate of seasoning varies among the different species. In general, hardwoods take longer to dry than softwoods, and the harder hardwoods are more difficult to dry than the softer species (see table 8–5).

Kiln Drying

Lumber may be dried much faster by kiln than by air drying. The time is reduced from several weeks or months to a week or less for some species. A further advantage of kiln drying is that conditions can be closely controlled to minimize both drying time and drying defects.

A dry kiln is simply an enclosure equipped with the apparatus necessary to create and control the drying conditions needed to season lumber in the shortest time possible. Lumber stacks are placed in the kiln by forklift or wheeled in on tracked carts. Once filled, the kiln is closed so that the conditions which influence seasoning can be varied as needed. These conditions are the same as for air drying, namely, temperature, humidity, and air movement. Inside the kiln, the temperature is raised by turning on heating elements (usually steam heated) and lowered by reducing the steam through the elements or turning off one or two elements at a time. Humidity is increased by releasing steam into the air inside the kiln and lowered by either turning off the outlet or venting some of the moisture-laden air. Air is circulated in the kiln by fans or by natural flow resulting from hot air rising through the stacks and cooler air sinking downward to be heated or vented. The schematic kiln cutaway in figure 8–8 shows a compartment kiln which utilizes fans to circulate air. All conditions in a kiln are controlled by a master unit called a recorder-controller, mounted outside the drying chamber. The kiln operator simply sets the controls at the desired levels, and the recorder-controller automatically operates the different elements which change the conditions as needed. It also records in graph form a continuous record of the temperature of the kiln.

The *Dry Kiln Operators Manual* (Rasmussen, 1961) classifies kilns as *compartment* or *progressive,* according to their construction and operation. Most woodworking and seasoning enterprises, especially smaller operations, make use of compartment kilns which operate on a batch basis. A load is placed in the kiln, dried to the desired moisture content, then removed to be replaced by another charge. Progressive kilns, on the other hand, operate continuously, and several stacks of lumber at different stages in the drying process may be in the kiln at one time. These kilns are long narrow buildings with tracks on which lumber carts travel slowly from the "green" end to the "dry" end. Drying conditions at the green end of the kiln are fairly mild, but increase in severity toward the dry end. The pace of the cart movement is such that by the time a stack has moved from one end of the kiln to the other, the lumber has reached the proper moisture content. Each time a dry load leaves one end of the kiln, a wet load enters at the other end.

Before a load of lumber is placed in a kiln, a *kiln schedule* must be prepared. This schedule is a chart showing the different sets of conditions which will be used to dry the lumber to the desired moisture content. The kiln operator changes the conditions by steps, on the basis of the moisture content of the lumber or by time intervals. Time schedules can be worked out through long experience with one kind of wood, but they are used primarily for softwoods.

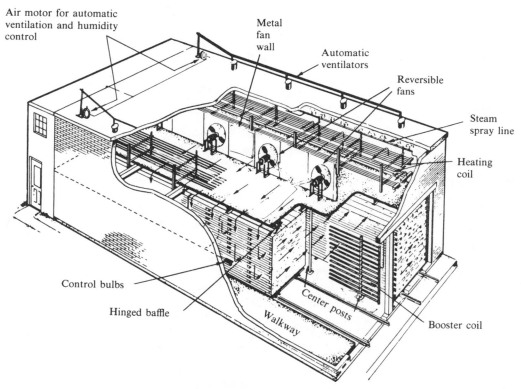

Air motor for automatic ventilation and humidity control

Metal fan wall

Automatic ventilators

Reversible fans

Steam spray line

Heating coil

Control bulbs

Hinged baffle

Center posts

Walkway

Booster coil

FIG. 8–8. *Schematic of track-type compartment kiln (bottom). Similar kiln being loaded by forklift (top). (Schematic courtesy of U.S. Forest Service, photo courtesy of Irvington-Moore.)*

An example of a moisture content kiln schedule is shown in table 8–6. It should be noted that the three factors included in the schedule are temperature, humidity, and moisture content. In the industry, temperature inside the kiln is called "dry-bulb" temperature, while humidity is indicated by the "wet-bulb" temperature or the "wet bulb depression." These terms are derived from the setup required to measure humidity, namely a thermometer in the open air (dry bulb) and a thermometer with its bulb cooled by a wet wick (wet bulb). The difference between the readings on the two thermometers can be used to calculate the relative humidity. Since there is a direct relationship between wet bulb depression and relative humidity, it is more convenient to use the former, without converting it to relative humidity values each time it must be used.

TABLE 8–6

Typical Kiln Drying Schedule

Temperature Step No.	Wet-bulb Depression Step No.	Moisture Content at start of step (Percent)	Dry-bulb Temperature (°F.)	Wet-bulb Depression (°F.)	Wet-bulb Temperature (°F.)
1	1	Above 40	130	5	125
1	2	40	130	7	123
1	3	35	130	11	119
2	4	30	140	19	121
3	5	25	150	35	115
4	6	20	160	50	110
5	6	15	180	50	130

SOURCE: U.S. Forest Service, *Dry Kiln Operator's Manual,* 1961, p. 122.

The dry-bulb temperature inside the kiln is controlled by the heating elements, while the wet bulb temperature is varied by introducing steam to increase the relative humidity or venting to reduce it. The kiln schedule in table 8–6 indicates changes in both of these by "steps." In "wet bulb depression step number 1," the conditions are mild, as a fairly low temperature and a high humidity (equivalent to a low wet-bulb depression) are used. The second step varies only the wet bulb temperature, so the "temperature [dry bulb] step" number is not changed. Whenever the lumber in the kiln reaches the moisture content specified in column three, either the dry or wet bulb temperature (or both) is changed. Using this schedule, the lumber would be dried to a final moisture content of 15 percent.

Normal kiln schedules seldom call for temperatures in excess of 180° F., but much higher temperatures can be used with certain species under controlled conditions. Interest in high-temperature drying, making use of temperatures in excess of 212°F., has revived in recent years because it shortens the drying time considerably. The main problem associated with high-temperature drying is increased degrade of the lumber, but much research has been carried out to find ways to alleviate the problem. Prefreezing and transverse compression prior to drying are two methods which show some promise of relieving degrade.

Other Drying Methods

In terms of time required and relative control possible, a process which falls between air and kiln drying is *forced air drying*. When this method is used, lumber is placed in an enclosed building and heated air is circulated by fans. Humidity can be controlled only to the extent of venting some of the moisture-laden air (Reitz, 1971).

Other methods which have received some attention in recent years are *radio-frequency* and *microwave drying*. High-frequency current or microwaves induce heat in boards, vaporizing the water and speeding up the drying process. Favorable results have been obtained by combining these methods with regular kiln drying (McMiller, 1961; Miller, 1971).

Chemical seasoning makes use of chemicals to protect wood against degradation while allowing faster drying. Few of these methods are widely used, because the problems caused by the chemicals generally more than offset the benefits gained (Hudson, 1969).

A method recently reported by the U.S. Forest Products Laboratory is *press drying*. This process is most suitable for thin lumber or thick veneer, and has the advantages of very fast drying and minimum degrade. Boards are placed between heated, vented platens and are slightly compressed during drying. Degrade due to warpage is practically eliminated because the boards are held completely flat until dry.

Drying Defects

When wood dries below the fiber saturation point, shrinkage occurs in two directions, across and tangent to the growth rings (see chapter 4 for complete discussion). Unless particular care is taken when drying lumber, defects of various kinds may accompany this shrinkage.

Warp. Warp is a defect which makes the machining of wood more difficult and results in considerable loss of wood as well. Four separate types of warp can be distinguished (fig. 8–9). *Cupping* describes a board curved across its width, and is caused by unequal shrinkage in the radial and tangential directions. It may be prevented by holding

FIG. 8–9. *Types of warp. (Courtesy of U.S. Forest Service.)*

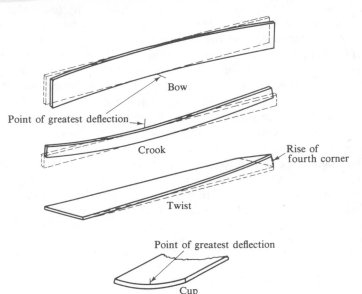

the board flat during drying. Boards near the bottom of a stack are held flat by the weight of the lumber on top, but upper layers must be weighted to prevent cupping.

Bow results when a board is curved in length flatwise. This defect is caused by cross grain or areas of abnormal wood. It may be minimized by proper stacking.

Crook is an edgewise curvature in the length of a board. It is caused by the same factors as bow. Crook is difficult to prevent in normal lumber drying operations.

When a board is placed on a flat surface and three corners touch, but the fourth is lifted, it is described as a *twisted* board. Twist is caused by spiral, interlocked, or other irregular grain patterns. Proper stacking is the best remedy for this defect.

Checks. The surface layers of a board dry first, because water in the inner portions must move through the wood cells to the surface before it can evaporate into the air, and moisture movement in wood is a fairly slow process. The result of this situation is that a *moisture gradient* is established, which means that the board is progressively wetter toward the center. If drying of the surface layer occurs too quickly, it may fall below the fiber saturation point and begin to shrink, while the inner portion of the board is still above the fiber saturation point, and hence has not begun to shrink. The resulting stress may cause small cracks called *surface checks* (fig. 8–10) to appear, usually in or near a ray. These checks may close up in later stages of drying when the inner part of the board falls below the fiber saturation point.

Since water travels much faster along the length of a board than across, the ends dry much sooner than the rest of the board and shrink, causing *end checks* (fig. 8–11). These may be reduced somewhat by use of an end coating to slow down moisture loss. Both types of checking are aggravated by too-severe drying conditions, especially during the early stages of drying.

Splits. When end checks extend deeper into the wood, larger cracks called *splits* open up. In some boards, what is called a *boxed heart split* develops when the center of the log is enclosed in a board.

Knots. Knots are not drying defects, but often during drying the difference between radial and tangential shrinkage in a knot will cause either *checked* or *loose knots* (fig. 8–12).

Collapse. Collapse of the cells in a board may not be noticeable unless it is quite severe, in which case the board may have a sunken or ridged surface. This defect is caused by too-high drying temperatures during early stages of seasoning.

Honeycombing. Honeycombing is internal checks in boards which occur when the "core" dries after the outer layers have dried and "set." This set resists the shrinkage of the core, causing the checks. A board may appear sound on the outside, but be severely honeycombed internally (fig. 8–13). This defect occurs most often in thicker boards of difficult-to-dry woods such as oak and walnut.

Casehardening. Casehardening is a condition produced when the drying of lumber reaches a stage similar to that described above, except that the internal stress is not high enough to cause honeycombing.

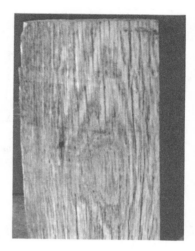

FIG. 8–10. *Surface checks.*

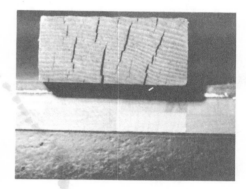

FIG. 8–11. *End checks.*

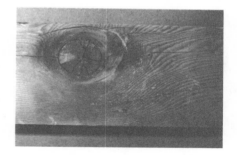

FIG. 8–12. *Loose and checked knot.*

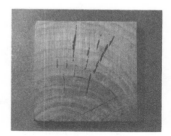

FIG. 8–13. *Four-inch walnut square severely honeycombed.*

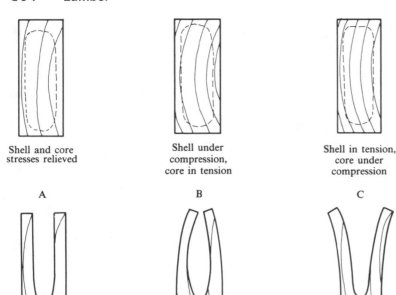

Shell and core   Shell under   Shell in tension,
stresses relieved   compression,   core under
                  core in tension   compression

A   B   C

Normal   Casehardened   Reverse casehardened

FIG. 8–14. *Effects of shell and core stresses.*

Referring to the "shell-case" illustration in figure 8–14b it will be seen that the core of the board is in tension (trying to shrink, but resisted by the shell which has set), while the shell is in compression (being "squeezed" by the core). If a sample is cut as shown casehardened lumber will curl inward. Reverse casehardening, which occurs at an earlier stage of drying, produces a sample as in figure 8–14c. The prongs of a normal sample remain parallel (fig. 8–14a).

Casehardening is a normal occurrence in lumber drying, and may not actually be a defect unless the lumber will be further cut up and manufactured. Softwood boards used "as is" are not degraded by casehardening, but when hardwood boards are ripped or surfaced, the stresses of casehardening may cause severe warpage. Casehardening can be reduced in the kiln by following the regular kiln schedule with a conditioning treatment which more nearly equalizes the moisture content throughout the boards.

Stain. Lumber being seasoned may be discolored by stains of two origins, that caused by fungi, mainly *blue stain* (see chapter 5), and that which is chemical in nature, the *brown stains.* Brown stains of this type are evidently caused by concentration and oxidation of extractive materials in the wood.

Resources

Brown, Nelson Courtlandt, and James Samuel Bethel. *Lumber.* New York: John Wiley and Sons, 1958.

Cech, M. Y. "Dynamic Transverse Compression Treatment to Improve Drying Behavior of Yellow Birch." *Forest Products Journal* 21 (February, 1971): 41–49.

Cech, M. Y., and D. R. Huffman. "High Temperature Kiln Drying of Spruce Joists." *Forest Products Journal* 21 (October, 1971): 55–60.

Cooper, Glenn A., Robert W. Erickson, and John G. Haygreen. "Drying Behavior of Prefrozen Black Walnut." *Forest Products Journal* 20 (January, 1970): 30–35.

Cuppett, Donald G., and E. Paul Craft. "Low-Temperature Drying of 4/4 Appalachian Red Oak." *Forest Products Journal* 21 (January, 1971): 34–38.

Erickson, Robert, et al. "Prefreezing Alone and Combined with Presteaming in the Drying of Redwood Dimension." *Forest Products Journal* 21 (July, 1971): 54–59.

Galligan, W. L., and D. V. Snodgrass. "Machine Stress Rated Lumber: Challenge to Design." *Forest Products Journal* 20 (September, 1970): 63–69.

Hallock, Hiram, and Lynn Galiger. *Grading Hardwood Lumber by Computer,* U.S. Department of Agriculture, Forest Service Research Paper FPL 157. Madison, Wisconsin: Forest Products Laboratory, 1971.

Hudson, Monne S. "Chemical Drying of Southern Pine Wood." *Forest Products Journal* 19 (March, 1969): 21–24.

Kennedy, D. E. "A New Look at Mechanical Lumber Grading." *Forest Products Journal* 19 (June, 1969): 41–44.

Koch, Peter. *Development of the Chipping Headrig.* Alexandria, Louisiana: U.S. Department of Agriculture, Forest Service, Southern Forest Experiment Station, 1967.

McAlister, William R., and Helmuth Resch. "Drying 1-inch Ponderosa Pine Lumber with a Combination of Microwave Power and Hot Air." *Forest Products Journal* 21 (March, 1971): 24–36.

McMiller, J. M., and W. L. James. *High-Frequency Dielectric Heating.* Madison, Wisconsin: U.S. Department of Agriculture, Forest Service, Forest Products Laboratory, 1961.

Miller, D. G. "Combining Radio-Frequency Heating with Kiln-Drying to Provide Fast Drying Without Degrade." *Forest Products Journal* 21 (December, 1971): 17–21.

National Hardwood Lumber Association. *An Introduction to the Grading and Measurement of Hardwood Lumber.* Chicago: National Hardwood Lumber Association, 1962.

National Hardwood Lumber Association. *Rules for the Measurement and Inspection of Hardwood and Cypress Lumber.* Chicago: National Hardwood Lumber Association, 1971.

Rasmussen, Edmund F. *Agriculture Handbook No. 188: Dry Kiln Operator's Manual.* Washington, D. C.: Government Printing Office, 1961.

Rietz, Raymond C., and Rufus H. Page. *Agriculture Handbook No. 402: Air Drying of Lumber.* Washington, D. C.: Government Printing Office, 1971.

Salamon, Marian. "High-Temperature Drying and Its Effect on Wood Properties." *Forest Products Journal* 19 (March, 1969): 27–34.

United States Department of Commerce, National Bureau of Standards. *American Softwood Lumber Standard: NBS Voluntary Product Standard PS 20–70.* Washington, D. C.: Government Printing Office, 1970.

Western Wood Products Association. *1970 Standard Grading Rules for Western Lumber.* Portland, Oregon: Western Wood Products Associaton, 1970.

Chapter Nine

Veneer and Plywood

The term veneer is often considered to mean a thin sheet of material or some form of a protective facing; however, when used in connection with the wood industry, it is defined as a thin sheet of wood which is rotary cut, sliced, or sawed from a log, bolt, or flitch (U.S. Department of Commerce, 1971). When pieces of veneer are assembled into a panel, each sheet is referred to as a ply. Plywoods are formed from the layering or stacking of these veneers (plys).

The art of veneering is centuries old and has been found depicted in Egyptian murals dated as early as 1500 B.C. Other historical accounts indicate that the Greeks and the Romans used veneer overlays to achieve decorative effects. From these times, centuries passed and little reference was made to veneering until the seventeenth and eighteenth centuries when artisans and craftsmen again began to utilize the technique in the construction of fine furniture. During the 1830s, plywood was first introduced in the making of pianos, and since that time, the uses of plywood have continuously expanded and become accepted (Hardwood Plywood Manufacturers Association, n.d.).

In the United States the plywood industry is divided into two segments, one concerned with the production of plywood from softwoods and the other with production of plywood from hardwood. The softwood plywood industry is primarily concerned with construction and industrial plywoods while the hardwood plywood industry gears its production to uses where esthetic characteristics are most important.

As the process of producing the veneer which makes up both softwood and hardwood plywood is basically the same, a brief general discussion of the manufacture of veneer will be undertaken in this chapter, followed by a discussion of both types of plywood with emphasis on their specific properties, grades, and uses.

Veneer and Plywood Production

It is helpful to gain an understanding of the various methods used in the cutting of veneer prior to discussing the process of producing plywood. The several methods of veneer cutting each produce a different grain configuration in the stock being cut, which along with basic characteristics of the wood itself provide varying patterns and effects.

Veneer Cutting Methods

Even though six methods of cutting veneer are used, over 80 percent of all the veneer cut is produced by rotary cutting. Used extensively in the softwood plywood industry, the rotary method accounts for virtually all of the softwood veneers produced.

Figure 9–1 provides a graphic illustration of the five most commonly used methods of of veneer cutting. The four slicing methods shown are used mainly for hardwood veneers. Slicing allows the flitch to be held in different positions to achieve the special grain patterns necessary for hardwood plywood and decorative panels. The sixth, sawn veneer, while the oldest method, is only used today to produce certain desired effects on such species as oak, red cedar, and Spanish cedar.

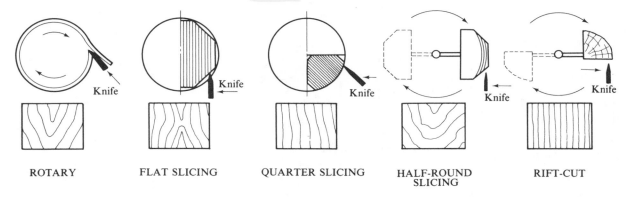

ROTARY	FLAT SLICING	QUARTER SLICING	HALF-ROUND SLICING	RIFT-CUT
The log is mounted centrally in the lathe and turned against a razor sharp blade, like unwinding a roll of paper. Since this cut follows the log's annular growth rings, a bold variegated grain marking is produced. Rotary cut veneer is exceptionally wide.	The half log, or flitch, is mounted with the heart side flat against the guide plate of the slicer and the slicing is done parallel to a line through the center of the log. This produces a variegated figure.	The quarter log or flitch is mounted on the guide plate so that the growth rings of the log strike the knife at approximately right angles, producing a series of stripes, straight in some woods, varied in others.	A variation of rotary cutting in which segments or flitches of the log are mounted off center in the lathe. This results in a cut slightly across the annular growth rings, and visually shows modified characteristics of both rotary and plain sliced veneers.	Rift cut veneer is produced in the various species of Oak. Oak has medullary ray cells which radiate from the center of the log like the curved spokes of a wheel. The rift or comb grain effect is obtained by cutting perpendicularly to these medullary rays either on the lathe or slicer.

FIG. 9–1. *Types of veneer cuts. (Courtesy of Fine Hardwoods-American Walnut Association.)*

During the cutting operation all veneer develops small "checks" at the point of the knife edge (fig. 9–2). This is caused by the "peeling back" action created at the point where the knife separates the veneer from the block. The underside (knife edge) is referred to as the loose

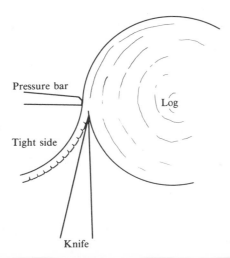

Pressure bar

Log

Tight side

Knife

FIG. 9–2. *Checks developed during cutting of veneer.*

side and the bark side (pressure bar side) is referred to as the tight side. The thicker the veneer is cut, the more noticeable the checks become. To prevent these checks from marring the appearance of a finished panel it is necessary to lay the outer ply of the panel with the tight side exposed (Demas, 1969). Depending upon use requirements and species, veneers may be cut in thicknesses ranging from approximately 1/100 to 3/8 of an inch.

Basic Plywood Manufacture

Veneer logs, once received at the plywood plant, are stored prior to use and are kept wet in order to prevent end-checking and splitting as they dry out. This is done several ways, the most common being storage in water (such as a pond) or piled storage where a continual misty spray is directed over the logs.

When the logs are ready for use, they must be debarked and cut to convenient lengths for processing. Debarking is a most important step in log preparation as it helps to eliminate the possibility of rocks or other objects imbedded in the bark from damaging the razor sharp veneer cutting knives at a later stage. In order to accommodate the plant processing equipment, the logs are cut into bolts of appropriate lengths (eight to ten feet is most common) for rotary slicing and further cut into half logs or flitches if other slicing methods are used.

Most manufacturers utilize one additional step prior to the actual slicing or cutting of the veneer. This step is sometimes referred to as "conditioning" and is accomplished by steaming or soaking the logs or flitches in hot water for a pre-determined length of time immediately prior to the slicing operation. This conditioning process serves to soften the wood fibers in the logs with the result that a smoother veneer will be produced and that checking or fracturing caused by the knife will be reduced.

Following the cutting operation (fig. 9–3), the veneer passes over a conveyor system to a machine called a "clipper" (fig. 9–4) where the sheets of veneer are trimmed, sized, and have waste or defects removed. If the veneer sheets are wet, they are cut oversize in order to compensate for shrinkage due to moisture loss during later drying. In most cases the veneer sheets do not go directly into the driers but continue along a conveyor where they are often pre-sorted. Still on a conveyor, the sheets enter large dryers where the moisture content is reduced to a level, generally below 10 percent, that is compatible with gluing and later usage. Temperatures reached in the dryer are in the 400° F. range and the time required to attain the desired moisture content is determined by such conditions as the veneer thickness, whether it is heartwood or sapwood, or which species is being dried. Once dried, the veneers are edge-glued to make full-size sheets if necessary. When defects are present at this stage they are often repaired thus improving the appearance or utility of the piece. Tapeless splicers, taping machines, and string tying are methods used to make up full-size sheets.

The veneer is now ready for build-up into the appropriate size panels. Softwood plywood is usually made of alternate crossbanded layers of veneer while hardwood plywood may use veneer plys as the core material or be made up of cores such as lumber, hardboard, or particleboard. The various veneer sheets or core materials are passed through a glue spreader or have the adhesive sprayed upon the appropriate faces. Primary adhesives used in the production of softwood plywood are blood, soybean, and phenolics, while hardwood plywoods most frequently utilize phenolic, urea, resorcinol, and melamine resins. The veneer is then stacked in the desired number of plys (3, 5, or 7 being most common) and placed in a multi-opening press (fig. 9–6). Both hot and cold presses are used, but the hot press is now most widely utilized. Heated platens (around 250° F.) and pressures of 150-300 psi are commonly used during the pressing operation.

Following pressing, the panels are sawn to dimension and sanded to thickness. Now ready for grading, they are inspected and then packaged and prepared for shipment.

It must be remembered that no two plants engaged in the production of veneer or plywoods operate exactly alike; however, production of most softwood and hardwood plywood is regulated by industry product standards PS 1-66 and PS 51-71, respectively.

FIG. 9–3. *Rotary cutting of veneer. (Courtesy of American Plywood Association.)*

FIG. 9–4. *Trimmed veneer leaving the clipper. Here a bank of three clippers is used. (Courtesy of American Plywood Association.)*

The Product Standard PS 1-66 was designed to establish nationally recognized standards for construction and industrial plywood made primarily from softwood species and defines softwood plywood as follows:

> Softwood plywood is a flat panel, built-up generally of an odd number of thin sheets or veneers of wood in which the grain direction of each ply or layer is at right angles to the one adjacent to it. Face and back plys and all odd numbered plys generally are oriented with grain direction parallel to the long dimension of the panel. The sheets of veneer are united under pressure by a bonding agent to create a laminated panel with an adhesive bond as strong as, or stronger than, the wood. The alternating of the direction of the grain of each contiguous layer of wood veneer and the odd numbered plys equalizes the strains, and minimizes shrinkage and warping of the panel and prevents splitting. Overlaid plywood is produced in a like manner with special resin treated surfacing material added over the panel faces (U.S. Department of Commerce, 1966).

Softwood Plywood

Softwood plywood is generally available in panel widths of 36, 48, and 60 inches and lengths from 60 to 144 inches in increments of 12 inches. Of these the most common sizes are 48 by 96 inches (4' X 8') and 48 by 120 inches (4' X 10'); however, other sizes may be made available through special orders. Thicknesses of sanded panels range from 1/4 inch to 1¼ inches, usually in increments of 1/8 inch. Thicknesses greater than 1¼ inch are also available by special order. In order to achieve uniformity of sizes, PS 1-66 lists an allowable tolerance of ± 1/32 inch of the specified width and/or length. Sanded panels have a thickness tolerance of 1/64 inch of the specified thickness, while unsanded, touchsanded, or overlaid panels must be within

± 1/32 inch for all panels up to 13/16 inch, and over 13/16 inch the thickness tolerance is ± 5 percent of the specified thickness.

TABLE 9–1

Summary of Veneer Grades Used in Softwood Plywood

Veneer Grade	Basic Characteristics
N	Special order "natural finish" veneer. Select all heartwood or all sapwood. Free of open defects. Allows some repairs.
A	Smooth and paintable. Neatly made repairs permissible. Also used for natural finish in less demanding applications.
B	Solid surface veneer. Circular repair plugs and tight knots permitted.
C	Knotholes to 1". Occasional knotholes 1/2" larger permitted providing total width of all knotholes within a specified section does not exceed certain limits. Limited splits permitted. Lowest grade permitted in Exterior-type plywood.
C Plgd	Improved C veneer with splits limited to 1/8" in width and knotholes and borer holes limited to 1/4" by 1/2".
D	Permits knots and knotholes to 2-1/2" in width and 1/2" larger under certain specified limits. Limited splits permitted.

SOURCE: American Plywood Association, *Plywood Properties and Grades* (Tacoma, Washington: American Plywood Association, 1971). Used by permission.

Softwood Plywood Grading

Grading of softwood plywood underwent significant changes when Product Standard PS 1-66 was accepted. In an attempt to clarify types of plywood needed for specific performance applications, a grade-use system of classification was developed. The grade-trademark stamped on each panel designates whether a panel's use is appearance-based or whether it has an engineered base (use in a variety of construction

FIG. 9–5. *Panels are built up as veneer emerges from glue spreader. (Courtesy of American Plywood Association.)*

or industrial applications where appearance is not an important factor). Based upon the American Plywood Association Bulletin No. 6 (1971), the following explanations should assist in developing an understanding of softwood plywood grades.

Type. Plywood is produced in two types—exterior, which has a 100 percent waterproof glue line and, interior, which has a moisture resistant glue line. Veneers used in the exterior type are of a higher grade than the minimum allowed in the interior type. For all applications to areas permanently exposed to the weather an exterior type should be specified.

Grade. Within each type (exterior or interior) there is a variety of appearance grades determined by the veneer grade (N, A, B, C, D) used on the face or back of the panel. Table 9–1 provides a summary of each of the veneer grades.

Group. As over fifty species of wood are used in the manufacture of plywood, they have been classed into five groups primarily on the basis of their strength properties. The group number appearing in the grade-trademark is based on the species used for the face and back of the panel, or the weaker species if face and back are different. Grouping of species may be found by referring to table 9–2.

Structural I, Structural II. This denotes unsanded sheathing grades both of which are made only with exterior glue. Structural I is limited

FIG. 9–6. *Built-up panels are often pre-pressed (center, foreground) before being placed in multi-opening hot press (background). (Courtesy of American Plywood Association.)*

TABLE 9–2

Classification of Species

Group 1	Group 2	Group 3	Group 4	Group 5
Birch	Cedar, Port Orford	Alder, Red	Aspen, Quaking	Fir, Balsam
Yellow	Douglas Fir 2**	Cedar, Alaska Yellow	Birch, Paper	Poplar, Balsam
Sweet	Fir	Pine	Cedar	
Douglas Fir 1*	California Red	Jack	Incense	
Larch, Western	Grand	Lodgepole	Western Red	
Maple, Sugar	Noble	Ponderosa	Fir, Subalpine	
Pine, Southern	Pacific Silver	Redwood	Hemlock, Eastern	
Loblolly	White	Spruce	Pine	
Longleaf	Hemlock, Western	Black	Sugar	
Shortleaf	Lauan	Red	Eastern White	
Slash	Red	White	Poplar, Western***	
Tanoak	Tangile		Spruce, Engelmann	
	White			
	Almon			
	Bagtikan			
	Maple, Black			
	Meranti			
	Mengkulang			
	Pine			
	Pond			
	Red			
	Western White			
	Spruce, Sitka			
	Sweetgum			
	Tamarack			

SOURCE: American Plywood Association, *Plywood Properties and Grades* (Tacoma, Washington: American Plywood Association, 1971). Used by permission.

  *Douglas fir 1 – Washington, Oregon, California, Idaho, Montana, Wyoming, British Columbia, Alberta
 **Douglas fir 2 – Nevada, Utah, Colorado, Arizona, New Mexico
***Also known as Black Cottonwood

to Group 1 species for all plys; Structural II permits Group 1, 2, or 3 species in all plys. These grades are recommended for heavily loaded applications where strength is of maximum importance.

Standard C-D Sheathing. This type is an intermediate sheathing grade recommended for sub-flooring, wall sheathing, and roof decking. It may also be obtained with an intermediate or a waterproof glue if panel may be temporarily exposed to weather. It is not designed for permanent exposure.

Identification Index. Many grade-trademarks (Standard C-D; Structural I, II; and C-C) bear a set of two numbers separated by a slash (see fig. 9–7). The number on the left indicates the maximum recommended spacing in inches for supports when used as roof decking with the face grain across the supports; the right-hand number indicates the recommended maximum spacing in inches for supports when used as subflooring with the face grain across the supports.

Class I, Class II. These are designations which apply only to Plyform grades intended for concrete form applications. Class I is a stronger panel than Class II.

As an aid to gaining a better understanding of specifications found on softwood plywood, figure 9–7 illustrates the use of type, grade, group, class, and identification index in four typical grade-trademarks.

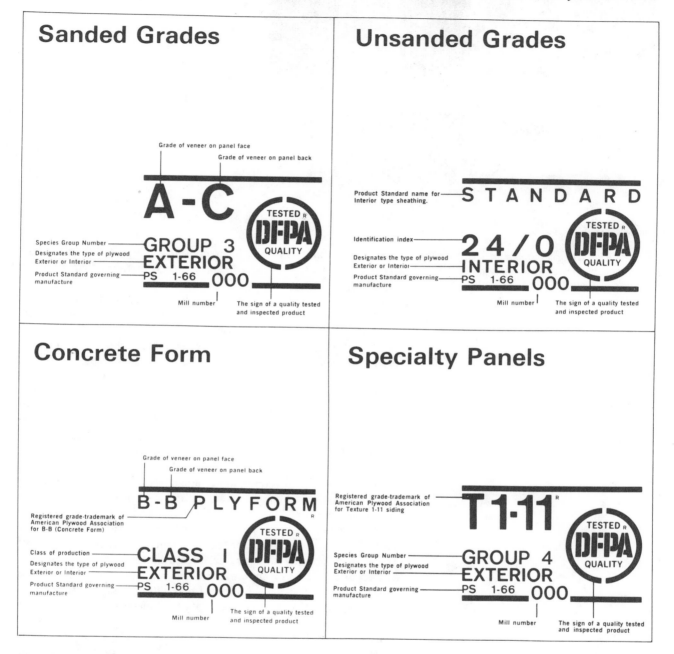

Sanded Grades

Grade of veneer on panel face
Grade of veneer on panel back

A - C

Species Group Number — GROUP 3
Designates the type of plywood
Exterior or Interior — EXTERIOR
Product Standard governing — PS 1-66 000
manufacture

TESTED R
DFPA
QUALITY

Mill number
The sign of a quality tested
and inspected product

Unsanded Grades

Product Standard name for — S T A N D A R D
Interior type sheathing.

Identification index — 24/0
Designates the type of plywood
Exterior or Interior — INTERIOR
Product Standard governing — PS 1-66 000
manufacture

TESTED R
DFPA
QUALITY

Mill number
The sign of a quality tested
and inspected product

Concrete Form

Grade of veneer on panel face
Grade of veneer on panel back

B - B P L Y F O R M
R

Registered grade-trademark of
American Plywood Association
for B-B (Concrete Form)

Class of production — CLASS I
Designates the type of plywood
Exterior or Interior — EXTERIOR
Product Standard governing — PS 1-66 000
manufacture

TESTED R
DFPA
QUALITY

Mill number
The sign of a quality tested
and inspected product

Specialty Panels

Registered grade-trademark of
American Plywood Association — T 1-11
for Texture 1-11 siding
R

Species Group Number — GROUP 4
Designates the type of plywood
Exterior or Interior — EXTERIOR
Product Standard governing — PS 1-66 000
manufacture

TESTED R
DFPA
QUALITY

Mill number
The sign of a quality tested
and inspected product

General Use Considerations

The popularity of plywood as a construction and industrial material has expanded greatly during the past two decades. Today it is possible to secure plywoods which are well adapted to fill the specific building needs of a wide variety of users.

Because of its cross-laminated construction, plywood possesses a high degree of strength and rigidity. Coupled with this is the fact that the impact resistance of plywood is greater than that of wood itself. Again, due to its cross-lamination, the dimensional stability of plywood is extremely high. This has been exhibited through tests which

FIG. 9–7. *Basic grade-trademarks found on softwood plywood. (Courtesy of American Plywood Association.)*

FIG. 9–8. *Plywood is used for both wall and roof sheathing. (Courtesy of American Plywood Association.)*

have shown that from oven-dry to complete saturation, plywood panels swell an average of only 2/10 of 1 percent (American Plywood Association, 1971).

Among the advantages enjoyed by users of plywood is the fact that it works easily and quickly with ordinary hand and power tools. Typical fasteners may be utilized in its fabrication and their holding power is very good. The fact that plywood does not split when fasteners are driven close to the edge is another positive factor.

Plywood is an economical material to begin with and, because it lends itself to faster fabrication, can reduce costs further. The size of the panels allows for rapid coverage and its light weight in relation to several other construction materials combine with labor savings to greatly enhance its use, especially in the construction industry. Also important is its capacity to be formed in simple curves.

Thermal insulating properties of plywood are high and its large panel size serves to reduce joints and their resultant drafts. Other properties such as chemical resistance and gas permeability, especially in the exterior and high density overlaid panels, are also good.

Developments in plywood sidings and decorative panels have created a new range of surface textures which lend themselves to both traditional and contemporary architectural uses.

Recent emphasis on the further development of both medium and high density overlays has increased many design possibilities. Essentially, these overlays are composed of paper sheets sufficiently impregnated with resin to form a continuous bond between the surfacing material and the plywood. Medium density overlays are designed to present a smooth, uniform surface suitable for high-quality paint finishes. The surfacing of the high density overlays is intended to be hard, smooth, and of such character that further finishing by paint or varnish is not necessary.

Applications

The uses of plywood have become so diverse in recent years that an exhaustive study of all of them would be next to impossible within the framework of this book. An attempt will be made, however, to categorize some of the applications under generalized headings and briefly discuss uses under each. Special attention will be given to several products (and their applications) which have just recently found their way into the market. At the close of this section, figures 9–11 and 9–12 provide a grade-use guide summary which may prove helpful in gaining a greater understanding of grades and uses for which they would prove suitable.

Sheathing. Probably the most widely recognized application of plywood is that of sheathing. This broad category includes sheathing used for walls, floors, and roofs. When used in walls the panels may be applied either vertically or horizontally. In most cases wall bracing and building paper can be eliminated if plywood wall sheathing is used. Often plywood panels are used as bracing at the corners and the remainder of the sheathing consists of insulation board. As a floor material, plywood is used extensively for both subflooring and floor underlayment. Recent developments permit the use of a one-layer floor when a tongue and grooved underlayment, used in conjunction with elastomeric adhesives, is fastened directly to the floor joist. The most common application with respect to roofs is that of sheathing which has replaced the use of roof boards in many localities. Plywood roof decking is adaptable to flat or low slope roofs as well as those of steeper slope.

Plywood components. A relatively new concept in the construction industry is that of using preassembled plywood components to erect buildings from parts rather than pieces. Among components commonly assembled are both flat and curved stressed skin panels (fig. 9–9) for use in floors, walls, or roofs; folded plate and/or radial folded plate roofs; box beams; and the more recently developed plywood joist.

Industrial uses. Among the myriad industrial uses, plywood is widely utilized in the construction of a variety of containers and crating. In the materials handling field, pallet bins and plywood decked pallets have gained widespread use. Plywood is also used extensively in the construction of traffic control and commercial signs. Especially acceptable are the medium and high density overlaid plywoods which provide ideal surfaces for painting or reflective sheeting. Other uses include dollies, linings for rolling stock, shelving and partitions, tote boxes, separator boards, cable reel heads, and many more.

Concrete forms. Specially made plywood (Plyform, Class I and Plyform, Class II) is widely utilized as form material during concrete construction. Plywood forms lend themselves to giant slip forms and complex shapes as well as the more conventional prefabricated components. The regular panels are mill oiled and may be reused several times. High density overlay plyform has the added advantage of a greater number of re-uses.

Paneling and siding. The development of textured sidings and paneling have, along with the development of medium and high density overlays, created new architectural applications for plywood. Panels are made in channel groove, kerfed, brushed, striated, texture one-eleven, fine line, and reverse board and batten surfaces (fig. 9–10). Use of overlaid panels has increased the adaptability of surfaces for painting and the use of vinyl films have made colorful scuff-resistant surfaces a reality. These newer developments have promise not only for paneling, but doors and other architectural uses as well.

Hardwood Plywood

In order to establish nationally recognized criteria for the principal types, grades, and sizes of hardwood and decorative plywood, Voluntary Product Standard PS 51-71 was initiated and became effective in 1971. The Standard states that the principal wood species used are hardwoods, although certain softwood species may also be used.

Hardwood and decorative plywoods are primarily intended for use as decorative wall panels where esthetic characteristics are important; for cut-to-size and stock panels used for furniture, cabinets, containers, and specialty products; and for certain marine applications.

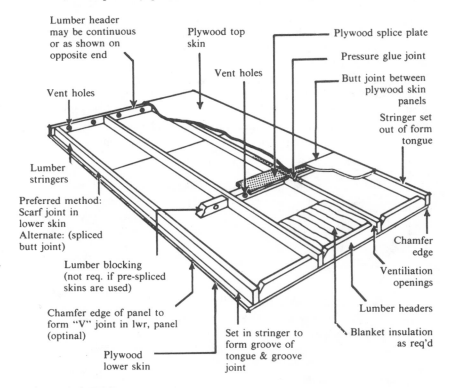

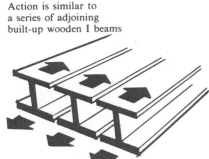

Action is similar to a series of adjoining built-up wooden I beams

Lumber header may be continuous or as shown on opposite end

Plywood top skin

Plywood splice plate

Pressure glue joint

Vent holes

Butt joint between plywood skin panels

Vent holes

Stringer set out of form tongue

Lumber stringers

Preferred method: Scarf joint in lower skin Alternate: (spliced butt joint)

Chamfer edge

Lumber blocking (not req. if pre-spliced skins are used)

Ventiliation openings

Chamfer edge of panel to form "V" joint in lwr, panel (optinal)

Set in stringer to form groove of tongue & groove joint

Lumber headers

Blanket insulation as req'd

Plywood lower skin

FIG. 9–9. *Flat stressed skin panel construction (top) and application (left). (Courtesy of American Plywood Association.)*

FIG. 9–10. *Contemporary architectural effects can be achieved with plywood siding. (Courtesy of American Plywood Association.)*

The most common panel sizes available are 48 by 84 inches (4' X 7'), 48 by 96 inches (4' X 8') and 48 by 120 inches (4' X 10') with thicknesses ranging from 1/8 to 3/4 inch. Tolerances for nominal dimensions of the panels are ±1/32 inch for the width and length. Thickness of unsanded panels is also a ±1/32 inch, while sanded panels have a tolerance of plus 0, minus 1/32 inch, except that sanded panels with a nominal thickness of 1/4 inch or more are permitted a tolerance of plus 0, minus 3/64 inch. Standard panels are considered to be four feet wide by eight feet long; however, some manufacturers have the capacity to produce panels five to seven feet wide and twelve feet long. It is possible to make panels as long as forty feet or more through the use of specialized scarfing equipment. Sizes this great, though, are highly dependent upon limitations imposed by such factors as handling and transportation. Thickness variations are not uncommon as witnessed by the fact that many aircraft and specialty use plywoods are 3/64 inch, while thicknesses of certain doors may be as much as 2¼ inches.

The product standard for hardwood plywoods lists the following constructions based on the kind of core:

1. Hardwood veneer core (3 ply, 5 ply, etc. in odd numbers of plys)
2. Softwood veneer core (3 ply, 5 ply, etc. in odd numbers of plys)
3. Hardwood lumber core (3 ply, 5 ply, and 7 ply)
4. Softwood lumber core (3 ply, 5 ply, and 7 ply)
5. Particleboard core (3 ply and 5 ply)
6. Hardboard core (3 ply)
7. Special core (3 ply or more)

The standard further states that panels shall be constructed with an odd number of plys and that all plys shall be combinations of species, thickness, and moisture content to produce a balanced panel. Inner plys must be in pairs with each ply placed on opposite sides of the core and with the grain of adjacent plys at right angles. Illustrated in figure 9–13 are several typical plywood constructions.

Appearance grades table.

Type	Use these terms when you specify plywood (2)	Description and Most Common Uses	Typical Grade-trademarks	Face	Back	Inner Plys						
Interior Type	N-N, N-A, N-B INT-DFPA	Cabinet quality. One or both sides select all heartwood or all sapwood veneer. For natural finish furniture, cabinet doors, built-ins, etc. Special order items.	N·N·G·1·INT·DFPA·PS 1·66 / N·A·G·2·INT·DFPA·PS 1·66	N	N,A, or B	C						3/4
	N-D-INT-DFPA	For natural finish paneling. Special order item.	N·D·G·3·INT·DFPA·PS 1·66	N	D	D	1/4					
	A-A INT-DFPA	For interior applications where both sides will be on view. Built-ins, cabinets, furniture and partitions. Face is smooth and suitable for painting.	A·A·G·3·INT·DFPA·PS 1·66	A	A	D	1/4		3/8	1/2	5/8	3/4
	A-B INT-DFPA	For uses similar to Interior A-A but where the appearance of one side is less important and two smooth solid surfaces are necessary.	A·B·G·4·INT·DFPA·PS 1·66	A	B	D	1/4		3/8	1/2	5/8	3/4
	A-D INT-DFPA	For interior uses where the appearance of only one side is important. Paneling, built-ins, shelving, partitions and flow racks.	A-D GROUP 1 INTERIOR DFPA	A	D	D	1/4		3/8	1/2	5/8	3/4
	B-B INT-DFPA	Interior utility panel used where two smooth sides are desired. Permits circular plugs. Paintable.	B·B·G·3·INT·DFPA·PS 1·66	B	B	D	1/4		3/8	1/2	5/8	3/4
	B-D INT-DFPA	Interior utility panel for use where one smooth side is required. Good for backing, sides of built-ins. Industry: shelving, slip sheets, separator boards and bins.	B-D GROUP 3 INTERIOR DFPA	B	D	D	1/4		3/8	1/2	5/8	3/4
	DECORATIVE PANELS	Rough-sawn, brushed, grooved or striated faces. Good for paneling, interior accent walls, built-ins, counter facing, displays and exhibits.	DECORATIVE·B·D·G·1·INT·DFPA	C or btr.	D	D		5/16	3/8	1/2	5/8	
	PLYRON INT-DFPA	Hardboard face on both sides. For counter tops, shelving, cabinet doors, flooring. Hardboard faces may be tempered, untempered, smooth or screened.	PLYRON · INT DFPA			C & D				1/2	5/8	3/4
Exterior Type	A-A EXT-DFPA (4)	Use in applications where the appearance of both sides is important. Fences, built-ins, signs, boats, cabinets, commercial refrigerators, shipping containers, tote boxes, tanks, and ducts.	A·A·G·4·EXT·DFPA·PS 1·66	A	A	C	1/4		3/8	1/2	5/8	3/4
	A-B EXT-DFPA (4)	For use similar to A-A EXT panels but where the appearance of one side is less important.	A·B·G·1·EXT·DFPA·PS 1·66	A	B	C	1/4		3/8	1/2	5/8	3/4
	A-C EXT-DFPA (4)	Exterior use where the appearance of only one side is important. Sidings, soffits, fences, structural uses, boxcar and truck lining and farm buildings. Tanks, trays, commercial refrigerators.	A-C GROUP 2 EXTERIOR DFPA	A	C	C	1/4		3/8	1/2	5/8	3/4
	B-B EXT-DFPA (4)	An outdoor utility panel with solid paintable faces.	B·B·G·1·EXT·DFPA·PS 1·66	B	B	C	1/4		3/8	1/2	5/8	3/4
	B-C EXT-DFPA (4)	An outdoor utility panel for farm service and work buildings, boxcar and truck lining, containers, tanks, agricultural equipment. Also as base for exterior coatings for walls, roofs.	B-C GROUP 3 EXTERIOR DFPA	B	C	C	1/4		3/8	1/2	5/8	3/4
	HDO EXT-DFPA (4)	Exterior type High Density Overlay plywood with hard, semi-opaque resin-fiber overlay. Abrasion resistant. Painting not ordinarily required. For concrete forms, cabinets, counter tops, signs and tanks.	HDO·A·A·G·1·EXT·DFPA·PS 1·66	A or B	A or B	C plgd		5/16	3/8	1/2	5/8	3/4
	MDO EXT-DFPA (4)	Exterior type Medium Density Overlay with smooth, opaque, resin-fiber overlay heat-fused to one or both panel faces. Ideal base for paint. Highly recommended for siding and other outdoor applications. Also good for built-ins, signs and displays.	MDO·B·B·G·2·EXT·DFPA·PS 1·66	B	B or C	C (5)		5/16	3/8	1/2	5/8	3/4
	303 SIDING EXT-DFPA (7)	Grade designation covers proprietary plywood products for exterior siding, fencing, etc., with special surface treatment such as V-groove, channel groove, striated, brushed, rough-sawn.	303 SIDING 16 o c GROUP 4 EXTERIOR DFPA	(6)	C	C			3/8	1/2	5/8	
	T 1-11 EXT-DFPA	Exterior type, sanded or unsanded, shiplapped edges with parallel grooves 1/4" deep, 3/8" wide. Grooves 2" or 4" o.c. Standard, other spacing optional. Available 8' and 10' lengths and MDO. For siding, paneling, fences, chimney enclosures.	T 1-11 GROUP 1 EXTERIOR DFPA	C or btr.	C	C					5/8	
	PLYRON EXT-DFPA	Exterior panel surfaced both sides with hardboard for use in exterior applications. Faces are tempered, smooth or screened.	PLYRON · EXT·DFPA			C				1/2	5/8	3/4
	MARINE EXT-DFPA	Exterior type plywood made only with Douglas fir or western larch. Special solid jointed core construction. Subject to special limitations on core gaps and number of face repairs. Ideal for boat hulls. Also available with HDO or MDO faces.	MARINE·A·A·EXT·DFPA PS 1·66	A or B	A or B	B	1/4		3/8	1/2	5/8	3/4

(1) Sanded both sides except where decorative or other surfaces specified.

(2) Available in Group 1, 2, 3, 4, or 5 unless otherwise noted.

(3) Standard 4x8 panel sizes, other sizes available.

(4) Also available in STRUCTURAL I (face, back and inner plys limited to Group 1 species).

(5) Or C-Plugged.

(6) C or better for 5 plys; C-Plugged or better for 3 ply panels.

(7) Stud spacing is shown on grade stamp.

FIG. 9-11. *Appearance grades of softwood plywood. (Courtesy of American Plywood Association.)*

	Use these terms when you specify plywood (2)	Description and Most Common Uses	Typical Grade-trademarks	Veneer Grade			Most Common Thicknesses (inch) (3)						
				Face	Back	Inner Plys							
Interior Type	STANDARD C-D INT-DFPA (1) (4)	Unsanded sheathing grade for wall and roof sheathing, subflooring; also industrial uses such as pallets. Also available with intermediate glue (9) or exterior glue. Specify intermediate glue where moderate construction delays are expected; exterior glue where durability is required in long construction delays. For permanent exposure to weather or moisture, only Exterior-type plywood is suitable.	STANDARD 32/16 INTERIOR DFPA / STANDARD 32/16 INTERIOR EXTERIOR GLUE	C	D	D	5/16	3/8	1/2	5/8	3/4	7/8	
	STRUCTURAL I C-D INT-DFPA and STRUCTURAL II C-D INT-DFPA (9)	Unsanded structural grades where plywood strength properties are of maximum importance. Structural diaphragms, box beams, gusset plates, stressed-skin panels, containers, pallet bins. Made only with exterior glue. STRUCTURAL I limited to Group 1 species for face, back and inner plys. STRUCTURAL II permits Group 1, 2, or 3 species.	STRUCTURAL I 32/16 INTERIOR DFPA EXTERIOR GLUE	C (6)	D (7)	D (7)	5/16	3/8	1/2	5/8	3/4	7/8	
	UNDERLAYMENT INT-DFPA (4) (1)	For underlayment or combination subfloor-underlayment under resilient floor coverings, carpeting in homes, apartments, mobile homes. Use UNDERLAYMENT with ext. glue where moisture may be present, such as bathrooms, utility rooms. Sanded or touch-sanded as specified.	UNDERLAYMENT GROUP 1 INTERIOR DFPA	C Plugged	D	C & D (8)	1/4	3/8	1/2	5/8	3/4		
	C-D PLUGGED INT-DFPA (4) (1)	For built-ins, wall and ceiling tile backing, cable reels, walkways, separator boards. Not a substitute for UNDERLAYMENT, as it lacks UNDERLAYMENT's punch-through resistance. Unsanded or touch-sanded as specified.	C-D PLUGGED GROUP 2 INTERIOR DFPA	C Plugged	D	D	5/16	3/8	1/2	5/8	3/4		
	2-4-1 INT-DFPA (5) (1)	Combination subfloor-underlayment. Quality base for resilient floor coverings, carpeting, wood strip flooring. Use 2·4·1 with exterior glue in areas subject to moisture. Unsanded or touch-sanded as specified.	2·4·1 GROUP 2 INTERIOR DFPA	C Plugged	D	C & D	(available 1-1/8" or 1-1/4")						
Exterior Type	C-C EXT-DFPA (4)	Unsanded grade with waterproof bond for subflooring and roof decking, siding on service and farm buildings, crating, pallets, pallet bins, cable reels.	C-C 32/16 EXTERIOR DFPA	C	C	C	5/16	3/8	1/2	5/8	3/4	7/8	
	UNDERLAYMENT C-C Plugged EXT-DFPA (4) and C-C PLUGGED EXT-DFPA (4)	For UNDERLAYMENT or combination subfloor-underlayment under resilient floor coverings where particularly severe moisture conditions may be present, as in balcony decks. Also use for tile backing where severe moisture conditions exist. For refrigerated or controlled atmosphere rooms, pallets, fruit pallet bins, reusable cargo containers, tanks and boxcar and truck floors and linings. Sanded or touch-sanded as specified.	UNDERLAYMENT GROUP 3 EXTERIOR DFPA C-C PLUGGED / C-C PLUGGED GROUP 4 EXTERIOR DFPA	C Plugged	C	C (8)	1/4	3/8	1/2	5/8	3/4	7/8	
	STRUCTURAL I C-C EXT-DFPA	For engineered applications in construction and industry where full Exterior type panels made with all Group 1 woods are required. Unsanded.	STRUCTURAL I C-C 32/16 EXTERIOR DFPA	C	C	C	5/16	3/8	1/2	5/8	3/4	7/8	
	B-B PLYFORM CLASS I & CLASS II (9) EXT-DFPA	Concrete form grades with high re-use factor. Sanded both sides. Edge-sealed. Mill-oiled unless otherwise specified. Special restrictions on species. Also available in HDO.	B-B PLYFORM CLASS I EXTERIOR DFPA	B	B	C					5/8	3/4	

(1) Also available with exterior or intermediate glue.
(2) All grades except PLYFORM available tongue and grooved in panels 1/2" and thicker.
(3) Panels are standard 4x8-foot size. Other sizes available.
(4) Available in Group 1, 2, 3, 4, or 5.
(5) Available in Group 1, 2 or 3 only.
(6) Special improved C grade for structural panels.
(7) Special improved D grade for structural panels.
(8) Ply beneath face a **special** C grade which limits knotholes to 1".
(9) Check dealer for availability in your area.

Classification of Species

Group 1	Group 2	Group 3	Group 4	Group 5
Birch Sweet Yellow Douglas Fir 1* Larch, Western Maple, Sugar Pine, Caribbean Pine, Southern Loblolly Longleaf Shortleaf Slash Tanoak	Cedar, Port Orford Douglas Fir 2** Fir California Red Grand Noble Pacific Silver White Hemlock, Western Lauan Almon Bagtikan Red Lauan Tangile White Lauan Maple, Black Mengkulang Meranti Pine Pond Red Western White Spruce, Sitka Sweetgum Tamarack	Alder, Red Cedar, Alaska Pine Jack Lodgepole Ponderosa Spruce Redwood Spruce Black Red White	Aspen Bigtooth Quaking Birch, Paper Cedar Incense Western Red Fir, Subalpine Hemlock, Eastern Pine Eastern White Sugar Poplar, Western*** Spruce, Engelmann	Fir, Balsam Poplar, Balsam

*Douglas Fir 1—Washington, Oregon, California, Idaho, Montana, Wyoming, British Columbia, Alberta.
**Douglas Fir 2—Nevada, Utah, Colorado, Arizona, New Mexico.
***Black Cottonwood.

FIG. 9–12. *Engineered grades of softwood plywood. (Courtesy of American Plywood Association.)*

Hardwood Plywood Types and Grades

Hardwood plywood is, essentially, marketed and specified through three essential aspects of its makeup; namely, the species and grade of the face veneer, and the type (glue bond requirements). A brief discussion of each follows, but those who wish more detailed information should consult the product standard PS 51-71.

Species. Panels shall be identified by the species of the face. The backs and inner plys may be any hardwood or softwood species. The species commonly used for veneers are listed in table 9–3 and are categorized according to specific gravity ranges.

TABLE 9–3

Categories of Commonly Used Species for Hardwood Plywood Based on Specific Gravity Ranges[a]

Category A species (0.56 or more specific gravity)	Category B species (0.43 through 0.55 specific gravity)	Category C species (0.42 or less specific gravity)
Ash, Commercial White	Ash, Black	Alder, Red
Beech, American	Avodire	Aspen
Birch, Yellow Sweet	Bay	Basswood, American
Bubinga	Cedar, Eastern Red[b]	Box Elder
Elm, Rock	Cherry, Black	Cativo
Madrone, Pacific	Chestnut, American	Cedar, Western Red[b]
Maple, Black (hard)	Cypress[b]	Ceiba
Maple, Sugar (hard)	Elm, American (white, red, or gray)	Cottonwood, Black
Oak, Commercial Red	Fir, Douglas[b]	Cottonwood, Eastern
Oak, Commercial White	Gum, Black	Pine, White and Ponderosa[b]
Oak, Oregon	Gum, Sweet	Poplar, Yellow
Paldao	Hackberry	Redwood[b]
Pecan, Commercial	Lauan (Phillippine Mahogany)	Willow, Black
Rosewood	Limba	
Sapele	Magnolia	
Teak	Mahogany, African	
	Mahogany, Honduras	
	Maple, Red (soft)	
	Maple, Silver (soft)	
	Prima Vera	
	Sycamore	
	Tupelo, Water	
	Walnut, American	

SOURCE: U.S. Department of Commerce, National Bureau of Standards, *Voluntary Product Standard, PS 51-71, Hardwood and Decorative Plywood* (Washington, D.C.: Government Printing Office, 1971).

[a] Based on ovendry weight and volume at 12 percent moisture content.

[b] Softwood

Veneer grades. Hardwood plywood is identified by the veneer grade of the face. In all, six grades of hardwood veneers are covered in the product standard as well as the specifications for certain decorative softwoods. Table 9–4 provides a brief and general summary of these grades. Further data may be obtained from PS 51-71.

Matching. When a particular piece of veneer is not large enough it may be matched with other pieces to form larger sizes. Many architectural uses require special patterns and these too may be achieved through matching. The veneer grade Premium (A) requires that veneers be either book or slip matched. These and several other matching patterns are illustrated in figure 9–14.

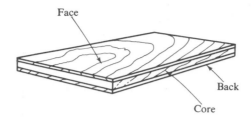

Three-ply veneer core construction

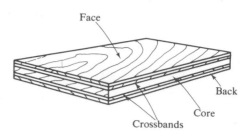

Five-ply veneer core construction

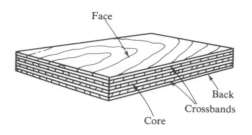

Multi-ply veneer core construction

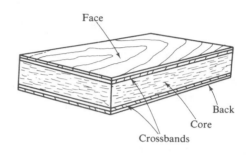

Five-ply particleboard core construction

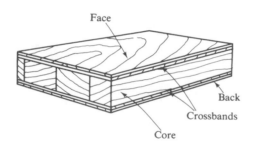

Five-ply lumber core construction

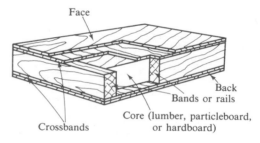

Five-ply construction
with banding or railing

FIG. 9–13. *Typical plywood constructions. (Reprinted from Voluntary Product Standard, PS 51-71, Product Standard for Hardwood and Decorative Plywood.)*

Types. The types as specified are related to the glue bond requirements. Four types are listed: (1) Technical Type plywood, (2) Type I plywood, (3) Type II plywood, and (4) Type III plywood. The Technical Type and Type I plywood must meet the same specifications and have great durability and possess a high degree of moisture resistance. Type III is a lower quality than Type II; however, neither is designed for prolonged exposure to moisture.

Hardwood or decorative plywood which conforms to the product standard must be so identified in either of the following ways (U.S. Department of Commerce, 1971):

1. Each panel shall be marked with the symbol of the Standard, PS 51-71; the name or recognized identification of the producer; the species and grade of the face veneer; the type of plywood; the symbol "CP," if container plywood; and the identity of the qualified inspection and testing agency, if applicable, or

2. The shipment or order shall be accompanied by a written certification which states that the panels conform to all of the requirements of the Voluntary Product Standard PS 51-71, and identifies the producer; the species and grade of the face veneer; the type of plywood; the qualified inspection and testing agency, if applicable; and the specific intended use if container plywood.

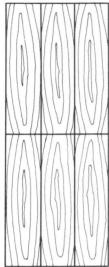

VERTICAL BUTT AND HORIZONTAL BOOKLEAF MATCH

Where the height of a flitch does not permit its fabrication into the desired height of panel, it may be matched vertically as well as horizontally.

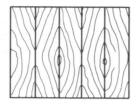

BOOK MATCH

All types of veneers are used. In book matching, every other sheet is turned over just as are the leaves of a book. Thus, the back of one veneer meets the front of the adjacent veneer, producing a matching joint design.

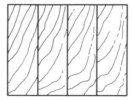

SLIP MATCH

In slip matching, veneer sheets are joined side by side and convey a sense of repeating the flitch figure. All types of veneer may be used, but this type of matching is most common in quarter-sliced veneers.

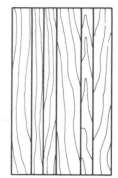

RANDOM MATCH

Veneers are joined with the intention of creating a casual unmatched effect. Veneers from several logs may be used in the manufacture of a set of panels.

SPECIAL   MATCHING   EFFECTS

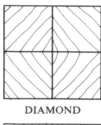

DIAMOND

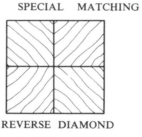

REVERSE DIAMOND

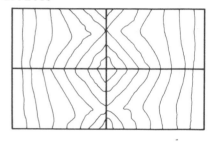

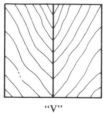

"V"

HERRINGBONE

FOUR-WAY CENTER AND BUTT

This type of match is ordinarily applied to Butt, Crotch or Stump veneers, since it is the most effective way of revealing the beauty of their configurations. Occasionally flat cut veneers are matched in this manner where panel length requirements exceed the length of available veneers.

FIG. 9–14. *Several types of veneer matches. (Courtesy of Fine Hardwoods— American Walnut Association.)*

General Use Considerations

Because of the natural warmth and beauty of hardwoods, hardwood plywood is one of the most popular materials used for architectural applications and for furniture. Perhaps one of its most important properties is that of its esthetic values. Among these properties are the wide range of colors which are found in fine hardwoods. This, coupled with the natural grain and figure patterns, often enhanced by matching, creates unlimited possibilities for the designer.

The basic properties of strength and dimensional stability which are inherent to plywood make it an ideal panel material for use in the furniture industry as well as other commercial uses.

The economies of using hardwood plywoods are another significant factor in their use considerations. Not only are the panels less costly than comparable sizes of solid wood, but the use of panels eliminates the need for costly operations such as gluing up and machining of

FIG. 9–15. *Fine hardwood panels enhance the interiors of many offices such as this. (Courtesy Fine Hardwoods-American Walnut Association.)*

solid stock. As with other plywoods, the material is easily worked with common tools and machines and is easily adaptable to a wide range of fastening techniques.

Other properties such as insulative values, splitting and impact resistance, and flexibility of use add to its acceptance as a prized material.

Applications

The range of specific use applications for hardwood and decorative plywoods is very extensive and, therefore, it is impossible to present an all-inclusive compilation of the products in which it is used.

TABLE 9–4

Summary of Veneer Grades Used in Hardwood Plywood

Veneer Grade	General Conditions
Premium Grade (A)	Veneer shall be smooth, tight cut, and full length. When used as a face and consists of more than one face, it shall be edge matched. Edge joints tight. Certain small defects allowed.
Good Grade (1)	Veneer should be smooth, tight cut, and full length. Edge joints shall be tight. Pieces need not be matched for color and grain, but sharp contrasts between adjacent pieces in grain, figure, and natural character markings is not permitted.
Second Grade (2)	Veneer shall be free from open defects. Matching for grain or color is not required.
Utility Grade (3)	Open defects are permitted—knot holes of 1″ diameter maximum, open splits or joints of 3/16″ for half the length of panel.
Backing Grade (4)	Similar to Utility grade except larger open defects are permitted—knot holes of 3″ maximum diameter, open splits or joints vary but may if 1/4″ extend for length of panel.
Specialty Grade (SP)	Includes veneer possessing characteristics unlike those of foregoing grades. Characteristics are as agreed upon by the buyer and seller. (Includes species such as wormy chestnut, birdseye maple. and English brown oak.)
Softwood Veneers	Certain decorative softwoods have face grades specified, others are graded under requirements for hardwoods.

SOURCE: U.S. Department of Commerce, National Bureau of Standards, *Voluntary Product Standard, PS 51-71, Hardwood and Decorative Plywood* (Washington, D.C.: Government Printing Office, 1971).

Architectural uses comprise one of the major markets for these panels. In both the residential and commercial applications a wide variety of wall panels are available. These applications range from the walls of the family room to board rooms of large corporations. Many forms of exterior sidings are available as are a wide range of hardwood veneer doors. Finish flooring of laminated blocks are also extensively used.

With respect to the furniture industry, hardwood plywood is widely used in flat panels as well as in curved and molded forms. Virtually all types of furniture such as chests, cabinets, desks, beds, and chairs are produced from it.

Exterior uses of hardwood plywoods are also found in the sporting goods industry. Skis, toboggans, golf clubs, tennis racquets, and small pleasure craft are but a few of its applications. Other uses include containers and a variety of items such as musical instruments, bowls, caskets, mobile homes, and tool handles.

Resources

American Plywood Association. *The American Plywood Association Presents U. S. Product Standard PS 1-66 for Softwood Plywood—Construction & Industrial, Together with DFPA Grade Trademarks.* Tacoma, Washington: American Plywood Association, 1966.

American Plywood Association. *Plywood Properties and Grades.* Tacoma, Washington: American Plywood Association, 1971.

Demas, Ted. *Basic Plywood Processing.* Tacoma, Washington: American Plywood Association, 1969.

Fine Hardwoods Association. *Fine Hardwood Veneers for Architectural Interiors,* AIA File No. 19F. Chicago: Fine Hardwoods Association.

Hardwood Plywood Manufacturers Association. *The Story of Hardwood Plywood.* Arlington, Virginia: Hardwood Plywood Manufacturers Association, n.d.

United States Department of Commerce, National Bureau of Standards. *Product Standard, PS 1-66, Softwood Plywood, Construction and Industrial.* Washington, D.C.: Government Printing Office, 1966.

United States Department of Commerce, National Bureau of Standards. *Voluntary Product Standard, PS 51-71, Hardwood and Decorative Plywood.* Washington, D.C.: Government Printing Office, 1971.

Chapter Ten

Wood
Composition Board

The term wood composition board is one of a generic nature and refers to panel products composed of wood (or other lignocellulosic material) which had been broken down into either small particles or wood fibers and then reconstituted to form the new product. The resulting panels retain some of the original properties of wood while gaining others which provide distinct advantages over the use of wood itself in many applications.

The increasing scarcity of high quality lumber and veneer has given increased emphasis to the production and use of wood composition board during recent years. Due to the small particles used in manufacture, it is possible to utilize non-logs and parts of trees formerly considered undesirable and also to use wood residues in the formation of the product; thus, greater "mileage" may be achieved from our forest resources.

Composition board is generally classified into two groups—fiberboard and particleboard. These categories are determined largely by the type of particle used in manufacture. Fiberboard is made from the fiber-like components of wood and utilizes the natural binding agent lignin, while particleboards are made from small wood particles and synthetic resins are utilized as the binding agents. Fiberboards are usually reclassified into two sub-groupings, insulation board and hardboard, and are so grouped on the basis of their density. Table 10–1 compares various types of wood composition boards.

As the major classifications of composition boards possess their own manufacturing processes, properties, and unique applications, each will be discussed in greater detail through the remainder of this chapter.

TABLE 10–1

Comparison of Wood Composition Boards*

Board Type	Basic Element	Density		Binding Agent	Common Board Thickness
		(G./cc.)	(Lb./cu. ft.)		
Insulation Board	Wood or other	0.02 to 0.50	1.2 to 31	Natural lignin	1/2 to 3 in.
Semi-rigid	lignocellulose	.02 to .16	1.2 to 10		
Rigid	fiber	.16 to .50	10 to 31		
Hardboard	Wood fiber	.50 to 1.45	31 to 90	Natural lignin	1/12 to 1/2 in.
Medium		.50 to .80	31 to 50	and/or other	
High		.80 to 1.20	50 to 75	adhesive	
Special		1.35 to 1.45	84 to 90		
Particleboard	Small wood components			Adhesives	1/8 to 2 in.
Low		Less than 0.59	Less than 37		
Medium		0.59 to 0.80	37 to 50		
High		More than 0.80	More than 50		

*Adapted from Wayne C. Lewis, *Insulation Board, Hardboard, and Particleboard* (Madison, Wisconsin: Forest Products Laboratory, Forest Service, U.S. Department of Agriculture, 1967).

Insulation Board

The oldest member of the fiberboard family is insulation board, first produced in 1914. Its development was the outgrowth of problems encountered by Edward W. Backus and Carl G. Muench. Backus, a paper manufacturer, was concerned with the growing amount of pulp residues which resulted from his papermaking operations and believed that more uses (other than burning) could be found for them. Muench, who worked for a refrigerator manufacturer, was convinced that a rigid insulating board made from wood fiber would be far superior to the flat straw product then in use. Through a mutual friend, Backus was persuaded to hire Muench and charged him with solving the problem of the ever growing piles of wood fiber which were being wasted (Insulation Board Institute, n.d.).

Assigned space in the basement of the paper mill, Muench designed a machine and within ten weeks had produced the first insulation board the world had known. Basically an adaptation of the papermaking process, his machine was capable of producing 3,000 square feet of board per day. Through continual refinements of his original process, insulation board plants today have achieved daily capacities in excess of 3 million square feet.

Properties

Prime among the advantages of insulation board are those properties which produce its high insulative values. Its low density provides a vast amount of tiny air pockets which greatly reduce the passage of either heat or cold through the product. In addition to its temperature regulating qualities, insulation board possesses acoustical values which, when used in ceilings, may absorb up to 70 percent of the excess noise which strikes it. The interlacing of fibers yields the additional advantage of strength and rigidity. This quality is put into widespread use as evidenced by the extensive application of insulation board as sheathing.

Manufacture

The two materials most widely used in the manufacture of insulation board are pulpwood and bagasse, a cellusosic by-product obtained during the processing of sugar cane. The first step in the process of producing insulation board is the moving of the pulp logs from storage areas to large chipping machines. In the chipper revolving knives reduce the material to uniform chips approximately 5/8 inch wide and 1 inch long. From the chipper, the material is moved to a refining section where it is further reduced to individual fibers. This process may utilize either steam or mechanical procedures and combines the fiber with water or other chemicals to prepare it for the mat-forming operation. The mat, a continuous blanket of interlaced and loosely formed fibers, is formed either wet or dry. A felter is used to produce a dry mat, whereas a fourdrinier (a machine which utilizes a type of wire screen upon which the liquid pulp is placed and some moisture extracted) or a cylinder machine (wet mat is laid, in measured amounts, on a screen and excess water is taken off) are used to produce a wet mat. Once the mats are formed, they undergo a cutting operation whereby sheets 16 to 26 feet long are produced and fed into large drying machines which reduce the moisture content to the desired level. After the dryer, the sheets are then cut and trimmed to the size of the specific product desired and packaged for shipment. If special use requirements dictate it, boards may be coated with asphalt after they are completed or may be impregnated with asphalt during the manufacturing process.

As the total consumption of the manufactured board is very closely linked to the requirements of the housing industry, production amounts may vary from year to year. The output of insulation board plants is currently measured in terms of billions of square feet annually if a 1/2 inch basis is used (Insulation Board Institute, n.d.).

Types and Uses

Insulation board products, practically all of which are construction oriented, are manufactured in accordance with the ultimate use for which they are intended; therefore, the types of products and uses are almost inseparable. The following types of products are now used extensively (Insulation Board Institute, n.d.):

Building board (wall board) is a low-cost, general-purpose product used most extensively as a covering for walls and ceilings. Most commonly produced sizes are 5/16 to 1/2 inch thick in 4 foot widths ranging in length from 8 to 12 feet. These panels are produced plain or may be purchased with flame-resistant surfaces in a variety of colors.

Insulating roof deck is a component product which serves as the roof deck, as the insulation, and as the finished ceiling. The material is available in panels 2' X 8' and in thicknesses of 1½, 2, and 3 inches. Each panel is nailed on top of the ceiling beams or joists and roofing materials may be applied directly to the weather side.

Roof insulation is designed for use on flat roof decks. Available in thicknesses from 1/2 inch to 3 inches and in sizes 23" X 47" or 24" X 48" it may be purchased plain or asphalt impregnated and either with or without a moisture resistant asphalt coating.

Ceiling materials are basically of two types, ceiling tile and lay-in panels. Ceiling tile usually comes in sizes of either 12" X 12" or 12" X 24" and 1/2 inch thickness, available in plain, perforated, and embossed surface features and in a variety of colors. They are applied directly to existing ceilings or fastened to furring strips. Various edge treatments allow for fastening by either adhesive or mechanical means. Lay-in panels are designed to fit within metal grids of suspended ceilings and usually are available in 2' × 2' or 2' × 4' panels 1/2 inch thick. A suspended ceiling allows for the lowering of a high ceiling and permits wiring, piping, or ductwork to be concealed above the panels.

Plank is generally used as an interim wall covering and applied in a vertical direction. Each plank is 1/2 inch thick, 12 inches wide and is available in 8 to 10 foot lengths. Available with tongue-and-groove edges and in colors, the planks provide a finished wall upon completion of the installation.

Sheathing is used to provide the covering for the exterior of stud walls and is commonly available in three types—regular density, intermediate, and nail base. As the most popular sheathing presently used in residential construction, insulation board sheathing provides effective thermal insulation and noise insulation, as well as structural bracing strength. Panels which are impregnated or coated with asphalt provide adequate water resistance and eliminate the need for using building paper. The most common type, regular density, is available in 1/2 or 25/32 inch thickness, in widths of 2 or 4 feet, and lengths of 8 to 9 feet. The 4 foot wide panels are applied in a vertical position while the 2 foot wide panels are applied horizontally. Intermediate density panels are designed to be used without corner bracing and are available in 1/2 inch thickness and either 4' × 8' or 4' × 9' sheets. The nail base sheathing is of a higher density than the other types and may be used as the backing for direct application of wood or asbestos cement shingles, and comes in the same sizes as the intermediate type.

Specially manufactured insulation boards are also available as shingle backers, formboards, and for use as sound deadening. Each comes in a variety of sizes and possesses square edges.

FIG. 10–1. *Insulation board is widely used for sheathing in residential construction. (Courtesy of the Celotex Corporation.)*

Hardboard

The development of the hardboard industry, like that of insulation board, came about through the concern of those who believed that some uses must be found for growing amounts of wood residue. In an attempt to produce a product somewhat similar to insulation board, William H. Mason discovered hardboard in 1924. Although the discovery came about quite by accident, his process became basic to the development of the hardboard industry. Mason, who later formed the Masonite Corporation, found that small wood chips could be exploded from their solid state into tiny wood fibers through the use of high pressure steam. The resulting fibers were then suitable for forming into a mat.

His accidental discovery took place when he placed a small mat of the wet fibers between the steam heated plates of a small press. Thinking only to dry the fibers, he applied pressure to the plates, shut off the steam and went out for lunch. When he returned after lunch, he found that a faulty valve had allowed the steam to continue its heating action on the plates during his absence. When he removed the fiber mat he found that it had been transformed into a hard, dense, dry, and grainless board—the first hardboard ever produced.

When the first hardboard plant in the United States was established in 1926 the total world production rate was less than 6 million square feet (1/8" X 12" X 12"). During the 1960s, the production of hardboard in the world had grown to over 4 billion square feet.

Properties

The definition of hardboard as expressed in the commercial standard CS 251–63 (U.S. Department of Commerce, 1967) gives some insight into the nature of the material:

> Hardboard is a generic term for a panel manufactured primarily from interfelted lignocellulosic fibers consolidated under heat and pressure in a hot press to a density of at least 31 pounds per cubic foot (0.497 grams per cubic centimeter).
>
> Other materials may be added during manufacture to improve certain properties, such as stiffness, hardness, finishing properties, resistance to abrasion and moisture, as well as to increase strength, durability, and utility.

This definition, then, indicates that hardboard is a hard, dense and grainless board which is composed of wood fibers and which possesses high tensile strength, density, and low water absorption.

Through engineering and manufacturing technology, wood fibers are reconstituted into a board which often has distinct advantages over wood itself. Because it has been compressed under tremendous heat and pressure, hardboard possesses greater hardness and weight per cubic inch than the wood from which it was made. Characteristics such as grain or knots are not evident in hardboard; therefore, problems associated with them are eliminated. In addition, hardboard is more resistant to abrasion and moisture than most forms of native wood.

More specifically, the American Hardboard Association lists the following advantages:

1. It may be easily worked with common tools and may be sawed, planed, sanded, drilled, or punched.
2. It accepts paints, stains, or other finishes readily by brushing, wiping, rolling, or spraying.
3. It is water-resistant.

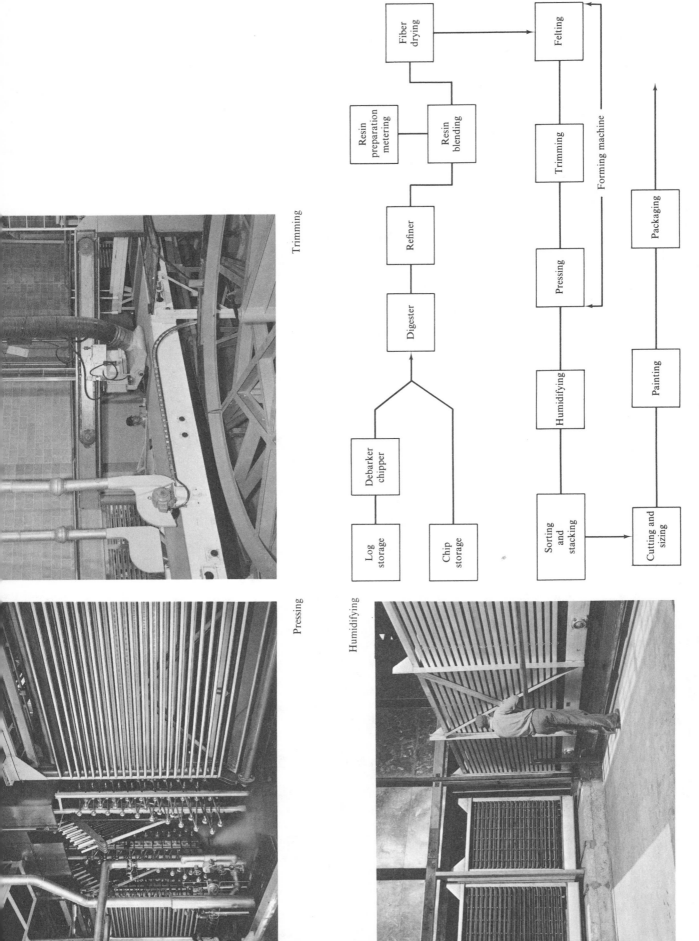

Trimming

Pressing

Humidifying

FIG. 10-2. Hardboard siding production. (Chart courtesy of Jim Walter Corporation, photos courtesy of American Forest Institute.)

4. It is available in flexible grades which may be bent or shaped to many contours.
5. It has uniformity of appearance and considerable strength, resists cracking, and will not split or splinter.
6. It possesses a high degree of dimensional stability.
7. It is available in a wide variety of patterns, colors, and textures.
8. It is economical and easy to use.

Manufacture

The actual process of producing hardboard is highly similar to that of producing insulation board, and in some instances, the same plant may produce both. Practically any species of wood may be used in the production of hardboard; however, in practice, individual plants lean heavily on species indigenous to their particular geographic area. In addition to pulpwood, residues or chips from sawmills and woodworking plants are extensively used as the source of raw material.

The process of producing hardboard begins when the raw material is sent through a chipper where the wood is cut up into small pieces, each approximately 5/8 inch wide and 1 inch long. The chips are then reduced to fiber bundles by defibering machines which tear the chips apart or through the use of steam pressure which is released suddenly, causing the chips to literally "explode" into fiber bundles. Following the breakdown of the chips into fiber bundles, machines called "refiners" are used to separate the bundles into individual fibers.

Once the fibers are separated, they are laid into a loosely formed and interlaced mat and then placed in a hot press. To produce hardboard, the mat is formed in one of several ways: (1) the mat is formed wet and pressed wet; (2) the mat is formed wet but dried before pressing; (3) the mat is formed dry but is wet and the moisture removed during pressing; or (4) the mat is formed dry and pressed dry. Basically, then, there are two methods of mat formation—wet and dry.

Wet forming is accomplished by either the continuous or batch method. Wet-continuous forming is highly similar to the process used for producing insulation board, except that a phenolic resin binder is mixed with the fibers in the headbox. In the batch method, rather than using a fourdrinier, the fiber, resin, and water mix flows onto a screen contained within a box (usually 4' × 8'). Suction is then applied to drain off the excess water and the sides of the box are raised, thus leaving a formed mat.

Dry forming is usually accomplished by spraying the fibers with a waterproof phenolic resin and then conveying the pulp through the air onto a slow moving screen. This process provides the advantage of allowing the fibers to interlace with each other in an infinite number of directions, whereas the wet process leaves the fibers oriented in a horizontal or layered direction. As a result, the dry formed board possesses a higher internal bond and the vertical tensile strength is increased considerably. Another advantage of the dry process is that, through the use of several felter heads, different length fibers may be laid down in layers with the smallest to the outside faces—thus producing a smoother face which provides a better base for paint or other finish.

Pressing may also be accomplished either wet or dry. Dry pressing requires that the fibers be reduced to a moisture content of 8 to 10 percent prior to the pressing operation itself. To accomplish this a fiber drier or kiln is used. Mats may then be pressed against a caul and emerge with two smooth sides. Wet pressing requires the use of a screen to allow an escape route for the excess water and steam as the board is being pressed. Boards of this type bear a characteristic screen imprint on the back.

Due to the tremendous heat and pressure generated during the pressing operation, the board produced is dryer than the surrounding atmosphere. To correct this, the board is placed into a humidifier where moisture is added and the board is stabilized to its surroundings. Once humidified, the board is then trimmed to size and readied for shipment.

To improve certain qualities of hardboard, it is often "tempered." Tempering, according to commercial standard CS 251-63, consists of "impregnating with a siccative material such as drying oil blends of oxidizing resin which are stabilized by baking or other heating after introduction." The result is a board which possesses improved properties of strength, hardness and water resistance over those of standard hardboard.

Types and Uses

According to CS 251-63, hardboard may be classified into three different types:

Standard. Standard hardboard is a product in substantially the same form as when it comes from the manufacturing press, except for minor processing steps such as humidification to adjust moisture content, and trimming to size. This is a hardboard of high strength and water resistance, and in most cases falls in a specific gravity range of .96 to 1.20 (60 to 75 lbs. per cu. ft.).

Tempered. Standard hardboard which has been impregnated with a siccative material such as drying oil blends of oxidizing resin which are stabilized by baking or other heating is termed tempered hardboard. This type has substantially improved properties of stiffness, strength, hardness, and resistance to water and abrasion as compared to Standard hardboard. In most cases its specific gravity falls in the range of 1.0 to 1.20 (62 to 75 lbs. per cu. ft.).

Service. This is a hardboard of moderate strength somewhat less than that of Standard hardboard. In most cases its specific gravity falls in the range of .80 to .96 (50 to 60 lbs. per cu. ft.). It is in substantially the same form as when it comes from the manufacturing press, except for minor processing steps such as humidification and trimming to size.

During the past several years medium density hardboards (31 to 50 lbs. per cu. ft.) have received increased attention on the markets. Medium density boards are homogeneous throughout and possess an even porosity. These characteristics allow for smoother machining and as a result minimize further finishing operations.

From these basic types the form of the finished board may be modified in various ways to produce a wide array of finished products.

Unlike insulation board, which is usually manufactured for specific end use requirements, hardboard is produced for a wider range of applications. Generally, the uses of hardboard can be divided into that developed for construction, furniture, cabinets and store fixtures, appliances and automotive or rolling stock (Lewis, 1967).

Applications in the construction industry include uses such as floor underlayment, facings for concrete forms, siding, door facings, and

FIG. 10-3. *The variety of finishes and other treatments to which hardboard is adaptable is illustrated by this collage of samples. (Courtesy of American Hardboard Association.)*

paneling. As the material may be purchased perforated, embossed, prefinished, and is available in a wide variety of surface treatments, it provides a very versatile material for both industry and the home craftsman.

In the appliance and furniture industries, hardboard is commonly used for furniture backs, panels, and drawer bottoms. Also extensively used as a core material, it may be overlaid with veneers or films and often serves as case material for chests, radio, television, or stereo cabinets.

Much of the hardboard used in automobiles or rolling stock is in the form of interior linings. Automobile door, side, and truck panels are often fabricated with hardboard as the backing material. Various types of prefinished or coated hardboards are often used as ceilings or interiors of station wagons and truck cabs.

In all, about one-half of the annual production of hardboard is used in the construction industry for the construction or remodeling of buildings. The other 50 percent is utilized for other industrial uses.

Particleboard

The youngest member of the composition board family is particleboard. Particleboard was developed in Europe near the end of World War II. Because of the havoc the war imposed upon the forests which served as the battlefields, a great scarcity of marketable timber products resulted. In the face of this critical shortage, a man-made product had to be developed which would make use of the broken or bent trees and turn them into a usable material. As European producers refined their products and processes, several small plants were started in the southern United States during the late 1940s. In 1951 the first large plant was placed in operation (National Particleboard Association, n.d.) As with insulation board and hardboard, the particleboard industry was born through a concern for greater utilization of growing amounts of wood waste. The production of particleboard increased to 125 million square feet in 1958, and by 1970 had risen to over 1 billion square feet.

FIG. 10–4. *Hardboard is widely used for siding, and many patterns and textures are available. (Courtesy of Jim Walter Corporation.)*

Properties

The commercial standard CS 236-66 (U.S. Department of Commerce, 1966) defines particleboard as:

> A panel material composed of small discrete pieces of wood bonded together in the presence of heat and pressure by an extraneous binder. Particleboards are further defined by the method of pressing. When the pressure is applied in the direction perpendicular to the faces as in a conventional multi-platen hot press, they are defined as "flat-platen pressed," and when the applied pressure is parallel to the faces, they are defined as "extruded."

Over 90 percent of the hardboard produced today is of the flat-platen pressed type. Extruded particleboard is characterized by a

FIG. 10–5. *Samples of even-textured (top) and multi-layered particleboard (bottom). Note coarser chips in center of multilayered board.*

TABLE 10–2

Particleboard Property Requirements

Type[1]	Density (Grade) Min. Avg.	Class[2]	Modulus of Rupture— Min. Avg. (psi)	Modulus of Elasticity— Min. Avg. (psi)	Internal Bond— Min. Avg. (psi)	Linear Expansion— Max. Avg. (percent)	Screw Holding— Min. Avg. Face (lbs)	Edge (lbs)
	A (High Density, 50 lbs/cu ft and over)	1	2,400	350,000	200	0.55	450	–
		2	3,400	350,000	140	0.55	–	–
1	B (Medium Density, between 37 and 50 lbs/cu ft)	1	1,600	250,000	70	0.35	225	160
		2	2,400	400,000	60	0.30	225	200
	C (Low Density, 37 lbs/cu ft and under)	1	800	150,000	20	0.30	125	–
		2	1,400	250,000	30	0.30	175	–
	A (High Density, 50 lbs/cu ft and over)	1	2,400	350,000	125	0.55	450	–
2		2	3,400	500,000	400	0.55	500	350
	B (Medium Density, less than 50 lbs/cu ft)	1	1,800	250,000	65	0.35	225	160
		2	2,500	450,000	60	0.25	250	200

SOURCE: U.S. Department of Commerce, National Bureau of Standards, *Commercial Standard CS 236-66, Mat-Formed Particleboard* (Washington, D.C.: Government Printing Office, 1966).

[1] Type 1. — Mat-formed particleboard (generally made with urea-formaldehyde resin binders) suitable for interior applications.

Type 2. — Mat-formed particleboard made with durable and highly moisture and heat resistant binders (generally phenolic resins) suitable for interior and certain exterior applications when so labelled.

[2] Class — Strength classifications based on properties of panels currently produced.

weakness across the length of the board and is subject to greater lengthwise swelling in the extruded direction. For these reasons it is most used as corestock.

Basically, the properties of particleboard are dependent upon the quality and shape of the particles and the amount and type of the resin binder which is used. In addition, density and moisture content affect the final use of a given panel which has been produced.

The size and shape of the individual particles, referred to as "particle geometry," and the resin used may be controlled to provide panels with given sets of properties. For example, many particleboards have cores of larger particles covered on each side with finer particles. These multi-layered boards therefore have a smoother surface while other panels which maintain greater and more uniform density throughout produce higher strength properties.

As revealed in table 10–2, the two types of mat-formed particleboard produced are so classed on the basis of the type of resin used as a binder. Type 1, primarily used for interior applications, is usually made with a urea-formaldehyde resin, while Type 2 panels using phenolic resins are suitable for interior and certain exterior applications.

Even though particleboard is an "engineered" product, it is a product made of wood and therefore is subject to moisture content changes with changes in atmospheric conditions. CS 236-66 requires that the panels at the time of shipment conform to one of the following requirements:

a. moisture content consistent with the known end use of the panel (usually around 7 percent ± a slight variance)
b. moisture content as specified by the purchaser
c. moisture content not in excess of 10 percent.

Specific use requirements for particleboard may be met through the production of panels which are engineered and through the application of special treatments or finishes. As such, particleboard surfaces may be embossed, primed or undercoated, and even treated with fire retardants or other chemicals to resist insects or fungi.

Manufacture

Because particleboard is a wood product, the basic ingredient in its manufacture is some form of wood particle. Presently, almost 90 percent of the material used is wood residues obtained from wood products processing plants. These materials take the form of planer shavings, sawmill chips, veneer wastes, and other such residues. In some areas where residues are not readily available, small logs are reduced to flakes and used in the manufacturing process.

Once the raw material has been gathered it is milled, generally through the use of flakers or hammermills, into the desired types of particles. The particles so produced are then either screened according to size or placed into large driers where the high temperatures drive off the excess moisture so that a uniform moisture content is attained. Huge storage bins hold the particles until they are required for the blending process. During the blending operation the synthetic binders (usually urea-formaldehyde or phenolic resins) and other chemical additives are sprayed onto the particles at a controlled rate to assure uniform distribution of the resin over the wood particles. Since many of the properties of the finished board are dependent upon proper resin bonds, extreme care is utilized during this step of the process.

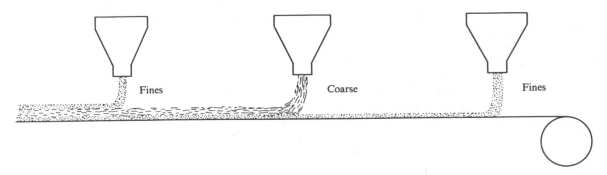

Fines   Coarse   Fines

FIG. 10–6. *Mat formation for multi-layer particleboard.*

After the particles are coated they are then ready to be formed into mats prior to pressing. Unlike insulation board and hardboard, all particleboard is made from dry formed mats. Inside the forming machine the particles are carefully metered and deposited onto belts or metal cauls. During this critical process the specific types and amounts of particles are "laid up" in the proper sequences to assure the desired uniformity during pressing.

Once the mats have been formed they are moved along conveyors to large heated hydraulic presses. These multi-opening presses have heated platens which cure the resin binder at temperatures ranging from 270° to 400° F. and at pressures up to 1,000 psi depending upon the resins used and the end product desired.

Following their removal from the press the newly formed panels are trimmed to the desired width and length and fed into large sanding machines. Through the use of several grit sizes, the panel is reduced to its final thickness and is given the desired degree of surface smoothness. The board is then conveyed to another section of the plant where it is either further cut and treated for specific uses, or packaged and prepared for shipment.

Types and Uses

In today's market approximately 40 percent of the particleboard produced is used as floor underlayment in the construction industry. The remaining 60 percent is used primarily as corestock material for furniture casegoods or for other architectural and industrial uses.

Because of its dimensional stability, relative low cost, smoothness, and workability, particleboard has become a dominant core material in furniture and casegoods production. Commonly used surface coatings or finishes include paints, enamels, stains, varnishes or lacquer and overlays of hardwood veneers, plastic laminates, hardboards or similar sheet materials (National Particleboard Association, 1967).

The National Particleboard Association (1967) lists the following types and uses of particleboard:

Floor underlayment—produced as a board with a hard, grain-free surface and designed as an underlay for resilient floor coverings or carpeting.

Corestock—products of flakes or particles bonded with synthetic resins and possessing various densities and related properties used for furniture, casework, architectural paneling, doors, and laminated components.

Wood veneered particleboard—corestock overlaid at the mill with selected wood veneers and used for furniture, panels, wainscots, and dividers.

Overlaid particleboard—panels faced with impregnated fiber sheets, hardboard, or other decorative plastic sheets or films and used for furniture, doors, paneling, sink or counter tops, cabinetry and store fixtures.

Embossed particleboard—surfaces are heavily textured in a variety of decorative patterns by branding with a roller and used for doors, paneling, wainscots, fixtures, and cabinet panels.

Filled particleboard—panels surface-filled, sanded, ready for painting and designed for printed end-products requiring firm, flat, and true surfaces.

Exterior particleboard—made with phenolic resins to provide resistance to weathering and designed for use as an exterior covering material.

Toxic-treated particleboard—treated with chemicals to provide resistance to insects, mold, decay producing fungi and designed for tropical applications or other areas where wood products require protection from insect attack or decay.

Primed or undercoated—factory painted base coats on filled or unfilled board of either interior or exterior quality and designed for any product to be printed or painted.

Fire retardant particleboard—particles are treated with fire retardants and panels are designed for use where building codes require low flame-spread materials.

Resources

American Hardboard Association. *The Story of Hardboard.* Chicago: American Hardboard Association, n.d.

Insulation Board Institute (now the Acoustical and Insulating Materials Association). *The Story of Insulation Board.* Chicago: Insulation Board Institute, n.d.

Lewis, Wayne C. *Insulation Board, Hardboard, and Particleboard.* Madison, Wisconsin: Forest Products Laboratory, Forest Service, U.S. Department of Agriculture, 1967.

National Particleboard Association. *Particleboard Design and Use Manual,* AIA File No. 23-L. Silver Springs, Maryland: National Particleboard Association, 1967.

National Particleboard Association. *The Story of Particleboard.* Washington, D.C.: American Forest Products Industries, Inc., n.d.

United States Department of Commerce, National Bureau of Standards. *Commercial Standard CS 251-63, Hardboard.* Reprinted with amendments, 1967. Washington, D.C.: Government Printing Office, 1967.

United States Department of Commerce, National Bureau of Standards. *Commercial Standard CS 236-66, Mat-Formed Particleboard.* Washington, D.C.: Government Printing Office, 1966.

Chapter Eleven

Modified Wood

Man has been trying to improve certain qualities of wood for centuries. In ancient days he found that by rubbing the surface of wooden implements with his hands the appearance of wood was enhanced. He later discovered that the application of surface finishes not only served to improve wood's appearance, but, to some degree at least, actually seemed to protect its surface. However, these surface treatments have only a retardant effect upon wood-moisture relationships. Only recently has man been able to achieve some success in making wood more dimensionally stable.

Due to the fact that wood is an anisotropic material, the changes resulting from moisture gain or loss have created many problems for wood users. Perhaps wood's most limiting characteristic is its relatively poor dimensional stability. In an earlier chapter basic wood-moisture relationships and the shrinkage and swelling of wood in different directions were discussed. These basic relationships are being considered as scientists seek ways to modify wood. Researchers have found that through the introduction of resins and other materials into the cellular structure of wood, certain properties (including dimensional stability) may be improved. Unfortunately, they have also found that improvement of some properties often results in a decrease of others. To this date only a few practical methods have been developed for modifying wood successfully. Even though some of these processes are used commercially, their applications are somewhat narrow in scope and their total impact on the wood industry is yet to be realized. Several processes of wood modification which have been developed or exhibit particular promise will be discussed in this chapter.

Impreg

Impreg is a term applied only to phenol resin-treated wood in which the resin has been cured in the cell-wall structure without the application of pressure. The production of impreg requires complete penetration of the resin. If only partial treatment were achieved, the bulking effect of the resin-forming chemicals would create stresses between the untreated and treated areas producing checking or honeycombing at that point (Seborg, 1962). Because penetration is difficult to achieve in larger specimens of wood, most impreg is made from veneers and later laminated.

Soaking wood in an aqueous phenol-formaldehyde system is the simplest method of treatment. A faster method is to immerse the veneer in a resinoid solution and place the container in a pressure cylinder. Depending upon the thickness and the species, different pressures are used for varying periods to attain a take-up of resin equal to 30–35 percent of the oven-dry weight of the specimen. Once impregnated, the speciman is cured through the use of heat, but without pressure (Seborg, 1962).

If impreg is treated to the 30–35 percent level, its shrinking and swelling may be reduced to 25 to 30 percent of normal and will exhibit marked reduction in grain raising and surface checking. Impreg has also shown considerable resistance to decay, termites, and marine borers; however, its changes in strength properties are not such that they justify its use for structural applications. Pattern and die models constitute the primary use of impreg today.

FIG. 11–1. *Die model of impreg used in the automobile industry. (Courtesy of U.S. Forest Products Laboratory, Forest Service, U.S. Department of Agriculture.)*

Compreg

Compreg, like impreg, is another resin-treated wood; however, it is compressed during curing. Phenol-formaldehyde has been found to be one of the most effective resins and the treatment process may be accomplished by the same means as used for impreg. Depending upon the properties sought, varying percentages of resin are used. If maximum dimensional stability is desired, a uniform 30 percent resin content (based on oven-dry weight of untreated specimens) is used while the attainment of maximum impact strength is achieved by 10–20 percent resin with greater amounts near the surface (Seborg, 1962).

Veneers treated at a resin level of 30 percent may be parallel laminated without the use of additional bonding resins between the plys as sufficient amounts of resin are squeezed out during compression. Those treated under this level and crossbanded require that the plys be dry and that a small amount of bonding resin be used. Compreg with a specific gravity of 1.3 to 1.4 can be produced by using pressures of 1000 to 1200 psi, a temperature of 300° F., and volatile resin contents between 2 and 4 percent. If compressed under this level, it is termed "semicompreg." Prior to compression the treated veneer must also be dried, but it is done at temperatures of 175° F. or less so that curing will not take place until the pressures are applied (Seborg, 1962).

Water absorption by compreg at a specific gravity of 1.35 is very low and other properties such as decay, termite resistance, strength, hardness, and abrasion resistance are increased. One of its most common uses has been for cutlery and tool handles, but its applications are far wider. Its improved strength properties make it extremely useful for dies and jigs as well as other uses such as water lubricated bearings, pulleys, electrical insulators and novelty items (Seborg, 1962).

FIG. 11–2. *Knife handles of compreg.*

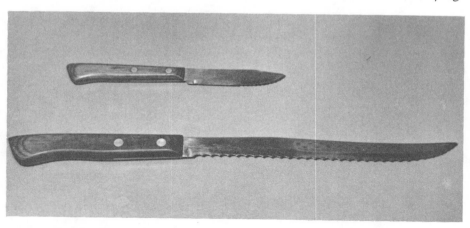

Staypack and Staybwood

Because compressed and uncompressed resin-treated woods, such as compreg and impreg, are more brittle than the original wood, the U.S. Forest Products Laboratory developed a compressed wood which contains no resin. This material, called staypack, is a heat-stabilized compressed wood produced by heating the wood to 320° C. and then compressing it at pressures from 400 to 4000 psi (Meyer, 1969). Its properties are achieved by modifying the compressing conditions to allow the lignin cementing material between the fibers to flow and thereby eliminate internal stresses (Seborg, 1962).

While not as water resistant as compreg, it does have high flexural and tensile properties and is much tougher. Its chief advantage is primarily in its increased impact strength. Today it is used in handles and often for desk legs (Meyer, 1969).

Staybwood is a heat-only stabilized wood which is produced by heating wood at temperatures of 150° to 300° C. While this process can reduce the amount of shrinking and swelling by as much as 40 percent, various mechanical properties are always affected. Both toughness and abrasion resistance are seriously curtailed and therefore its applications are severely limited.

Acetylated Wood

In seeking ways to modify wood which would reduce the embrittling effect peculiar to resin treating, the chemical process of acetylation has been developed. Using an active agent such as acetic anhydride with pyridine as a catalyst, the process is carried out in an airtight chamber. The specimen is first dried and then, with the chamber air intakes closed, the liquid agent and catalyst are introduced. Air is then circulated throughout the chamber at temperatures between 80° and 120° C. until acetate groups are formed. The liquid is drained out and heated air again circulated throughout. A condenser removes the excess agent, catalyst, and the acetic acid which has been formed, and the circulation continues until the wood is free from odor (Meyer, 1969; Seborg, 1962).

This process, now used to treat veneers and stock up to 2" X 6" X 48", provides very good dimensional stability. Shrinking and swelling can be reduced to as little as 20 to 30 percent of normal while the specific gravity is increased only 6 to 12 percent. Unlike resin treatments, the wood is not darkened; however, high resistance to termites and decay is attained. While most strength properties are unaffected, its toughness and impact qualities may be increased by as much as 10 to 20 percent (Meyer, 1969; Seborg, 1962).

Polyethylene-Glycol

A very successful method of wood stabilization has been achieved through the use of the water-soluble bulking agent polyethylene-glycol, which has a molecular weight of 1000 (PEG-1000). The process of PEG-1000 treating is actually quite simple, although the time period required to achieve the desired uniform uptake of 25 to 30 percent of chemical may be lengthy. Essentially, treatment consists of immersing either green or dry wood in a solution of PEG-1000. It has been found that heating the solution increases the rate of its uptake; however, the nature of the stock being treated largely determines the length of time required. For example, thin cross-sectional pieces may be treated in a day or two, while thicker longitudinal pieces may require several weeks. As PEG-1000 is a water soluble material, continued exposure to water could result in its again going into solution and leaving the wood; therefore, polyurethane varnishes are often applied to serve as a surface water barrier.

PEG-1000 is effective in preventing checking of green wood during drying. Several of its major applications have been in the preservation of old wood, protection of carvings, and in the treatment of gunstocks. One of its most unusual applications was in the preservation of the centuries old Swedish ship *Wasa*. Raised from the harbor bottom, the vessel underwent several years of PEG-1000 treatment to reduce the excessive cracking and distortion which would have otherwise resulted from drying.

FIG. 11–3. *Swedish warship* Wasa *in dry dock during restoration. (Courtesy of Statens Sjöhistoriska Museum and warship* Wasa.)

Irradiated Wood

During recent years a great deal of research has been carried out to determine the possibilities of using gamma rays to polymerize (combine small molecules to form larger molecules) certain plastics which have been introduced in wood. The results have been encouraging and certain wood-plastic combinations (WPC) have been developed to the point where they are being utilized commercially. Much of the work in this area was sponsored by the Atomic Energy Commission and carried out at West Virginia University under the direction of Dr. James Kent (Ellwood, 1969).

In the AEC sponsored program the following four monomer systems were selected for the testing: (1) methyl methacrylate, (MMA); (2) methyl methacrylate (88%) and phosgard (12%), (MMA & P); (3) styrene (60%) and acrylonitrile (40%), (SA); and (4) ethyl acrylate (80%) and acrylonitrile (20%), (EA) (Ellwood, 1969). The wood used was obtained from four species (loblolly pine, eastern white pine, yellow poplar, northern red oak), dried to a moisture content of 12 percent, and the specimens cut slightly oversize. Once the specimens were prepared the process of impregnation was conducted as follows:

All the monomer systems used in the study presented handling problems by virtue of toxicity, odor, flammability, etc. This was particularly true for ethyl acrylate-acrylonitrile (EA) and accordingly a specially designed and fabricated "closed" impregnating apparatus was used for this monomer. The sticks were impregnated with EA in this closed apparatus inside the irradiation container. An "open" system was used for the other monomers where the test sticks were not impregnated in the irradiation containers.

The impregnation equipment and the irradiation containers were sized so that a set of material could be treated and irradiated as a unit. Though there were some important mechanical differences between the open and closed system, the impregnation process consisted primarily of:

1. moving the set of specimens from the conditioning room to the impregnation chamber,
2. evacuating the system to 1% of atmospheric pressure for 30 minutes,
3. increasing the chamber pressure for a period of time to a pressure dependent on the desired loading and the monomer,
4. introducing the monomer into the chamber,
5. reducing the pressure and letting the excess monomer drain off,
6. again raising the chamber pressure for a period of time,
7. reducing the pressure,
8. placing specimen in the irradiation container.

Steps 6 and 7 were omitted and steps 3 and 4 reversed for fully loaded specimens (Ellwood, 1969).

Using cobalt-60, the specimens were irradiated with gamma rays for twenty hours and once treated were cut to final test size prior to testing. Numerous tests of physical and mechanical properties were conducted and yielded a variety of results. These data were used to show that the greatest improvements in the properties of the polymer treated wood were: (1) up to an eleven-fold increase in side hardness; (2) up to a seven-fold increase in abrasion resistance; and (3) up to a six-fold increase in compression perpendicular to the grain. High anti-swell efficiencies were also realized, especially with the styrene-acrylonitrile treated specimens (Ellwood, 1969).

One realm in which wood-plastic combinations have thus far proven commercially successful is in the area of wood flooring. Acry-

FIG. 11–4. *The* Wasa *undergoing treatment with PEG 1000. Note spray nozzles indicated by arrow. (Courtesy of Statens Sjöhistoriska Museum and warship* Wasa.*)*

lic wood flooring has achieved some popularity not only due to its natural wood beauty, but also because of its abrasion resistance, easy maintenance, and cost with respect to certain other quality floor coverings. As the full potential of wood-plastic combinations has not yet been achieved, further research and development will undoubtedly open up many additional markets. Examples of other processes which may hold promise for modifying wood include aqueous polyurethane treatments (Hartman, 1969), vapor phase chemical treatments (Barnes, 1969), and those using heat and suitable catalysts to achieve polymerization (Meyer, 1965).

Ammonia

Unlike the previously discussed methods of modifying wood which were primarily aimed at achieving greater degrees of dimensional stability, treatment through the use of ammonia processes are aimed at temporarily making solid wood "plastic" so that it can be shaped or formed. Presently, most industrial methods of forming bent wood products utilize lamination or a process of either hot water soaking or steam to soften the wood until it is pliable enough to shape over a form. The water or steam methods require that stock be retained in molds or forms for rather lengthy periods to allow for drying. In addition, due to the heat of the water or steam, certain physical properties are reduced. Further limitations of the steam forming process include the small number of species that are suitable for the process, the fact that shapes are not always permanent, and the high breakage rate (Davidson, 1970).

FIG. 11–5. *Parquet flooring of acrylic WPC. (Courtesy of Seery Hill Associates and Arco Chemical Company, Perma Grain Division.)*

Recent experimentation with anhydrous ammonia in both liquid and gaseous states has shown that wood may be plasticized through

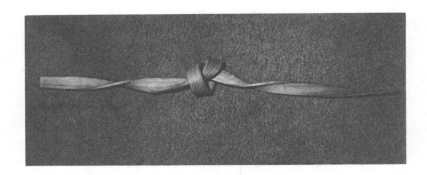

FIG. 11–6. *This small strip of maple was literally tied in a knot after being plasticized in gaseous ammonia.*

treatment, and, once dry, regains its original properties and retains the new form. While some form of restraint is required for a short period, there is only a slight tendency for the wood to spring back to its original form (Schuerch, 1964). Researchers believe that the greater plasticity of the ammonia-treated wood is due to the ability of the ammonia to penetrate the cellulosic structure and create a temporary plasticization of the lignin (Davidson, 1970).

The liquid treatment process involves the direct soaking of the wood in a tank containing anhydrous ammonia. The soaking time is dependent upon the species used and the thickness of the specimens being treated; however, soak periods of from one to three hours for stock up to 3/4 inch have been effective with certain woods such as maple and cherry. Not only is it possible to form simple bends with this process but compound curves and embossed objects may be made as well. Small strips of wood have even been tied in knots. Because liquid ammonia has a boiling point of approximately –33° C., it is necessary to incorporate a refrigeration unit with a reservoir system in order that the temperature of the liquid be kept below this point. Precooling of the stock to be treated prior to immersion has also proven helpful in reducing excessive boiling of the ammonia. As ammonia fumes are extremely strong and irritating, protective clothing should be worn and adequate exhaust provision should be made or a gas mask worn whenever this system is used (Geiger, 1969).

The gas treatment process is accomplished by placing the wood to be treated into an airtight chamber, evacuating the air from the chamber, and filling the chamber with anhydrous ammonia in a gaseous state. The length of time required for treatment varies with the species and size of stock, although 1/4" X 2" X 24" maple stock has been treated in 1½ to 2 hours. Once treatment has been effected, the gas is evacuated from the chamber and the stock, upon removal, may then be formed to the desired shape. After a minimum amount of restraint the wood will retain its new shape without any significant change in its basic properties. Again, due to the hazardous nature of working with anhydrous ammonia, suitable protective devices and exhaust provisions should be utilized.

The commercial uses of the various processes of forming wood with anhydrous ammonia are not yet fully developed; however, it is anticipated that the potential for these processes is great and further development will occur. Experimental products which have been made include bowls, novelty items, sporting equipment, lamps, picture frames, and various furniture parts.

Resources

Barnes, H. M., E. T. Choong, and R. C. McIlhenny. "An Evaluation of Several Vapor Phase Chemical Treatments for Dimensional Stabilization of Wood." *Forest Products Journal* 19 (March, 1969): 35–39.

Davidson, R. W., and W. G. Baumgardt. "Plasticizing Wood with Ammonia —A Progress Report." *Forest Products Journal* 20 (March, 1970): 19–25.

Ellwood, Eric, Robert Gilmore, James A. Merrill, and W. Kenneth Poole. *An Investigation of Certain Physical and Mechanical Properties of Wood-Plastic Combinations.* Report for Division of Isotope Development, U.S. Atomic Energy Commission, Contract AT-(40-1)-2513, Task 20, completed at Research Triangle Institute, Research Triangle Park, North Carolina. Springfield, Virginia: Clearinghouse for Federal Scientific and Technical Information, National Bureau of Standards, U.S. Department of Commerce, May, 1969, pp. ix-4, 11.

Geiger, William H. "Plasticizing Wood with Liquid Ammonia." Unpublished research problem. Richmond, Kentucky: Eastern Kentucky University, 1969.

Hartman, Seymour. "Modified Wood with Aqueous Polyurethane Systems." *Forest Products Journal* 19 (May, 1969): 39–42.

Meyer, J. A. "Treatment of Wood-Polymer Systems Using Catalyst-Heat Techniques." *Forest Products Journal* 19 (September, 1965): 365–69.

Meyer, John A., and Wesley E. Loos. "Process of, and Products from, Treating Southern Pine Wood for Modification of Properties." *Forest Products Journal* 19 (December, 1969): 32–33.

Schuerch, Conrad. "Wood Plasticization." *Forest Products Journal* 14 (September, 1964): 377–81.

Seborg, R. M., Harold Tarkow, and A. J. Stamm. *Modified Woods.* Report No. 2192 (Revised). Madison, Wisconsin: Forest Products Laboratory, U.S. Department of Agriculture, 1962.

Chapter Twelve

Wood Building Products

Lumber and other wood products continue to be the most popular basic materials used in the field of residential construction. In addition to this type of utilization, other construction uses create additional markets for these materials. Prime among the reasons for the continuing importance of wood products are such factors as availability, ease of handling and fabrication, relatively low cost, and their adaptability to a wide range of applications. Practice in recent years has brought about changes in how certain products are utilized. For example, declines in the use of lumber for sheathing and flooring have occurred, but there have been concurrent increases in its use for framing, millwork, and trim. In other instances a change in the type of wood product used in specific applications has taken place, as evidenced by the increased use of panel materials for sheathing and subflooring.

FIG. 12–1. *Dimension lumber used as framing members in residential construction.*

FIG. 12–2. *A combination of vertical and diagonal wood siding creates an interesting effect on this apartment complex. (Courtesy of Western Wood Products Association.)*

Lumber in General Construction

A large portion of all lumber produced is used for residential and commercial construction. Most lumber used in these respects is that which is termed dimension lumber (see chapter 8). While some hardwoods are used in the finishing aspects of construction, softwoods account for most of the lumber used. The framing members are almost exclusively made from softwoods. The term *framing members* includes all those components which constitute the framework or skeleton of a building. Among these are girders, sills and plates, joists, studs, and rafters, each of which is briefly discussed below.

While steel "I" beams are sometimes used as *girders,* either solid or built-up wood girders are extensively used. The built-up girder is the most popular and has as its intended purpose the provision of a bearing surface for the joists and a reduction of the span. Generally, they are made from three 2" × 10" or 2" × 12" nominal size pieces of lumber nailed together. The *sill* is designed to be laid around the top of the foundation and is used as a base for the support and fastening of the floor joist. Commonly made of 2" × 6" or 2" × 8" stock, the sill is often fastened to the foundation by means of anchor bolts.

The *floor joists* are placed on top of the sill with their center portions being supported on the girder. The size of the joists is determined by the span, the load to be carried, and the spacing between them. Most normal residential uses call for the use of 2" × 8", 2" × 10", or 2" × 12" joists spaced 16 or 24 inches on center, depending upon design factors. The joists are intended to span the distance between the foundation walls and carry the loads of the remainder of the building. Once in place the subfloor is fastened directly to the joists.

The *studs* are the vertical members, usually 2" × 4", which constitute the walls of a building. The sheathing or siding is applied to them on the outside, and paneling or wallboard is installed on the inside. They are held in place by the plates (top and sole) and are usually spaced 16 inches on center, although the spacing may be as much as 24 inches, again dependent upon the system being employed.

Ceiling joists are used to span the distances across the top of the studs and to provide a nailing base for the finished ceiling. *Rafters* are used to support the roof and are supported by the top plate at the outside perimeter. As with all framing members, their size and spacing are determined by such factors as span and load. Rafters used in residential construction are generally in the range of 2" × 6" or 2" × 8" and spaced either 16 or 24 inches on center. When truss rafters are used, the lower chord also serves as the ceiling joist.

Once the frame of a building has been erected the outside of the structure is covered with a variety of materials which are termed sheathing or siding. Sheathing is most often referred to as the first or base covering applied directly to the stud walls. Siding is most often

Sheathing and Siding

FIG. 12–3. *Wood shingles and shakes lend themselves to either traditional or contemporary designs. (Photos courtesy of Red Cedar Shingle and Handsplit Shake Bureau.)*

thought of as the outermost or finish covering which is applied on top of the sheathing. Some materials, usually those sold in sheet form, are designed to serve both as the siding and sheathing in one application.

Sheathing gives rigidity to a frame building and serves to minimize air infiltration and provide insulation. Lumber was once extensively used as a sheathing material, but it has largely been replaced by the use of plywood and structural insulation board. Often plywood and insulation board are used in combination to cover the exterior. In these instances the plywood is used at the corners to provide additional bracing strength and the insulation board is used as the remainder of the covering. Each of these materials has been covered in more detail in previous chapters.

Siding, the outermost covering, has important influences not only upon the final appearance of the building, but upon the maintenance and weatherability of the structure as well. In addition to masonry and plastic sidings a wide variety of wood and wood-base materials are available. Wood products used for siding include lumber, plywood, wood composition boards, shingles and shakes, and combination materials. These products are available in a wide range of patterns and textures and may be purchased unfinished or prefinished.

Lumber sidings are predominantly manufactured from softwood species, including redwood. Depending upon the types, these sidings may be applied either horizontally or vertically. While wood siding

FIG. 12–4. *Workman splitting shakes from a block with a froe. (Courtesy of Red Cedar Shingle and Handsplit Shake Bureau.)*

is available in a number of grades, it is usually found to be of a higher grade and generally free from knots, pitch pockets, and other such defects. Much of that used is in the Number 1 or 2 common grade ranges. Typical types available include those called board, channel, drop, bevel, tongue and groove, dolly varden (a variation of bevel), and log cabin. The various lumber sidings are generally applied with rust resistant nails to prevent staining or discoloration. If unfinished sidings are used they may be stained, painted, or otherwise treated in accordance with acceptable finishing standards.

Sheet materials such as composition boards and plywoods are extensively utilized for siding materials. When these products are used as siding they are of the exterior type and designed to stand up under exposure to the weather. Plywood sidings are available in several textures and surface treatments. They may be rough sawn, kerfed, grooved, striated, fine lined, or otherwise textured. Medium density overlaid plywood in a variety of styles is now being extensively used, especially when further painting is required. Composition boards, such as hardboard and particleboard, are also available in a range of styles and are being widely used for sidings. Typically these materials come in a primed or prefinished state. Further discussion of these sheet materials may be found in chapters 9 and 10.

Shingles and Shakes

Once one of the most extensively used roof coverings, wood shingles and shakes gave way to other materials; however, in recent years they have again become an extremely popular form of covering material. In addition to roof coverings they are widely used as a siding material because of the unusual architectural effects they present. While they are usually applied in the natural or unstained state, certain sidewall shakes are available in colors. The essential difference between shakes and shingles is that shingles are sawn and shakes are split, thus giving the shakes a more uneven or textured surface.

Shingles and shakes are made primarily from western red cedar, although other species such as northern white cedar, baldcypress, and redwood are sometimes used. Red cedar shingles are available in four grades, Numbers 1, 2, 3 and 4. The grades range from Number 1 (premium) grade which is 100 percent heartwood, 100 percent clear, and 100 percent edge-grain, to the Number 4 grade (undercoursing) which allows a wider range of defects. The Number 4 grade is only used as the under and covered course in double sidewall applications or for certain interior applications when they are desired for accent purposes. Shingles are made in three standard lengths (16, 18, and 24 inches) with each length possessing a different butt thickness, 0.40, 0.45, and 0.50 inches respectively. Depending upon the exposure to the weather, four bundles, laid at five inches, will cover one square (100 sq. ft.) (Red Cedar Shingle and Handsplit Shake Bureau, 1967).

Shakes are made from the Number 1 grade and range in length from 15 to 32 inches with butt thickness ranging from ¾ to 1¼ inches. Coverage is in the range of five bundles per square. Shakes are available in three styles—split and resawn, tapersplit, and straightsplit. Split and resawn, the most popular, have split faces and sawn backs. They are made by cutting cedar logs to the desired length and then splitting blanks (or boards) of proper thickness. The split blank is then diagonally bandsawed to produce two shakes from the one blank.

Tapersplit shakes are produced largely by hand through the use of a steel froe (a sharp cleaving tool) and a mallet. The taper is achieved by reversing the block end-for-end after each split. When shakes are cut by always splitting from the same end, the straightsplit shake is produced (Red Cedar Shingle and Handsplit Shake Bureau, 1967).

Wood Flooring

Flooring materials may generally be classified into two categories—subflooring and finish flooring. The subflooring, which constitutes the base for application of the finish floor, is usually made of wood or a wood product. While other materials such as carpeting and vinyl have made inroads into the finish flooring market, wood continues to enjoy considerable popularity.

Subfloors

Wood subfloors are important in construction because they provide a solid base for other flooring materials, and because they lend bracing strength to the structure and provide an additional barrier against cold and dampness. Ordinarily the subfloor is fastened directly to the floor joists, providing a high degree of rigidity and assisting in the elimination of floor sags and squeaks. At present, the most commonly used materials for subfloors include lumber laid diagonally and plywood.

If lumber is used in conjunction with strip flooring, nominal sizes of 1" X 6" and 1" X 8" are the most desirable because they tend to reduce the amount of shrinking and swelling due to variations in moisture content and humidity. Even so, they should not be laid tightly together, but rather should be laid so that slight gaps exist between adjacent pieces. They are laid diagonally for greater bracing strength and because the diagonal pattern will allow the strip flooring to be laid in any direction. All end joints should be made over a bearing surface and each board should be nailed to each joist.

Plywood when used as subfloor is laid at right angles to the direction of the joists. In general use, it is recommended that a minimum thickness of 1/2 inch be used for plywood subfloors. Because plywood does not shrink and swell as much as regular lumber, it may be laid with adjacent edges closer together, although some space still must be left between panels. Whether using nails or adhesives, plywood should also be fastened over each joist.

Finish Flooring

If the finish floor is to be made of carpeting or linoleum, for example, the subfloor is usually covered with an underlayment such as particleboard to which the covering may then be directly applied. If wood strip flooring is to be applied, it is fastened directly to the subfloor. When strip floors are to be laid over concrete it is necessary to fasten wooden "sleepers" or "screeds" to the concrete in order to provide a nailing base for the finished flooring.

In general, finished wood flooring is available as *strip flooring, plank flooring,* and *block and parquet flooring.* The most commonly used hardwoods for finish flooring are oak, maple, beech, birch, and pecan. Grading is done according to species and is regulated through rules established by the National Oak Flooring Manufacturers' Association and the Maple Flooring Manufacturers' Association.

FIG. 12–5. *An interesting application of hardwood strip flooring. (Courtesy of Bangkok Industries, Inc.)*

Strip flooring is the most extensively used of all the wood flooring products. It is made with tongue and groove on the sides and at the ends, or as square edge strips. The tongue and groove strips are generally available in random lengths with thicknesses of 1/2, 3/8 and 25/32 inches, and widths of 1½, 2, 2¼, and 3¼ inches. The most commonly used size is 25/32 inch thick by 2¼ inches wide.

Plank flooring is perhaps the oldest type of hardwood floor; however, that used today is vastly superior to its predecessor. As with strip flooring, plank flooring is available with either tongue and groove or square edges. The tongue and groove variety is usually made in 25/32 inch thickness while the square edge is most commonly found in 5/16 inch thickness. The width of each type is in a range from 3 to 9 inches at 1 inch intervals. Unlike strip flooring which is generally blind nailed along the tongue, plank flooring is blind nailed along the edges and screws are used at each end and at intervals along the length. The screws are counterbored and flush plugged.

Block and parquet floorings are used when definite patterns are desired in the finished floor. The major difference between block and parquet flooring is that block flooring is laminated or preassembled to a given size at a flooring manufacturer, whereas parquet flooring is made of pieces cut to exact dimensions and laid separately. Most parquetry is manufactured in a thickness of 25/32 inch, in widths ranging from 1½ to 3 inches and in lengths usually based upon a multiple of the width (2¼" wide = 6¾, 9, 11¼ long, etc.). Block flooring is usually 1/2, 25/32, or 33/32 inches thick. The overall block size is dependent upon the width of the individual strips and whether the block is square or rectangular. These types of wood flooring may be tongue and grooved or square edged and are either nailed or laid in mastic.

Wood floors must be finished just as any other wood product, the exceptions being some of the recently developed prefinished block flooring or those made from wood plastic combinations. Procedures for finishing may include sanding, staining, filling, sealing, topcoats, and final waxing.

Moulding and Millwork

Moulding and millwork constitute an important contribution of wood in building applications. Alone or in combination, they are designed to be used in conjunction with the so-called "finished" aspects of construction. Ranging from simple pieces of unpainted trim to preconstructed and prefinished components, they cover a wide range of specifically designed products.

FIG. 12–6. *Tasteful use of wood moulding adds greatly to the decor of this room. (Courtesy of Western Wood Moulding and Millwork Producers.)*

Moulding

Often termed "trim" by those in the trades, mouldings are extensively used to create a wide variety of architectural details as well as to provide a more finished appearance. Painstakingly created by the hands of skilled craftsmen, mouldings in construction were at one time largely limited to only those who could afford such luxury. Today, mouldings are produced by precision machines and their cost is within the range of all.

The majority of stock mouldings available on the market today are produced from softwood species and are typically allowed to contain only slight defects. Sizes of mouldings vary according to patterns but in general are available in lengths ranging to twenty feet. Availability of such long lengths is directly attributable to the development of precision cut finger joints which allow for end jointing. The various moulding patterns are achieved by sending precut strips through high speed machines called moulders, which contain precision ground knives in a cutter head, and which operate similarly to the cutting principles of a spindle shaper or portable router.

A wide variety of patterns are available and range from those which are rectangular in cross-section to those which possess intricate combinations of flats and curves. Specific types of mouldings, each available in a variety of patterns, include such products as crown and bed, casing and base, drip cap, stop, chair rail, and brick mouldings.

Millwork

The term "millwork" is generally ascribed to those wood products and components which are produced in a manufacturing plant and transported to a construction site where they are installed. Specific products included under this term are such items as doors, windows,

FIG. 12–7. *This attractive entry is a good example of millwork. (Courtesy of American Forest Institute.)*

frames, stairs and stair parts, mantels, shutters, and a variety of cabinets. As with mouldings, the majority of stock items have been made from softwood species, although specific types are often made of hardwoods. Millwork companies are very much like furniture factories in that the equipment and processes used are often the same.

Some items, such as window and door units, are manufactured by large plants that specialize only in these items. Wood window units are the most popular types used in residential construction. They come in a variety of sizes and styles among which are the double hung, casement, sliding, awning, and hopper. The units are completely made up at the plant and packaged for shipment. Once received on the job, the window unit is installed into the rough opening by the carpenter. The only additional work needed to complete the installation is the application of the window trim, a job done after the walls have been prepared. Doors are also made in a variety of stock sizes and styles. They are made for either exterior or interior uses and may be built of solid wood members or a combination of materials in a sandwich type construction. Basically, door styles are of three types—panel, flush, and louver. Each type is available in several stock sizes. For interior doors the most common thickness is 1⅜ inches and for exterior doors the most common size is 1¾ inches. The height of a door may vary, but the most widely used is 6' 8". Door widths are the most variable; however, a range of from 2' 4" to 3' 6" includes those most commonly used in typical installations. Bifold and other novelty styles are usually somewhat smaller. Entrance doors are often made up as preassembled units which include the frame, the door, and various architectural treatments such as side lights, facings, pilasters, and pediments.

Stairs and stair parts are manufactured and assembled or adapted at the site. Included here are not only the treads and risers but the hand rail, balusters, newel posts, nosing, and other items. Mantels and shutters are available in a wide array of styles and constitute yet another kind of millwork.

Millwork in the form of cabinetwork is often used in a variety of applications. Corner cabinets, kitchen cabinets, and other similar storage units are often purchased as completed units and simply installed on the job. Production of these items is often done in plants specializing only in this type of work and follows the processes common to the furniture industry.

Structural Glued Laminated Timbers

The use of glued laminated timbers in all types of structures has gained increasing economic importance during recent years. Structural uses of these timbers range from the construction of small dwelling units and churches to massive arenas and convention centers. The best definition of these timbers is found in Commercial Standard CS 253-63 and is cited as follows:

> The term "Structural Glued Laminated Timber" as employed herein refers to an engineered, stress-rated product of a timber laminating plant, comprising assemblies of suitably selected and prepared wood laminations securely bonded together with adhesives. The grain of all laminations is approximately parallel longitudinally. The separate laminations shall not exceed 2 inches in net thickness. They may be comprised of pieces end joined to form any length, of pieces placed or glued edge to edge to make wider ones, or of pieces bent to curved form during gluing.

Advantages

Perhaps the major advantage of using glued laminated timber lies in the fact that it is an engineered product. This, coupled with the basic properties of wood, makes it adaptable to a wide range of structural applications. Building systems based upon laminated timbers are both structurally sound and aesthetically pleasing. Their design and use have enabled the construction of buildings which have spans over three hundred feet with no load bearing columns or partitions to

FIG. 12–8. *Laminated beams form the main framework of this large coliseum. (Courtesy of Eastern Kentucky University.)*

FIG. 12–9. *Laminated beam plant. The beam on which the men are working is nearly ready for finishing. (Courtesy of Weyerhauser Company.)*

either obstruct views or hinder space utilization. Other advantages include safety, strength, durability, and economy. Because of the slow burning of wood in massive forms, laminated timbers are actually more resistant to heat and flame than steel. The corrosion resistance of wood also makes it more appropriate for use around chemicals and fumes than many forms of metal, and at a much lower cost.

Manufacture

In general the quality of laminated timber products is dependent upon and determined by the quality of the lumber and the adhesives used coupled with the adequacy of the fabrication techniques. The American Institute of Timber Construction (AITC) is an agency concerned with the development, production, and marketing of glued laminated structural timbers. Through its quality control and inspection programs, the Institute seeks to assure the maintenance of quality products in accordance with the Commercial Standard CS 253-63 and other specified criteria. In so doing, the AITC has become one of the foremost spokesmen for the industry in the production and use of laminated beams and arches.

Whether a lamination is straight or curved, the basic fabrication processes are similar. The species used include both hardwoods and softwoods; however, only those for which allowable unit stresses have been developed may be used (see CS 253-63). While certain non-stress graded material may be used in laminates fabricated for purely decorative or non-structural areas, most beams and arches are constructed of stress graded lumber. The moisture content of the lumber generally used does not exceed 16 percent, except that when use conditions are at an e.m.c. of 16 percent or more, the moisture content at gluing may be as high as 20 percent.

In the production of laminated members either 1 inch or 2 inch nominal thickness lumber may be used. Most straight beams are constructed of 2 inch stock while curved members are most often built up from the 1 inch stock. Individual full length laminations are made by end gluing either scarf or finger-jointed pieces. The members are then surfaced to achieve a uniform thickness and a uniform full-length coating of adhesive is applied. The individual glued pieces are then laid up into the full-sized structural member and formed, as a package, by bending and/or clamping at high pressures (100-250 psi) until the adhesive is cured. After curing, the laminated member is surfaced on each side and trimmed to its final shape. It is then inspected and any minor surface defects are filled prior to sanding and shipment.

Adhesives used in the fabrication of laminated units are classed as either dry or wet use types. Dry use adhesives are those which will perform satisfactorily under use conditions at moisture contents up to 16 percent and often include the casein types. Wet use adhesives may be used in all laminations but are required when the moisture content of the wood exceeds 16 percent during prolonged or repeated periods of service. Among the wet use adhesives are those of the phenol, resorcinol, and melamine types.

Laminated beams and arches are manufactured in three appearance grades—Industrial, Architectural, and Premium. The industrial grade is ordinarily suitable for use in warehouses, garages, or other places where appearance is not of primary concern. The laminations may contain the natural characteristics of the lumber grade and void filling is not required. Architectural grades are ordinarily suitable in construction where appearance is an important requirement. In this grade voids may be either filled or replaced with clear wood inserts. Under conditions where the finest appearance is required, the premium grade is used. In this grade the face laminations are selected for appearance. Defects such as knots are limited to specifications, closing of voids is carefully controlled, and all exposed surfaces are smoothed and eased.

FIG. 12–10. *Unique and appealing architectural effects are possible by using laminated beams. (Courtesy of Laminated Timbers, Inc., London, Kentucky.)*

Resources

Anderson, L. D. *Wood-Frame House Construction.* Agriculture Handbook No. 73, Forest Products Laboratory, U.S. Department of Agriculture. Washington, D.C.: Government Printing Office, 1970.

Maple Flooring Manufacturers Association. *Grading Rules for Hard Maple, Beech, and Birch Flooring.* Oshkosh, Wisconsin: Maple Flooring Manufacturers Association, 1967.

National Oak Flooring Manufacturers' Association. *Specification Manual.* A.I.A. File No. 19-E-9. Memphis, Tennessee: National Oak Flooring Manufacturers' Association, 1966.

Red Cedar Shingle & Handsplit Shake Bureau. *Red Cedar Shingles, Handsplit Shakes, and Grooved Sidewall Shakes.* A.I.A. File No. 19-D-1. Seattle, Washington: Red Cedar Shingle & Handsplit Shake Bureau, 1967.

Southern Pine Association. *Southern Pine Technical Bulletin.* A.I.A. File No. 19-B-3. New Orleans: Southern Pine Association.

United States Department of Commerce, National Bureau of Standards. *Commercial Standard CS 253-63, Structural Glued Laminated Timber.* Washington, D.C.: Government Printing Office, 1963.

Chapter Thirteen

Secondary Wood Products

Secondary wood products are those which are manufactured from raw materials such as wood or wood base materials. They are termed "secondary" because they are composed of a wood material which has already been processed in some form (i.e., lumber, plywood, or wood composition board) and has been reprocessed or fabricated to create a new product. Included in this category are a wide range of products such as furniture, cabinets, recreational equipment, containers, pallets, and specialty items. Wood and wood products in the manufacture of furniture and cabinetry constitute the greatest segment of these secondary products in terms of the volume consumed and the value of goods produced. Other secondary products when grouped together also constitute an important segment of the wood industry.

Furniture and Cabinetry

Furniture and cabinetry is the most readily identified industry in the area of secondary wood products. Every day each of us comes into contact with and uses furniture and cabinetry made from wood. The value of these products to the wood industry amounts to billions of dollars annually. Firms specializing in the manufacture of furniture or cabinetry range from small custom producers to large multi-product line operations. While production materials, set-ups, and the amount and types of equipment in use vary greatly from one plant to another, certain commonalities exist throughout the industry. These commonalities stem from three sources: (1) all products are based upon certain styles, (2) all product styles are produced from basic construction types, and (3) all production follows a similar basic sequence. Each of these common elements is discussed in the remainder of this section.

FIG. 13–1. *The simple beauty of contemporary design emphasizes both utility and appearance (top), while a more traditional style lends a touch of elegance. (Top photo courtesy of Jens Risom Design, bottom photo courtesy of Drexel Heritage.)*

Styles

All furniture and cabinetry is available in a wide range of styles. Over the years many styles have been introduced—some have been short-lived, others have endured for centuries, and others have yet to stand the test of time. In a sense all styles may be termed contemporary as this is what they were when they were introduced and if they are in use today they are, in fact, contemporary. In general usage, however, styles are commonly classified as being of two types—traditional and contemporary.

Traditional. Styles termed "traditional" are usually thought of as those which have been introduced at a given point in history and which still have acceptance today. The titles of these styles have in general evolved from the names of the reigning monarch at the time of their introduction or from the particular artisan who designed and produced the pieces. As a result we have come to know certain styles as Queen Anne, Louis XV, Victorian, Chippendale, Duncan Phyfe, or Sheraton. The so-called "provincial" styles are basically simplified interpretations of the traditional styles which had regional influence upon given groups of people; therefore, we have styles designated as French Provincial or Colonial (Doan, 1969).

TABLE 13–1

Selected Furniture Styles and Characteristics*

	Style	Characteristics	Chief Woods Used
TRADITIONAL	Gothic	Massive and ornate, vertically high pointed arches and geometrical forms, use of trefoil and quatrefoil motif, heavily carved, ecclesiastically inspired.	Oak
	Queen Anne	Use of curved lines and graceful proportions, extensive use of cabriole leg, chairs have splat backs and tops are curved, simple carving (usually shell or leaf), spoon or ball and claw feet.	Walnut
	Louis XV	Elaborate ornamentation, cabriole legs, extensive carving often in form of curled endive leaf, minimal use of stretchers.	Mahogany, oak, walnut
	Louis XVI	Return to classical principles, straight lines predominate, fluted columns, legs usually tapered, fluted or twisted, delicate carving often in form of wreaths or flower basket.	Mahogany
	Chippendale	Latticed and ribbon back chairs, surface carving, back legs often straight, fretwork decoration, early pieces with cabriole legs—later straight.	Mahogany
	Hepplewhite	Slender tapered and fluted legs, spade feet, shield back chairs, concave corner construction, simple unbroken curves.	Mahogany
	Sheraton	Inlay extensively used for ornamentation, often square backs on chairs, convex corner construction, round, slender legs common.	Mahogany
	Duncan Phyfe	Extensive use of lyre as motif, legs fluted and gracefully curved, chair backs low, brass tipped claw feet, top rails curled over.	Mahogany
	Victorian	Oval or horseshoe backed chairs, spool turnings popular, carved scrolls and leaves common, marble tops.	Rosewood and walnut
	French Provincial	Simple cabriole legs, curved and shaped aprons, bun feet, some carving, simple and graceful lines.	Fruitwoods and native species
	Italian Provincial	Lines predominantly rectangular, neo-classical inspired, straight square tapered legs, moldings used to decorate.	Walnut, mahogany
	Mediterranean	Massive and solid appearing, darkly stained, rectangular shapes, carving or moulding follow geometric forms.	Oak
	Early American	Simple forms, legs usually round and turned, spindles and stretchers turned, curved scrolls, some use of raised panels.	Maple, pine
CONTEMPORARY	Scandinavian	No ornamentation, legs round or square tapered, simple curves, sculptured edge treatments.	Walnut, teak
	Shaker Modern	Little ornamentation, surfaces plain, straight gracefully tapered legs, construction details often visible.	Cherry, maple

*Adapted from *Seng Furniture Facts*, 22nd ed., edited by Franklyn E. Doan (Chicago: The Seng Company, 1969). Used by permission.

Contemporary. These styles are often referred to as "modern." The term modern denotes style that is in the process of development and reflects the current influences upon it. For example, the terms Swedish Modern or Danish Modern denote styles which are presently produced and bear slightly variant characteristics due to the influences of different designers. A case could be made to name such styles as Early American or Mediterranean "contemporary" because they are current adaptations of traditional styles. Most authorities, however, would accept the concept that contemporary style is modern in the sense that it is evolving.

As a rule, most traditional designs are characterized by a variety of details such as carving, inlay, pediments, or other forms of surface enrichment and their basic design has been fixed in a historical sense. Contemporary style, on the other hand, is difficult to describe, but usually it may be characterized by the use of clean and simple lines and the elimination of ornate types of surface decoration. Table 13–1 has been developed to present some of the major characteristics associated with selected styles of furniture.

Construction Types

The woodworker has a variety of joining techniques available to use in the fabrication of furniture or cabinets. These techniques range from simple to complex and are used to varying degrees depending upon the nature of the product being produced. Most items are produced from single or duplicate members joined in various ways to make up component parts, which in turn are assembled into a completed product.

Casegoods are loosely defined in the industry as those non-upholstered products which are used for storage and include such specific items as chests, dressers, night stands, buffets, and similar pieces. Furniture like tables, chairs, and beds are assembled from basic leg and rail or frame construction while casegoods may include a combination of several component types.

In general, it may be helpful to typify furniture as being *one member, duplicate part, frame, leg and rail,* or *case* construction. Using a variety of joining techniques, alone or in combination, it is possible to categorize most furniture as one of these types.

FIG. 13–2. *A chest is typical of furniture produced by case construction. (Courtesy of Thomasville Furniture Industries, Inc.)*

Production Sequence

Even though the size and layout of all production plants vary, the basic production sequence in each case is similar. Essentially, the sequence consists of (1) preparing the raw materials, (2) cutting and shaping component pieces, (3) sub-assembly and assembly of component parts, and (4) finishing the assembled product. The methods and procedures used during each of these sequences is dependent upon the products being produced and the sophistication of the equipment which is used; however, no matter what the size of the operation, all production is characterized by these sequences.

Rough milling. This is the name most frequently used to describe the area where the initial cutting and sizing of the raw materials is accomplished. These materials, whether they be lumber, plywood, veneer, or composition products, are ripped and cut to appropriate dimensions for later processing. Lumber used in furniture production is usually purchased as either standard grades or dimension stock. Many plants operate their own kilns and others purchase ungraded stock which is cut and graded in accordance with their own production needs. Cutoff saws are used to cut the lumber into pieces of suitable length for the component parts needed. This operation is one of the most critical, because the saw operator must be able to recognize defects and be able to obtain the highest number of usable pieces of stock from a length of lumber. From the cutoff saw the pieces travel along a conveyor where they are fed into ripsaws and further sized. Many production schedules require that stock be ripped prior to cutting to length; in all cases care is exercised to keep waste to a minimum. If thickness planing is required (some stock is purchased already surfaced to the proper thickness), it is done prior to either the cutoff or ripping stages.

Mill room. The mill or machine room describes the area where the stock prepared in the rough mill is cut or otherwise machined to its final shape and dimension. Typical operations accomplished during this phase include turning, boring, cutting of joints (tenons, mortises, grooves, etc.), shaping, routing, dovetailing, and sanding. Production machines used to accomplish these varied operations include: turning

FIG. 13–3. *Frame construction is used for items such as this chair, which will be upholstered. (Courtesy of Drexel Heritage.)*

FIG. 13–4. *Stock being planed to thickness prior to further sizing.*

lathes (profile and back knife), tenoners (single and double end), mortisers (single and multiple spindle), routers, bandsaws, moulders, shapers, boring machines, dovetailers, carving machines, and sanders. A detailed discussion of these production machines may be found in Rudolph Willard's publication *Production Woodworking Equipment.*

Assembly room. Operations carried out in the assembly room include the fabrication of the component parts into sub-assemblies as well as the total assembled product. Here the completed parts are glued and clamped and fitting of doors, drawers, and hardware is accomplished. The sophisticated clamps, jigs, and fixtures used in assembly are geared to the type products being assembled and are often designed

FIG. 13–5. *Mill room operations include the cutting of curved parts on the bandsaw.*

FIG. 13–6. *Parts cut to size and shaped in the mill room make up the components used here to assemble this chest. (Courtesy of Thomasville Furniture Industries, Inc.)*

specifically to accommodate particular components. Fasteners and adhesives used are also selected with reference to the specific item being assembled. After complete assembly the product is carefully inspected to make sure it is ready to be finished.

Finishing room. In this area, furniture receives a finish appropriate for the articles being produced. The overall purposes of finishing include appearance and protection. To achieve these purposes, stains, fillers, sealers, and top coats are applied in accordance with the styles and intended use of the product. In larger furniture plants the finishing process is achieved through assembly line techniques while the smaller facilities utilize less sophisticated processes. The material and methods of furniture finishing are discussed more fully in chapter 17.

Recreational Products

The use of wood in the production of items intended for recreational use is widespread. Ranging from golf tees to large pleasure craft, the diversity of products is truly amazing. Production techniques for individual products vary widely because of this diversity, and any discussion of them is beyond the scope of this text. However, it is hoped that some understanding of the uses of wood in these products can be realized.

Toys and games constitute but one segment of the recreational uses of wood. Increased use of plastics has made vast inroads in this area but wood is still widely used. Wood is often preferred for toys used by small children because it is an economical and durable material. Wooden toys have lasted through generations of use without breaking and if broken are often easily repaired. Wagons, cars and trucks, pound-a-sets, puzzles, and play furniture are but a few examples of such products. Games of the table top variety are commonly made of wood, and wood croquet and shuffleboard sets are still preferred by many.

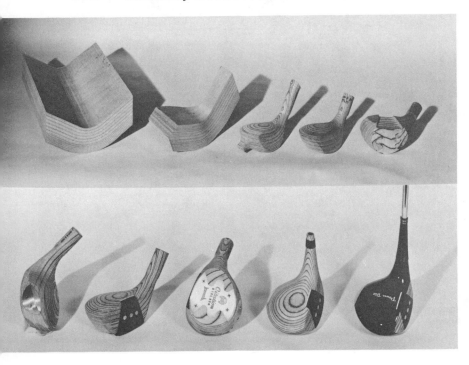

FIG. 13–7. *A golf club head is formed from a curved block of thin laminated veneers. The layers of veneer are accented by dark-colored lines of waterproof glue. (Courtesy of Hillerich & Bradsby Company, Inc.)*

Sports equipment of many varieties is often made of wood. While materials such as metal or plastic are also used, the natural properties of wood make it more suitable for many items. Among these properties are its weight-strength ratio, bending strength, stiffness, and toughness. Because of these properties, wood baseball bats continue, by far, to be the most popular. Laminated wood has achieved wide acceptance in the fabrication of such equipment as golf club heads, snowshoes, toboggans, and archery equipment. Other sports equipment commonly made of wood include arrows, hockey sticks, tennis racquets, skis, pool cues, ping pong paddles, bowling pins, fishing equipment, and gun stocks.

Marine products, particularly boats, account for a large segment of the uses of wood for recreational purposes. While aluminum and fiberglass pleasure craft have gained widespread popularity during recent years, wood continues to be in demand as a boat-building material and is considered by many to be the aristocrat of all materials. The preference for wood is based upon the properties of wood previously discussed as well as its corrosion resistance. Both solid and laminated wood are used in the construction of pleasure craft which range in size from the runabout to the cabin cruiser. Supplementary uses of wood for marine recreational purposes include docks and floats, as well as oars, paddles, water skis, and other products.

Musical instruments made of wood form another area which might be considered in the domain of recreational use. No material has yet been found that is superior to wood in the construction of certain musical instruments. Fashioned by the hands of craftsmen, wood instruments such as the Stradivarius violin have endured for centuries and are cherished for their outstanding tonal qualities. In addition to these qualities, wood is easily worked and fabricated and therefore preferred by those who produce the instruments. String instruments, such as the violin, viola, cello, bass, guitar, and banjo are almost exclusively made of wood. Pianos and organs are yet another example of wood instruments and their manufacture constitutes a significant aspect of the industry.

The manufacture of wood containers, barrels, and pallets is a specialized, yet important, segment of the wood industry. In general, containers and pallets are produced from the lower grades of either hardwood or softwood lumber, although certain products such as barrels may require the use of higher-grade hardwood stock. While plastic and paper containers have increased in popularity during recent years, a variety of wooden boxes, crates, and barrels are still manufactured for specific uses. Pallet manufacture, on the other hand, is an industry which has grown rapidly in recent years due to advances in materials handling.

Pallets are extensively used for materials handling, shipping, and storage in a wide variety of manufacturing and distributive industries. Demands for pallets have doubled in recent years and projections indicate that over 200 million units will be required by the 1980s (Forest Products Laboratory, 1971). Generally the manufacture of pallets is conducted in a specialized plant, although their production may be but one product line of a larger, more diversified operation.

Since economy is an important consideration in their use, pallets and pallet containers are usually simple in design and construction. They are typically made from lower grades of lumber (#2 or #3 common) or from plywood, and fabrication is usually achieved through nailing, although the use of adhesives has shown some promise. Sizes and types of pallets are determined by their intended use; however, they are often categorized as being *expendable* (non-returnable), *general*, or *special purpose*. The expendable type is designed primarily to facilitate shipping and once used is discarded. The general purpose pallet is designed for re-use and is of the type most frequently used in warehousing operations. Special purpose types are designed for specific products or uses and include the bin or box pallet and such specialty pallets as those used in the shipping and handling of ammunition.

FIG. 13–8. *One of the early stages in the assembly of a barrel is termed "raising." (Courtesy of Louisville Cooperage Company.)*

FIG. 13–9. *Wood pallets allow quick and easy handling of merchandise in a large warehouse. (Courtesy of Begley Drug Company.)*

The various types are designed so that their assembly will allow clearance for the tines of fork lift trucks, slings, or other devices used during lifting and transportation. Usually this clearance is provided in such a way as to allow the handling equipment to pick it up from opposite sides (two way entry) or from all four directions (four way entry).

Wood containers is a general term used to describe a wide range of products including such items as crates, boxes, baskets, bins, and cooperage. Containers of these types are used extensively for the transit and storage of items ranging from fruits and vegetables to large transformers or heavy machinery. During recent years the annual shipment value of these products has averaged over $500 million (Bureau of Domestic Commerce, 1971).

Economy is often an important concern in the production of crates, boxes, and baskets; therefore, their design and fabrication are kept simple. To further this end, the shook (individual pieces) for certain types of wooden containers are often resawn from lower grade lumber or stock unsuitable for other purposes. Assembly of these products is usually accomplished by using simple fasteners such as staples, nails, or wire applied by automatic machines. Prime advantages of wooden containers are their high strength-weight ratios, durability, rigidity, and ability to retain their properties.

Cooperage is a generic term for a wide range of products such as barrels, kegs, storage vats, and other items made from staves. When containers of this type are designed to hold liquids they are often referred to as tight cooperage, while those designed to contain solids are generally referred to as slack cooperage. Manufacture of cooperage varies in accordance with the intended use of each item; however, most cooperage is assembled from staves, heads, and hoops. The staves and heads are made from a variety of species including both hardwoods and softwoods. For example, barrels used in the production of bourbon whisky are made from the higher grades of white oak while smaller kegs used to ship fish or seafood products are often made of southern yellow pine. Hoops for tight cooperage are made from steel; however, both wire and wood hoops are extensively used when assembling certain types of slack cooperage. In general, cooperage is assembled in one plant from components which have been produced elsewhere.

An exhaustive treatment of the wide array of manufactured wood products is neither possible nor practical in this text. Literally thousands of wood-base items are in general use and we come in contact with many of these every day with little thought of their origin. The following brief listing provides but a few examples of such products:

Miscellaneous Secondary Products

bowls	pencils
buttons	picture frames
clothespins	plaques
desk sets	puzzles
dowels	shuttles
ice-cream sticks	spools
jewelry	tongue depressors
lamps	tool handles
matches	toothpicks
name plates	utensils

Resources

Bureau of Domestic Commerce, U.S. Department of Commerce. *Industry Profiles 1958–1969.* Washington, D.C.: Government Printing Office, 1971.

Doan, Franklyn E., ed. *Seng Furniture Facts.* 22nd ed. Chicago: The Seng Company, 1969.

Forest Products Laboratory. *Wood Pallet Manufacturing, U.S.D.A. Forest Service Research Note FPL-0213.* Madison, Wisconsin: Forest Products Laboratory, Forest Service, U.S. Department of Agriculture, 1971.

Willard, Rudolph. *Production Woodworking Equipment.* Rev. ed. Raleigh, North Carolina: Department of Industrial Engineering, North Carolina State University, 1966.

Chapter Fourteen

Other Products of Our Forests

People tend to think of lumber and, perhaps, plywood as the only products of our forests. While these products do consume tremendous amounts of this natural resource, an amazing variety of other products are derived from this source. We come in contact with forest-related products every day, seldom stopping to think of their origin. The paper upon which this book is printed is but one example. Other examples run the gamut from fuels to foodstuffs. Some of these products bear only slight economic significance, but others such as paper have great economic or even cultural dimensions. This chapter is included in an attempt to create an awareness of some of the diverse products which stem from our forests. It is hoped that some understanding of their scope will be realized from this selective discussion.

Poles, Piles, Posts, and Ties

Millions of trees are consumed each year to meet the demands for wooden poles, posts, piles, timbers, and ties. Some of this number is attributable to replacements for poles or posts which are no longer serviceable; however, much of the consumption is due to increased demands and the renewed popularity of such construction techniques as pole and post structures.

Approximately one-half of all our electrical powerlines and telephone and telegraph lines are carried on wood poles (Forest Service, 1961). Increased needs for more power and services to provide for expanded consumer demands will continue to create markets for poles. Among the species used for poles are the southern yellow pines, Douglas fir, and western redcedar. These species are suitable for this purpose because their basic strength properties are sufficient to withstand heavy loads and resist the stresses of winds and storms. Most

FIG. 14–1. *Because wood is non-corrosive, this large warehouse is being constructed of pressure-treated poles. (Courtesy of Koppers Company, Inc.)*

poles now installed receive preservative treatments which, when effectively applied, can provide poles giving useful service for as much as a third of a century.

Wood pilings continue to play an important role in today's structural applications. Even though many steel and concrete piles are found in service, wooden piles are still extensively used for foundations, docks, piers, bridges, breakwaters, jetties, and similar uses. Because wood piles are tough and have high resistance to crushing along the grain they can withstand the heavy impact of the pile drivers and, once in place, they are capable of supporting tremendous loads. Proper preservative treatments allow the piles to perform for years without the need for costly maintenance or replacements. Piles are produced in a similar manner to poles, and yearly production and use estimates are in the millions.

While not used in numbers required previously, wood posts are still in great demand for fences, guard rails, and signs. Demands for wood posts create markets for several hundred million units every year. Although certain species such as cedar, chestnut, and locust are often used for years without significant deterioration, preservative treatments can extend the service life of posts to several decades. Wood posts are still favored by many because they maintain good bearing in the earth and because it is easy to fasten wire and other materials to them using common tools.

FIG. 14–2. *Pressure-treated wood is one of the few materials suitable for building docks, piers, and wharves. (Courtesy of Koppers Company, Inc.)*

Ties and timbers are yet another important product of our forests. While railroad passenger service has declined during the past years, railroads continue to be one of the major means employed for the shipment of a wide variety of products. The thousands of miles of track require several hundred thousand ties as replacements each year. To this date no other material has been found that can equal wooden ties in service, mainly because the tie itself is cheap, strong, shock resistant, long lasting, and easily maintained. Structural timbers are extensively used in a variety of construction applications and are still a preferred means of providing the framework and shoring required in a wide range of mining activities.

Wood and Charcoal Fuel

Wood and charcoal have declined as major sources of heating fuel during the twentieth century; however, a considerable demand presently exists for these products.

No accurate estimates are available to measure the amounts of raw wood that are actually used for heating. Many wood industry plants continue to use slab wood and residues as a source of heat and while oil, gas, or electricity are the prime means used to heat our homes, the fireplace remains a cherished item in millions of homes. Firewood has become a lucrative business in many areas of the country because it is readily available. Wood suitable for fuel can come from thinnings, from the tops and limbs of trees cut for other purposes, or even from mill wastes. Preferences tend to run in favor of hardwoods, but well-seasoned and conveniently cut lengths of almost any species will usually find enthusiastic buyers.

Charcoal has long been used as a fuel for both domestic and commercial uses. While charcoal was of prime importance in the production of iron and steel, its use for such purposes has dwindled significantly since the beginning of the century. In turn, the growing demand for charcoal to use in outdoor cooking has created a vast new market.

Charcoal is made by the partial burning of wood under controlled atmospheric conditions until it is carbonized. This process is accomplished by placing a wood charge in a kiln and bringing the temperature up to 400° to 500° F. Then, by controlling the amount of air allowed to enter the kiln, the wood begins to carbonize at temperatures approaching 900° F. Once carbonization has taken place the kiln is sealed off, the fire smothered, and the charcoal which has been formed is allowed to cool—a process which is accomplished in about a two week period. After cooling the charcoal may be taken to a briquetting plant or it is sometimes packaged for lump sales. Briquetting is accomplished by pulverizing the wood charcoal and then compressing the resulting powder in the form of briquettes. Because the equipment needed for making briquettes is more expensive, kiln operators often take their charcoal to a briquetting plant which processes the outputs of many small kilns (Jarvis, 1960).

Naval Stores

The term naval stores is descriptive of the various products obtained from the gums (oleoresins) of several yellow pines. Historically the term can be traced to the days when pitch and tar were obtained from

FIG. 14–3. *An addition to this large international airport is being built on a foundation of treated wood piles. (Courtesy of Koppers Company, Inc.)*

these trees and used to caulk the seams of wooden sailing vessels. While the uses of the so-called naval stores have changed over the years, this is still a significant industry in the South Atlantic and Gulf Coast states.

The most important products produced today are turpentine and resin. These products are obtained by distillation of the gums which exude from chips or slashes which are cut into living trees, from resin laden stumps, or from byproducts of sulphate pulp obtained during papermaking. The most important species of trees used as sources for these resins are the longleaf and slash pines.

After the resins have been collected from the trees they are taken to central processing plants where the crude gum is converted into rosin and turpentine. Yield per tree has been increased through chemical stimulation of the chipped area. Stimulation is accomplished by spraying the wounded area with sulfuric acid, thereby opening the ends of the resin canals and allowing the gum to flow more freely and for a longer period of time. Weekly treatments of this type have been found to increase the yield by 50–60 percent (Forest Service, 1961).

Turpentine has long been used as a thinner for paints and varnishes, and while much is still used for this purpose increasing amounts are now being used for other industrial purposes. Rosin, familiar to the violinist and baseball player, is chiefly used in the manufacture of a wide range of industrial products such as finishing materials, synthetic rubber goods, and printing inks. A high proportion of all rosin produced is consumed in the production of paper where it is used as a sizing material.

In addition to turpentine and rosin, many other extractive products are obtained from our forests. Among these extractives are other resins, oils, tannins and dyes, pharmaceuticals, sugars, and syrups.

Synthetics have largely replaced certain natural extractive resins although their use still continues. Canada balsam, a clear resin obtained from the balsam fir, has been extensively used as a cement for optical lenses and the mounting of microscopic slides because it possesses a refractive index in the range of optical glass. From the sweetgum tree, storax, which contains cinnamic acid, has been used in such products as chewing gum, salves, and even flypaper.

Production of maple syrup and sugar remains an important element in certain localities of the country. While the total production today is lower when compared with past years, considerable demand still exists for these products. Obtained primarily from the sugar maple and the black maple, the "sugaring" operation is a relatively uncomplicated process consisting of tapping the tree, collecting the sap, and "boiling" it down until it becomes a syrup. Sugar content of the sap in maple trees ranges up to 10 percent with the average being in the range of 2–3 percent (Forest Service, 1961). To collect sap, small holes are drilled horizontally into the sapwood portion of the tree two or three feet above the ground. A spile (spout) is inserted into the hole in order to hold the collection container and to allow the sap to drain into the container. As the sap is collected it is taken to a central location and placed in larger tanks where, through the application of heat, the water is evaporated to produce the syrup or sugar. Most sugaring operations are conducted in the northern states where maple

FIG. 14–4. *Much maple sap is still collected in traditional buckets, but plastic bags are now being used as well. (Courtesy of Agency of Development and Community Affairs, Vermont Department of Agriculture, and U.S. Forest Products Laboratory Forest Service, U.S. Department of Agriculture.)*

trees grow in substantial numbers. As the best time to tap trees is in late winter when the days are warmer and the sap tends to flow more readily, the process is especially profitable to farmers who are normally unable to conduct other farming operations during that period.

Tannins obtained from the bark of trees continue to play an important role in the production of leather. Many synthetic tannins have been developed, but vegetable tannins are still widely used. Principle sources of tannin in the United States had been from the bark of species such as chestnut oak, eastern hemlock, and chestnut, but as these supplies began to dwindle, increasing amounts had to be imported. Today, most of the vegetable tannins are obtained from imports of the South American quebracho tree and the Italian chestnut. When hides are soaked in tannin solutions, an insoluble substance is formed in the leather and imparts durability and other desirable wearing qualities (Forest Service, 1961).

Historically, trees have provided an important source of dyes and stains; however, only a small amount of these products are so derived today. Almost entirely replaced by chemical dyes, vegetable dyes may be obtained from the bark or fruits of certain trees. The coffeetree, osage orange, butternut, black oak, and walnut are American trees which have provided sources in the past.

Forest extractives which possess medicinal properties are used in the preparation of various pharmaceutical products. The so-called patent remedies at one time were largely derived from the bark or roots of trees. Although medical and chemical science have created an astounding array of compounds for use in medicines, certain extractives are still widely used for medicinal purposes. Among those currently used in economically important quantities are Cascara bark, ginseng root, storax gum, and witch hazel bark. Cascara bark, for example, is often used in the preparation of laxatives while the bark and leaves of the witch hazel tree are frequently used in the preparation of widely used astringent products (Forest Service, 1963).

Yet another example of extractive products are a variety of aromatic oils which are extracted from the leaves, bark, or roots of trees. Many of these have been commercially used in the production of soaps, perfumes, or polishing oils while others have been used as flavoring materials. The commercial importance of these products is not great but most individuals will recognize extractives such as oil of cedar, oil of hemlock, pine oil, oil of sassafrass, or oil of wintergreen.

Seasonal Wood Crops

A variety of tree crops which possess economic significance are harvested annually in the United States. Ranging from nuts to Christmas trees many of these products are cultivated while others are derived from natural growth.

The growing and harvesting of Christmas trees has long been a lucrative business pursued throughout the northern tier of states. Trees harvested from both natural woodlands and the so-called Christmas tree farms constitute a multi-million dollar industry. Some of the most popular species include the Scotch pine, balsam fir, blue spruce, and Douglas fir. The introduction of artificial trees during recent years has had a significant effect upon the market; however, many individuals prefer the real tree and markets will probably con-

tinue. Closely associated with the Christmas tree industry is the production of evergreen wreaths and boughs or decorations made from holly. Even the harvesting of the forest parasite mistletoe has some local economic significance.

Nuts harvested from the forests and those commercially cultivated constitute economically important products. Most important of these are pecans and walnuts, while others such as hickory nuts, butternuts, beechnuts, chestnuts, and pinyon nuts possess varying degrees of significance. The only nut cultivated on a large scale is the pecan and

FIG. 14–5. *Christmas trees can be a profitable crop for many farmers. (Courtesy of American Forest Institute.)*

FIG. 14–6. *Long rows of pecan trees present a picturesque vista. (Courtesy of Extension Horticulture Department, University of Georgia.)*

extensive orchards may be found in the southern states with most ranging between Georgia and Texas. Many nuts are marketed unshelled but those that are processed and shelled are considerably more expensive due to the difficulty of extracting the meats in an unbroken condition. Cracking machines have been developed and improved during recent years and as a result shelling has been improved and yields increased.

Other edible products of the forest, often in demand in local areas, include the wild grape, blackberry, and strawberry as well as the wild plum, paw paw, or persimmon. These items are no longer of great economic importance; however, they remain yet another example of the diversified nature of forest products.

Wood Chemical Products

Modification of wood through chemical processes is another method whereby the potential of our forests may be realized. The principal product achieved through chemical conversion of wood is pulp and paper, although certain fibers and plastics are produced. Pulp and paper products constitute the most extensive aspect of these processes and are the only ones which constitute a continuing growth pattern. Fibers and plastics chemically derived from wood are becoming less important as the competition from synthetic and other materials has increased during recent years.

People have become so accustomed to the use of pulp and paper products that they do not think of them as products of our forests. In reality, however, these products constitute one of the major uses of wood. In the first half of this century, pulpwood rose from only one-fiftieth of the total of all industrial wood to approximately one-third of the total and consumption today continues at a similar level (Forest Service, 1961). While some paper is produced from other materials such as flax or rags, about 97 percent comes from wood (American Forest Products Industries, 1968). The majority of pulp

FIG. 14–7. *Great quantities of pulpwood are consumed by the paper industry. (Courtesy of American Forest Institute.)*

FIG. 14–8. *The mat is formed on a fourdrinier paper machine, and finished paper is wound onto a large roll as it leaves the machine (above). (Courtesy of American Forest Institute.)*

and paper products have been produced from softwood species; however, it is now possible to use almost any species.

Pulp is the raw material from which paper and other products are made. The process of transforming the raw wood into pulp is accomplished through the use of one of three basic processes—mechanical, chemical, and semi-chemical—all designed to separate the cellulosic fibers so that they may be rearranged to produce an entirely new product.

The mechanical process of pulping is used to produce the cheaper grades of paper products such as newsprint or various paper boards, and uses primarily softwood species. The process is accomplished by literally tearing apart raw wood and separating it into fibers through a grinding process. Chemical pulping processes (sulfite, sulfate, and soda) are accomplished when the dissolving action of the chemicals in connection with steam pressure removes all the constituents of wood except the fibers. The third pulping process, semi-chemical, is the most recently developed. Essentially, this process first uses chemicals to partially dissolve and soften the raw wood chips and then completes the reduction to fibers through mechanical means. The chemical process is adaptable to both softwoods and hardwoods and can be used to produce a variety of grades and products while the semi-chemical process is primarily used for hardwood pulps made into corrugated board, newsprint, and specialty boards.

Once the raw wood has been converted into pulp, the fibers are cleaned to remove leftover chemicals and other impurities. The fibers are then further separated in a beater and coloring, sizing, and fillers are added as required. The next step in processing takes place in a machine called a Jordan where the treated fibers are further separated and cut to the required size. Now ready to be made into paper, the wet pulp is run onto a wire screen (fourdrinier machine) where much of the water is extracted and the mat is then passed through rollers which press and further dry the sheet. Calandering rolls are then used to impart the required degree of smoothness necessary for the finished product prior to its being rolled or otherwise processed for the consumer (American Forest Products Industries, 1968).

As previously mentioned, the chemical conversion of wood is almost exclusively directed at the production of wood pulp and paper products. The market for cellulose fibers, used primarily in the production of rayon, accounts for a distant second in terms of wood pulp consumed. Pulp as a source of cellulose resins for the plastics industry constitutes a third area of the chemical modification of wood. Such resins as cellulose acetate, cellulose acetate butyrate, cellulose nitrate or ethyl cellulose are commonly used in the plastics industry. In general these resins possess good electrical properties and are among the toughest of the plastics. Research is constantly being conducted into other aspects of the chemical modification of wood and, therefore, only the future will be able to reveal those which may become feasible for use.

Resources

American Forest Products Industries. *The Story of Pulp and Paper.* Washington, D.C.: American Forest Products Industries, Inc., 1968.

Forest Service, United States Department of Agriculture. *Products of American Forests, Miscellaneous Publication No. 861.* Washington, D.C.: Government Printing Office, 1961.

Forest Service, United States Department of Agriculture. *Special Forest Products for Profit, Agriculture Information Bulletin No. 278,* Washington, D.C.: Government Printing Office, 1963.

Jarvis, J. Pitts Jr. *The Wood Charcoal Industry in the State of Missouri.* Columbia, Missouri: Engineering Experiment Station, University of Missouri, 1960.

Panshin, A. J., E. S. Harrar, J. S. Bethel, and W. J. Baker. *Forest Products: Their Sources, Production, and Utilization.* 2d ed. New York: McGraw-Hill Book Company, 1962.

Part Three

Wood-Related Products and Processes

Chapter Fifteen

Wood Gluing and Adhesives

Adhesives have enhanced the value of many materials of industry, opening avenues of usefulness not available through the use of mechanical fasteners. Foremost among these materials is wood, probably the oldest beneficiary of the favors bestowed by adhesives as well as the chief reason for many developments in modern adhesive technology. Without adhesives, plywood, particleboard, furniture, and thousands of other wood products would not be possible, or would be very limited in form and application. Anyone interested in wood, therefore, should know something about the adhesives used to join wood to wood.

The Function of Adhesives

Why are adhesives needed? Why cannot a broken solid be restored simply by fitting the pieces back together again? Bikerman (1961) provides the following explanation.

Whenever a solid, such as a glass rod, is broken and the ends fitted together again, we know that not only is the original solid not restored, but that the mutual attraction of the two pieces is practically zero. This phenomenon is explained by two factors, both having to do with the surface of the solid. First, the surface is rough, consisting of miniature jagged peaks and valleys, and due to the plastic deformation of the material just before it broke, as well as the relief of stress in it, the hills of one piece do not have the same shape as the valleys from which they were torn. Thus, the fit between the two pieces is not nearly as exact as it may appear to the naked eye (see fig. 15–1). Also, when the solid is broken in open air, the surfaces are immediately covered with molecules (mostly water) from the air. Therefore, the pieces fitted back together actually make very little or no surface-to-surface contact.

Solid material is held together by forces of attraction between adjacent molecules. These forces are inversely proportional to the distance separating the molecules, which means that the force decreases rapidly with increasing distance, and that molecules must be very close together for the attraction to be of any consequence. In view of this fact, one might reason that two solids could be made to adhere simply by smoothing the mating surfaces until the molecules would be as close when the two were pressed together as they were in the material itself. Theoretically, this is true, and some surfaces have been ground to such an extent that considerable force was required to separate them when they were placed in contact. In reality, however, even these surfaces are made up of hills and valleys which are as much as two hundred times as large as the biggest molecule; consequently the strength of the joint is only a very small fraction of the strength of the material.

While it is very difficult to bring the surfaces of two solids into intimate contact, no such problems are encountered in bringing together a liquid and a solid. Since a liquid will readily fill up the valleys of a rough surface, all that is required is to spread a sufficient amount of the liquid on each surface to fill up the valleys, and press the two surfaces together to form an adhesive joint.

Unfortunately, there is more to the process than that. First of all, the liquid must be a special type, namely, one that will solidify under certain conditions. Furthermore, the substance formed when the liquid solidifies must be relatively strong, or the joint would break apart between the molecules of the solidified adhesive substance. Actually, there are several other limiting factors, but before these are discussed, it should be helpful to examine more closely why adhesives work.

FIG. 15–1. *Contact between two solid surfaces (greatly magnified).*

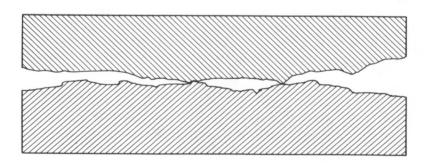

The Theory of Adhesion

Since the surfaces of solids are rough, full of hills and valleys, the solidified adhesive can be viewed as a thin film between the two surfaces, with small "arms" or hooks reaching into these recesses. Because of this fact, it was once believed that the mechanical holding or hooking effect of the adhesive gave the joint strength. This theory, called the mechanical adhesion theory, under closer investigation, has been found to account for only about 10 to 20 percent of the total holding force of an adhesive joint. One exception is adhesive bonds between very fibrous materials such as paper and cloth, in which mechanical adhesion is the major holding factor. In most materials the majority of the adhesive force is attributed to *specific adhesion,* a term which is interpreted to mean attraction due to intermolecular forces between the adhesive and the adherend. This type of attraction is possible because the adhesive in liquid form flows easily into the irregularities of the surfaces to be joined, even to the extent that bonds will be formed between the molecules of the adhesive and the adherend. The exact nature of what happens between the adhesive and the adherend is not fully understood, but authorities presently attribute adhesive action to various types of physiochemical bonds between atoms and molecules.

Types of Adhesives

Classifying adhesives so that they may be described in relatively brief terms is a difficult task, because modern technology has created a wide array of new adhesive products. In the past, mostly "standard" adhesives were manufactured and it was necessary to select from those available one which would most nearly fit the needs of a given situation. While standard adhesives are still available, the trend is increasingly toward formulation of special-purpose adhesives which will provide the user with the optimum properties for his particular needs. These special formulas usually involve modifications and combinations of more common adhesives, however, so rather than attempt to discuss all the individual adhesives, this text will be concerned mainly with more common, generally available adhesives which are widely used for wood gluing.

Adhesives may be classified according to origin, as either *natural* or *synthetic*. Natural adhesives include animal, casein, blood, and vegetable glues, while the most common on the rapidly expanding list of synthetics are polyvinyl acetates, urea resins, melamine resins, phenol resins, resorcinol resins, and rubber-based adhesives. Before World War II, glues of natural origin were predominant, and all types were widely used for wood gluing. Since that time, however, synthetics have taken over much of the market, and now hide and casein glues are the only natural adhesives of appreciable commercial importance.

Adhesives may also be classified according to their manner of setting or curing. One type of adhesive must be heated to fairly high temperatures before becoming liquid, so a bond is formed by the *cooling of a molten liquid.* These adhesives are called hot-melts. A second type becomes a solid by *releasing a solvent,* which may be water or some other liquid compatible with the solid component of the adhesive. Included among these are hide, polyvinyl, and casein glues. Phenols, urea resins, and melamine resins belong to a group which set by *polymerization,* the formation of large molecules (polymers) from smaller ones (monomers). Adhesives which cure by means of solvent release are used mainly for porous substrates (such as wood) which will absorb the solvent, but polymerizing resins may be used for either porous or non-porous materials.

Properties of Adhesives

The most important properties of several common adhesives are presented in table 15–1. It should be pointed out that the properties listed apply only to standard formulations of each adhesive; modifications of standard formulas are often made to produce changes in one or more properties of the adhesives. Also, some of the glues, such as urea and phenol resins, are available in either liquid or powder form, and the different forms may exhibit different properties. In other words, the table is not intended to be exhaustive, but only representative of the more common adhesives. Complete coverage of the properties of each adhesive family, including the variations of each type, would consume more space than the subject justifies in this text.

TABLE 15–1

Properties of Adhesives

Adhesive	Form	Setting Time & Temperature	Method of Set	Water Resistance	Main Advantages	Main Limitations
Hide	Flakes or beads	2–4 hrs. at 70–80°F.	Cooling and solvent loss	Low	Quick setting: good strength; non-staining	Short open assembly time; low water resistance
Hide	Liquid	12–24 hrs. at 70–80°F.	Solvent loss	Low	Longer open assembly; non-staining	Slow setting; low water resistance
Casein	Powder	8–12 hrs. at 70–80°F.	Solvent loss	Good	Good gap-filling properties; sets at low temperature; clear glue line	Stains many woods; abrasive to cutting tools
Polyvinyl	Liquid	2–4 hrs. at 70–80°F.	Solvent loss	Low	Colorless glue line; low cost	Low water resistance; tendency to creep under load
Urea Resin	Liquid or powder	6–8 hrs. at 70–80°F.; faster at higher temp.	Polymerization	Good	Good open assembly; non-staining; can be used at room temperature or in hot press	Requires close-fitting joints; dries brittle
Phenol Resin	Liquid or powder	Time varies with temp. 250–300°F.	Polymerization	Waterproof	Good water and heat resistance	Suitable only for hot press applications; dark colored glue line
Melamine	Powder	5–15 minutes at hot press temp. (240–260°F.)	Polymerization	Waterproof	Colorless glue line; good water and heat resistance	Expense; limited to hot press applications
Resorcinol	Liquid	8–12 hrs. at 70–80°F.; faster at higher temp.	Polymerization	Waterproof	Very good water and heat resistance	Expense; dark colored glue line

Handwritten margin notes: "NATURAL", "MILK", "WHITE ACETATE TITEBOND", "THERMAL SETTING", "WATER RISTANCE", "WATER PROOF"

In addition to the adhesives listed in the table, two more categories of adhesives have some importance in wood utilization. *Rubber-based* adhesives include a great number of individual formulations made from both natural and synthetic rubber. One of the important advantages of rubber-based adhesives is the ease with which their properties can be modified using different rubbers and by the addition of tackifiers, resins, plasticizers, and other materials (Skeist, 1962). The properties of these adhesives are therefore difficult to describe, as they vary in the bond from very plastic and flexible to quite hard and stiff.

Most rubber-based adhesives do not cure or set in the same sense as the ureas or phenolics. The adhesive thickens by loss of solvent until it becomes a more or less plastic substance, but never becomes completely hard. A bond of this type is not rigid, and will exhibit a certain amount of "give" under stress. Rubber-based adhesives can be made to cure by the addition of phenolic resins, in which case the cured bond will be harder and less flexible.

Two rubber-based adhesives often used with wood are the *contact adhesives* and the elastomeric *construction adhesives.* Contact adhesives, or contact cements, are used extensively to bond plastic laminates to wood substrates. The adhesive is spread on both surfaces, the solvent allowed to evaporate, then the two surfaces are pressed together, making the bond upon contact. Construction adhesives are applied from a tube in a conventional caulking gun. They are used to install paneling of all types without nails, and have recently been utilized for structural applications, especially the gluing of subfloors to joists. Use of adhesives instead of, or in addition to, nails greatly increases the rigidity of a structure, and in floor systems, squeaks are eliminated. In general, neither contact nor construction adhesives are highly moisture-resistant, although some are considerably better than others in this regard. All are sufficiently durable for the interior applications for which they are recommended.

Another type of adhesive which differs from both the common woodworking and rubber-based adhesives is the *hot-melts*. These adhesives are thermoplastic solids which liquify when heated, and set by simple cooling. Hot-melts have only recently achieved importance in the woodworking industry, where they excell as edge-banding adhesives. The very rapid cooling of hot-melts severely limits open assembly time, so much that practically all applications must be performed by machines which melt the glue, apply it to the surfaces, and then apply pressure immediately. These adhesives are not utilized for other wood gluing applications for this reason.

Factors Affecting Adhesive Joint Quality

An adhesive joint consists of five "links" (fig. 15–2), and the strength of the joint depends upon the performance of the weakest link.

The weakest link in most types of joints may be determined by testing a sample joint to failure and observing the location of the rupture. If the adhesive itself fails, it is called a *cohesive failure*, because the cohesive strength within the adhesive was less than the adhesive strength of the bond between adhesive and adherend. If failure occurs at the *interface* (a theoretical line between the adhesive and the substrate), it is termed an *adhesive failure*, because the adhesion between adhesive and adherend failed. An *adherend*, or *substrate*, *failure* occurs only when both the cohesive strength of the adhesive and the adhesion between adhesive and substrate exceed the cohesive strength of the substrate.

A proper adhesive joint with wood as the substrate should always have a high percentage of wood failure when tested to rupture. The wide availability of high-quality adhesives applicable to wood gluing practically eliminates cohesive failures if the proper adhesive is chosen for the job, so the area of greatest concern is the interfaces. It will be noticed that the factors affecting joint quality relate mostly, if not entirely, to the nature of the interface.

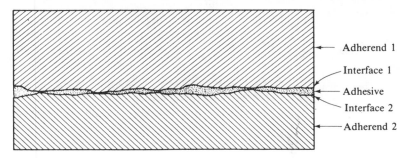

FIG. 15–2. *Components of an adhesive joint.*

Surface Topography of Wood

Surface texture is one of the most important factors that affect adhesion for any type of surface, and this is especially true for wood. Even if the surface of a piece of wood could be planed perfectly flat, which it cannot, the surface still would not be smooth, because wood is a porous material, the cells being nothing more than hollow shells. This unique structure has a definite effect on the gluing process. While the porosity of the material and roughness of the surface prevent perfect contact between adherends, these factors actually aid in forming a strong adhesive joint. Because of surface irregularities, the true area of a solid surface is actually much greater than the area as we normally measure it. Consequently, there is more area to which the adhesive can bond than if the surface were smoother. Which is to say that, within a certain limit, stronger adhesive joints can be formed when the surfaces are relatively more irregular. The limit to this statement in the case of wood gluing is that a rougher surface usually indicates more damaged fibers, which detract from joint strength. Any machining operation leaves damaged fibers, but on a planed surface produced by a jointer or planer, this damage does not seriously impair the strength of the joint. Certain types of circular saws also produce cuts smooth enough to allow gluing, but the blade must be kept sharp and free of vibration.

In addition, surface roughness is generally accompanied by increased porosity in the adherend and a consequent decrease in its strength. When this strength decreases to a certain point, the wood itself will be the weakest part of the joint. Surfaces which are too rough require more glue to fill the irregularities, resulting in a thick, expensive glue joint.

Penetration

Before an adhesive can form bonds with the adherend surface, it must come into intimate (molecular) contact with the surface. In a porous material such as wood, the adhesive must penetrate the hollows of the cells and make contact with the cell walls. If the adhesive does not penetrate, too little contact is made, and the joint will fail at the interface. On the other hand, if too much penetration occurs, too much of the adhesive is carried away, leaving a "starved" joint.

The extent to which an adhesive fills the pores of wood and comes into intimate contact with cell walls is determined in part by the degree to which the adhesive will "wet" the surface of the adherend. Wetting actually indicates the affinity of a liquid for a solid, and can be described as follows: If a drop of water is placed on a smooth solid surface, it will immediately begin to spread over the surface until the edges of the drop have reached a certain equilibrium angle with the surface; if this angle, called the *contact angle,* is low, it means that the water has high affinity for the solid, that the water will spread over a large area, and that good wetting takes place (fig. 15–3); on the other hand, a high contact angle indicates that the water has remained almost in a round drop, and very little or no wetting takes place.

Another factor which affects penetration is the *viscosity* of the adhesive. Viscosity is correctly defined as the resistance to flow, but in common use it is equated with the consistency of a liquid. Before

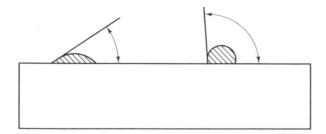

FIG. 15-3. *Low and high contact angle.*

an adhesive can adequately wet a surface, it must flow easily over that surface. An adhesive of high viscosity will not flow easily and therefore will not wet the surface and bring about good penetration.

Pressure

Pressure can overcome some of the difficulties encountered when one or more of the above factors are not favorable. Pressure not only brings the two surfaces into closer contact, but also brings about better penetration by forcing the adhesive into the pores of the wood. Thus an adhesive of somewhat higher than optimum viscosity can be used if sufficient pressure is applied to the joint.

Moisture Content of Wood

In general, the moisture content of wood at the time of gluing should be very near that which will be attained in service. Some adhesives will tolerate a fairly wide moisture content range, while others have a quite narrow zone for optimum bond formation. If the moisture content is not correct at the time of gluing, the wood will subsequently pick up or lose moisture, placing stress on the glue line when the wood swells or shrinks. Also, too-wet wood will obviously not absorb water as rapidly from an adhesive which cures by water loss, thus slowing down the rate of cure.

Resources

Bikerman, J. J. *The Science of Adhesive Joints.* New York: Academic Press Inc., 1961.

Brown, H. P., A. J. Panshin, and G. C. Forsaith. *Textbook of Wood Technology.* Vol. II. New York: McGraw-Hill Book Company, Inc., 1952.

Eley, D. D. *Adhesion.* London: Oxford University Press, 1961.

Houwink, R., and Salomon, G., eds. *Adhesion and Adhesives.* New York: Elsevier Publishing Company, 1967.

Proceedings of the Conference on Theory of Wood Adhesion. Sponsored by the National Science Foundation and the School of Natural Resources, Department of Wood Science and Technology. Ann Arbor: University of Michigan, 1961.

Skeist, Irving, ed. *Handbook of Adhesives.* New York: Reinhold Publishing Corporation, 1962.

Synthetic-Resin Glues. U.S. Forest Service Research Note FPL-0141. Madison, Wisconsin: Forest Products Laboratory, 1966.

Vick, C. B. "Elastomeric Adhesives for Field-Gluing Plywood Floors." *Forest Products Journal* 21 (August, 1971): 34-42.

Chapter Sixteen

Wood Preserving

The field of wood preserving has developed through attempts to protect wood from certain destructive agents which attack it, causing deterioration and thereby decreasing the serviceability it might otherwise provide. Preservatives are effectively used to protect wood against such agencies as fungi, insects, marine borers, fire, and weather. Many preservatives and processes have been developed to help combat these agencies with each type possessing specific properties and meeting specific needs.

While the initial cost of preservative treated products is slightly higher, their extended periods of serviceability far outweigh this consideration. The costs of repair and replacement of deteriorated wood products would prohibit their use if suitable preservatives were not available. Marine pilings, for example, will give long service only if they are well impregnated with a suitable preservative. Marine borers have been known to destroy untreated pilings in periods as short as one year, while properly treated piles may be expected to remain serviceable fifteen times as long.

The Importance of Preserved Wood

Many people are prone to think of preservative treatments as being applicable only to poles, pilings, or other heavy structural members, but in reality the scope of wood preservation includes many applications, even in their own homes, of which they are unaware. Such preservative treated wood products as window sash, doors, frames, trim, siding, and framing members are often found in residential construction. The renewed popularity of pole buildings and the recent development of wood foundations are further examples of increased use of treated wood in the construction industry. Treated wood has provided savings to homeowners from three to five times its original cost and greatly increased the life span of homes.

The field of wood preservation has also made great contributions in terms of the conservation of our forest resources. It has been estimated that the crossties used by American railroads number over 1 billion (approximately 40 billion board feet). The railroads have calculated that treated ties reduce replacements by as much as 70 percent, an equivalent savings of about 2.5 billion board feet each year. This savings in lumber would be enough to construct 200,000 new homes each year (if each used about 13,000 board feet). The contributions of wood preserving may be viewed in yet another way if we consider that there are over 100 million wood poles in use by telephone, telegraph, and electrical companies. As each of these poles represents a tree and figures indicate that treated poles last six times longer than untreated poles (an average of about thirty years), we then realize a savings in the neighborhood of 80 million trees every five years (Roche, 1965).

Experiments to measure the effectiveness of various methods of treating wood products are conducted on a continuing basis by the U.S. Forest Service and member agencies of the American Wood Preservers' Institute. Through efforts such as these, new methods and materials of wood preservation are constantly being evaluated with the goal of improving the serviceability of wood products.

In chapter 5 the various destructive agencies which can attack wood were discussed. In the remainder of this chapter some of the more commonly used preservatives and methods of treatment which are utilized in efforts to minimize the effects of these destructive agencies will be examined.

Preservatives

Wood preservatives are substances that possess toxic properties or repellent effects upon the organisms which attack wood or have a retardant effect upon other agencies such as fire. Each type of preservative possesses its own characteristics and suitability of application but, according to Hunt and Garratt (1967), in general use the preservative should be toxic to the destroying agent, permanent, penetrative, safe to use and handle, economical, and harmless to both wood and metal. They further indicate that certain uses may require the preservative to be clean, moisture repellent, fire resistant, colorless or odorless, capable of receiving a surface finish, or, in some cases, a combination of several of these properties. Unfortunately, to this time at least, no one preservative has been developed which would prove effective in all use situations.

Basically, standard wood preservatives may be grouped into three categories: (1) creosote, (2) oil-borne preservatives, and (3) water-borne preservatives (Southern Pine Association). A brief discussion of each of these categories follows.

Creosote

Creosote and various creosote solutions are used for situations where protection from decay and other wood-destroying organisms is of primary importance. They are not used where painting or other surface finishes are required, nor where slight odors might prove objectionable. Creosote, creosote-coal tar mixtures, and creosote-

FIG. 16–1. *Octagonal pole pressure treated with creosote supports street light as well as carrying electric power and telephone lines. Poles were installed in 1898 on Staten Island. (Courtesy of Koppers Company, Inc.)*

petroleum mixtures are the three general types found under this category.

Creosote. Creosote is the most widely used of all the preservatives and, in general, is still one of the most effective materials for all-around protection from destructive organisms. Creosote is a bulk distillate of coal tar and is distilled out at temperatures ranging from approximately 175° C. to 400° C. It has been found that of the 162 known chemical compounds in creosote, those that distill out above 235° C. are the most effective in providing protection. The effectiveness of creosote is attributed to the individual toxicity of many of the compounds found in it. Retention rates of twenty or more pounds per cubic foot make creosote suitable for service in lumber and timbers in coastal areas. Retention rates of approximately twelve pounds per cubic foot or lower make it suitable for use in lumber, timber, ties, piles, poles, and posts where contact with fresh water or the ground will be experienced.

Creosote-coal tar mixtures. Creosote-coal tar mixtures are the most widely accepted preservatives for marine or salt water installations. At retention rates of about 20 lbs./cu. ft., they are the most effective agent for use in waters where marine borers are active. Against the destructive Limnoria, treatments at 25 lbs./cu. ft. are successful. Creosote-coal tar mixtures are made by the simple blending of creosote and coal tar. Four mixtures, ranging from 50 percent creosote-50 percent coal tar to 80 percent creosote-20 percent coal tar, are generally blended. While the addition of the coal tar tends to reduce the cost of the preservative it is effective in reducing the water absorption rate and therefore cutting down checking and splitting, a quality especially important for railroad crossties.

Creosote-petroleum mixtures. Creosote-petroleum mixtures are used primarily where economy is one of the most important factors. They are not designed for marine installations. Usually the mixtures are made up in a 50-50 ratio of creosote and petroleum. As the prime reason for the addition of petroleum is the reduction of cost, the user often specifies and has the mixture blended to his needs. Similar to creosote-coal tar mixtures, the creosote-petroleum mixtures are suitable for crossties, posts, and for many structural uses. Poles are not usually preserved with this mixture because it leaves an oily film on the surface of the treated member.

Oil-Borne Preservatives

Oil-borne preservatives may be used in almost any type of installation, except for those in contact with salt water. If the proper petroleum oil solvents are used and the treated wood then undergoes seasoning to remove the solvents, the wood may be suitable for painting and may remain both clean and odorless. Because they are chemical compounds, concentrations of these solutions may be varied and the toxicity to certain fungi and insects controlled in relation to its application. The American Wood Preservers' Association has included the oil soluble chemicals pentachlorophenol, copper napthenate, and solubilized copper-8-quinolinolate in its Standard P9-67.

Pentachlorophenol. Pentachlorophenol (penta) is the most widely used of the oil-borne preservatives. It is insoluble in water and therefore highly permanent, as well as being very toxic to both fungi and insects. Pentachlorophenol is formed by the chemical reaction of chlorine upon phenol and its concentration in the treating solution should be between 4.5 percent and 5.5 percent by weight. Penta is more readily soluble in heavier petroleums, having less solubility in lighter solvents such as kerosene or fuel oils. These lighter petroleum solvents must be used in connection with an auxiliary solvent which does not exceed 5 percent of the total of the combined solvents. The lighter solvents are used when cleaner surfaces, such as those required for various types of millwork, are desired. Penta solutions may be irritating to the skin under conditions of prolonged use, but if normal precautions are followed few, if any, harmful effects will be realized. Penta treatments may be achieved through either pressure or non-pressure processes and are widely applied by dip, soak, and even brushing techniques. Penta can be used with creosote as the solvent. This type of treatment is often used for poles and posts. Oil-borne penta solutions are effective for the general treating of lumber and structural timbers, poles, piles, and posts; however, they are not effective in salt water nor are they effective against marine borers. Because of their "clean" properties, penta solutions are widely used in the treatment of sidings, plywoods, sash, and a variety of millwork.

Copper napthenate. Copper napthenate is a chemical salt obtained by combining copper and napthenic acids. Copper napthenate has a decidedly green color and its use creates a green color in the wood being treated. Usually applied through non-pressure methods, it has been used effectively in the treatment of poles, posts, and other structural applications. Due to a waxy characteristic, copper napthenate is not recommended where painting or other surface finishes are desired.

Copper-8-quinolinolate. Copper-8-quinolinolate is a chemical compound containing elements of nickel and copper. Because of the copper, it also possesses a green color which is transmitted to the material being treated. Its chief advantage lies in the fact that it possesses low toxicity to humans and therefore may be used in treated wood such as fruit and vegetable crates, truck or refrigerator linings, or other applications where it may come in contact with foodstuffs. It is not extensively used in exterior applications or in treatment of wood for general construction.

Water-Borne Preservatives

Water-borne preservatives are most often used for installations off the ground; however, they are used to a limited extent where ground contact occurs if painting is required. Because the preservative is water soluble, it is subject to leaching and therefore is not adaptable to use where contact with moisture is prolonged. The chief advantage of water-borne preservatives is their lower costs, primarily due to the solvent itself. Other advantages include the fact that they penetrate well, are clean and may be painted, and that they are toxic to fungi and insects but not to humans. The primary disadvantage of the water-borne preservatives lies in the fact that the water causes the wood to swell. As a result, the treated wood must be redried, through either an air or kiln drying process, until the proper moisture content is again achieved.

The water-borne preservatives are chemical salts which are usually obtained through the combination of several chemical elements, the most common of which are copper, zinc, chromium, and arsenic. The combinations of the different compounds vary and the percentages are listed in the American Wood Preservers' Association Standard P5-68. Table 16–1 lists eight water-borne preservatives, their symbols, and their trade names. The standard must be consulted for specific formulations and treatment retentions.

TABLE 16–1

Water-Borne Preservatives—Symbols and Trade Names

Preservative	Symbol	Trade Name
Acid Copper Chromate	ACC	Celcure*
Ammoniacal Copper Arsenite	ACA	Chemonite*
Chromated Copper Arsenate, Type A	CCA – Type A	Erdalith* Wolman* Salts CCA
Chromated Copper Arsenate	CZC	Boliden* K–33 Greensalt Osmose* K–33
Chromated Zinc Chloride	CAC	
Copperized Chromated Zinc Arsenate	CuCZA	Copperized Boliden Salts*
Fluor Chrome Arsenate Phenol, Type A	FCAP – Type A	Tanalith Wolman Salts* FCAP Wolman* Salts FMP
Fluor Chrome Arsenate Phenol, Type B	FCAP – Type B	Osmosalts* (Osmosar*)

SOURCE: American Wood Preservers' Association, *AWPA Standards, M9–67* (Washington, D.C.: American Wood Preservers' Association, 1967). Used by permission.

* Registered, U.S. Patent Office

Fire Retardant and Water-Repellent Preservatives

Wood in service often must be treated to retard either fire or moisture. While it is not possible with our current technology to make wood absolutely fire or waterproof, effective treatments have been achieved which can significantly retard the severity of damage incurred through these agents.

Fire retardant treatments generally use water-borne fire-retardant chemicals which are impregnated into the wood through a pressure process. Most of the chemicals used for this treatment have the advantage of leaving the wood clean, odorless, and paintable. Among the most effective chemicals are ammonium phosphates, aluminum sulfates, and chromated zinc chlorides. As with other chemical compounds, the formulations used for the specific qualities desired are quite critical. The American Wood Preservers' Association Standard P10-68 lists four types (Types A, B, C, D) of fire retardants and the chemical formulation for each and should be consulted for specific information. The key to effective fire-retardant treatments lies in their ability to prevent the spread of flame and not support combustion once the source of heat is removed. High retention and good penetration of these chemicals are necessary if effective treatments are to be realized. Chemical salts which are toxic to fungi and insects may be added to fire-retardant chemicals in order to achieve both objectives. Most chemicals used for these purposes are water soluble; therefore, they are subject to leaching if they are exposed to the weather or are in contact with wet ground. Recently, fire-retardant paints have been introduced which serve to create a barrier between flame and the wood. While these paints will eventually break down under prolonged exposure to fire, they do prove effective as fire-retardants.

Water-repellent treatments usually use oil-borne preservatives. The primary water-repellent preservative in use today is pentachlorophenol to which other oils, resins, and waxes are added. The chief use of water-repellent preservatives has been in the treatment of various forms of millwork such as doors and window sash. Because penta solutions are non-swelling, toxic, and, depending upon the solvent, clean, they have received the greatest applications for these purposes. Generally, the method of treatment used is a non-pressure process such as the dip or soak method. As pointed out in an earlier chapter, various forms of modified wood are also available which greatly reduce the undesirable effects of moisture.

FIG. 16–2. *The rigorous conditions under which railroad ties are used demand a creosote pressure treatment. The ties in the center stacks above are untreated.*

Essentially there are two methods of impregnating wood with a preservative substance—pressure treating and non-pressure treating. Of the two methods, far superior results may be achieved through the use of pressure treating. The effectiveness of any preservative used is determined by the uniformity and depth of penetration achieved. This, coupled with the application or the protection which is desired, usually dictates which treatment process is used. In general the non-pressure processes are of lower cost; however, the treatments tend to be superficial and the degree of protection is therefore lower.

Pressure Treating Methods

The vast majority of preservative treated wood in the United States is impregnated by pressure processes. Basically the various methods consist of placing the wood into a closed cylinder, introducing the preservative, then subjecting the contents to high pressures. Standard pressure treating processes are the only means by which deeper penetration and uniform distribution of the preservative may be realized. In general, pressure treating may be categorized by what is termed a full-cell process or an empty-cell process, although other variant processes are also in use.

Empty-cell processes are most generally employed for treatments using creosote or preservative oils and are categorized as either the Lowry or Rueping methods. Essentially the empty-cell process is accomplished by subjecting the wood to high air pressures prior to the introduction and the injection of the preservative under even greater pressures. When the pressure is released, the expanded and trapped air in the wood cells expels the excess preservative from the cells, thereby reducing the net retention of the preservative. This method provides greater uniformity and penetration than is possible with the full-cell process and is extensively used in the treatment of poles, posts, and piles.

Full-cell process is the term applied to the method used when the major purpose is to retain the maximum amount of preservative within the cell cavity as well as in the cell walls. The wood is not subjected to higher pressures prior to the introduction of the preservative; rather, the wood is placed in the treating cylinder and a slight vacuum is pulled to remove the air from the cell cavities. The preservative is then introduced, and when subjected to high pressure, the solution is forced into the cell structure. Unlike the empty-cell process, excess preservative is not driven off and that which has been introduced will remain. When creosote or its solutions are used, there

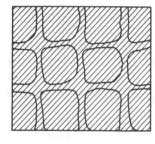

Full cell

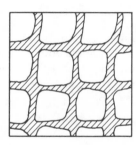

Empty cell

FIG. 16–3. *Comparison of full and empty cell processes. Shading indicates preservative retention in both cell wall and lumen for full cell process, whereas in empty cell process, retention is in or on the cell wall.*

is a tendency toward unclean surfaces and many treating plants utilize a slight final vacuum to clean and dry the exterior of the treated wood. The full-cell process is also widely utilized for treatments using the water-borne preservatives and fire-retardant chemicals.

Variant processes are also used whereby it is possible to treat only specified local areas of wood such as the butt end of a timber or post, or to impregnate the area around holes which have been bored. A type of pressure process recently developed, termed the Cellon process, utilizes liquid petroleum gas as the carrier for the preservative penta. Due to a lower viscosity, the solution is capable of deeper penetration and leaves the wood water repellent, free of raised grain, and paintable.

Non-Pressure Treating Methods

When wood is used under continuously dry conditions and not subject to insect or fungi attack, preservative treatment is unnecessary; however, in cases where the wood is generally dry but may be exposed to moisture for limited times and at varying intervals, added protection may be achieved through the introduction of preservatives by non-pressure treatments. The non-pressure treatments are ineffective when conditions of service are more severe. The various methods available may be used for all types of preservatives; however, oil-borne preservatives such as penta or copper napthenate are among the most widely used.

Brush or spray applications should be made on thoroughly dry wood as penetration is dependent upon capillary action taking up the preservative. The preservative should be very freely applied in order to fill all the checks or cracks in the surface.

Dip and soak applications consist simply of submerging the wood in the preservative for varying periods of time. The term dip is used for immersion periods of up to approximately fifteen minutes, while soaking refers to longer periods of immersion. Much of the treatment of doors, window sash, and other millwork is accomplished by the dip method with submersion periods of three to five minutes being quite common. Soak applications are often measured in terms of days and are frequently used in treating wood for fences and posts.

Hot and cold bath treatments consist of heating the wood in the preservative in an open tank for several hours, and then quickly submerging it in cold preservative and allowing it to remain for several more hours. The results achieved are not always consistent; however, they may be excellent under proper conditions and this process has been widely used to treat poles and posts.

Vacuum process is a non-pressure treatment whereby a preliminary vacuum is used to evacuate the air from the wood and the preservative is injected under normal atmospheric pressure. This process is suitable for the application of water-repellent preservatives such as penta to lumber which will be subjected to relatively low decay hazards and insect attack.

Diffusion processes are used where a concentrated water-borne chemical salt is allowed to penetrate into the wood through the free water within the wood. The double-diffusion method consists of soaking the wood first in one chemical solution and then in another. As the chemicals are water soluble they diffuse into the free water in the

FIG. 16–4. *Far left—operator loads pallet of machined wood window parts in dip-tank for preservative, water-repellent treatment. Center (door 2)—load having completed dip cycle is drained of excess fluid before removal. Right—load of parts just being immersed in tank. (Courtesy of Anderson Corporation.)*

wood and react with one another to form a relatively insoluble compound that has little tendency to leach out. This process has been used successfully for the treatment of posts and similar items.

Resources

American Wood-Preservers' Association. *AWPA Standards, P9-67.* Washington, D.C.: American Wood-Preservers' Association, 1964.

American Wood-Preservers' Association. *AWPA Standards, M9-67.* Washington, D.C.: American Wood-Preservers' Association, 1967.

American Wood-Preservers' Association. *AWPA Standards, P5-68.* Washington, D.C.: American Wood-Preservers' Association, 1968.

American Wood-Preservers' Association. *AWPA Standards, P10-68.* Washington, D.C.: American Wood-Preservers' Association, 1968.

Hunt, George M., and George H. Garratt. *Wood Preservation.* 3d ed. New York: McGraw-Hill Book Company, 1967.

Roche, James N. *Wood Preservation—An Important Factor in Conservation.* Paper presented at American Wood-Preservers' Association Convention, St. Louis, Missouri, 1965.

Southern Pine Association. *Southern Pine Architects Bulletin No. 6.* A. I. A. File No. 19-A-1. New Orleans: Southern Pine Association.

Chapter Seventeen

Wood Finishing

Wood finishing is a generic term which may be applied to the materials and procedures utilized in coating wood with a substance basically designed to either protect or enhance the appearance of wood surfaces. Unlike preservative treatments, which depend upon penetration into the wood, wood finishes are considered to be primarily in the realm of surface coatings. The type of finish which may be applied to any given wood product is initially determined by the function that product is designed to serve. The application of paint to wood siding, for example, has as its primary purpose the protection of the wood from the effects of moisture and weather with a secondary purpose of enhancing its appearance. While the paint coating does not prevent moisture from entering the wood, it does retard the rate at which this happens and thereby reduces the tendencies of the material to warp, check, crack, or swell.

Simply stated, finishes of all types are held to the wood through adhesion which is created through physical or physiochemical attraction of the finishing material to the wood itself. Physical (mechanical) adhesion is attained to the degree that the finish is allowed to enter into the fibrous structure or into the many small cavities found in the surface of the wood and physically fill and hold to these areas. Physiochemical adhesion is attained through the attraction of the molecules in the finishing film to those in the wood itself. Adhesion of finishes is much the same as that found in the adhesion of glues to wood, the main difference being the number of wood surfaces involved. Further discussion of the theory of adhesion may be obtained by referring to chapter 15.

The topic of wood finishing is extremely broad in its scope—not only in terms of the range of applications, but in the various materials and processes utilized as well. A prime factor in the success of any finishing endeavor is the condition of the wood prior to the application of the finish itself. The surface must be clean and dry if effective finishing is to be achieved and if, as in furniture manufacture, the surface is not well sanded and smooth a poor appearance will result. Too often proper surface preparation is ignored with the resultant effects of wasting time, energy, and materials, not to mention the serious depreciation of aesthetic qualities.

This chapter attempts to present some of the most commonly accepted materials used in wood and wood products finishing as well as a description of some of the general processes used in the actual application of the materials.

Finishing Materials

A wide variety of finishing materials are found on the market today. Many of the materials being used are the same ones that have been in use for years; however, recent advances in chemical technology have produced a wide range of synthetic materials which possess many superior qualities and which are gaining rapid commercial acceptance. In order to facilitate presentation, the basic finishing materials have been categorized as (1) stains, (2) fillers, (3) wash coats and sealers, (4) toners, bleaches and shading stains, (5) topcoats, and (6) paints, each of which is briefly treated below.

Stains

Stains may be defined as coloring agents used to change the color of wood which is to be finished and basically are composed of finely divided pigments in suspension or chemicals in solution. Stains are used not only to change the color of wood, but to beautify and accent some of the woods' features such as figure and grain. Stains are commonly classified according to the carrier, or solvent, used and are categorized as (1) water stain, (2) oil stain, (3) non-grain-raising stain, and (4) spirit stain. Of the four groups the oil and non-grain-raising stains are used most extensively.

Water stains. These stains are made from dyes which are soluble in water and have the prime advantage of promoting evenness of color. The intensity of the stain may be regulated by the proportions of the powdered dye added to the water during mixing. The major disadvantages of water stains lie in the facts that they will raise the grain of the wood and that they are considered to be slow drying. To counteract the tendency to raise the grain, it is necessary to either sponge the wood with water or apply some type of wash coat prior to staining. The object will then require a light sanding prior to the staining operation. In order to attain the greatest uniformity, water stains are best applied by spraying. Sometimes included under the category of water stains are many of the so-called chemical stains. These stains are made from water-based substances, such as ammonia or carbonate of potash, and create color changes not by staining, but rather by reactions with the chemical traces found in the wood itself. Chemical stains are not widely used and are effective only in the hands of experienced finishers.

Oil stains. Oil stains are generally further divided into two groups—pigmented oil stains and penetrating oil stains. Pigmented stains, sometimes termed wiping stains or uniforming stains, are probably the second most widely used stain in the furniture industry. These stains are made from finely ground pigments suspended in oil and thinned in hydrocarbon solvents such as naptha or mineral spirits. Their chief advantages are that they are relatively inexpensive and may be applied using a variety of methods, including spraying, brushing, and dipping. After application they are allowed to dry for a brief period and then are wiped to remove any excess pigment and to achieve uniformity. Penetrating oil stains are made from oil-soluble dyes and use such vehicles as naptha, turpentine, or benzol. Often referred to as volatile stains, they are available in powder or liquid form. Usually applied by spraying or dipping, they penetrate more deeply than pigmented stains and do not show laps or streaks; however, they have a tendency to bleed into successive coats and must, therefore, receive a sealer or wash coat.

Non-grain-raising stains. NGR stains are one of the most recently developed types of stains, and, as the name implies, have little or no tendency to raise the grain of the wood. For this reason, as well as the fact that they are permanent and non-bleeding, these stains are used extensively on high grade furniture and other types of wood cabinetry. NGR stains are made from dyes of the so-called acid-dye type which are similar to those used in the older water stains. Normally NGR stains contain methyl alcohol (methanol) or a related solvent. Other solvents are sometimes used to augment the methanol in holding the dyes in solution. A short drying time (fifteen to thirty minutes) makes these stains very adaptable for assembly line finishing techniques. The method of application most widely used is that of spraying; however, these stains may also be applied through the dipping technique.

Spirit stains. These are made of coal-tar dyes (aniline dyes) which are soluble in alcohol. Because the alcohol evaporates so rapidly spirit stains are difficult to apply. They have a tendency to lift and mix with the filler and wash coats, thereby creating an unclear or muddy appearance. More expensive than water stains, the chief use of spirit stains is for touch-up and/or repair work.

Fillers

Wood fillers are used to produce a smooth surface by filling the pores and to enhance the beauty of the wood by accenting the grain pattern. Filling is one of the most important phases of the finishing operation and, if improperly done, can be a source of untold problems. Essentially, wood fillers are high solid mixtures of pigments carried in a vehicle such as turpentine or other similar solvent.

Usually a filler is purchased in a paste or semi-paste form and thinned to proper consistency through the addition of solvents. Open grained or large pore woods are filled with a thick bodied filler while closed grain woods are better filled with a thinner consistency filler. All fillers should be agitated thoroughly prior to use in order to prevent the pigment particles from settling to the bottom of the container.

Depending upon the articles to be finished, fillers may be applied by brushing, spraying, or dipping. Items such as chairs are often dipped, whereas various case goods are generally sprayed. The brushing technique may be used in a variety of instances; however, it is a slower method and not appropriate for production finishing due to the higher labor costs incurred. Once applied, the filler should be worked into the pores while still wet, and then within a few minutes it must be wiped off to remove the excess.

After application the adequate drying of the filler is a most important consideration. Failure to properly dry the filler prior to subsequent finishing may result in shrinkage, graying, and possible loss of adhesion of the successive coats.

Wood fillers are often classified according to their relative drying speed. The most common types used in production finishing are (1) overnight fillers, (2) fast dry fillers (approximately four hours), and (3) quick dry fillers (approximately an hour or less). The fast dry fillers are often force dried in low temperature ovens and are widely used to achieve acceptable production schedules. Because of their rapid drying time, the quick dry fillers are difficult to wipe off and have not gained wide acceptance by the industry.

Wash Coats and Sealers

A wash coat is usually applied to a wood surface after it has been stained and prior to the application of the filler. Sealer coats are generally applied on top of the stain or filler and serve to provide a smooth foundation for the successive top coats.

Wash coats consist of a thin coat of material such as a shellac solution or a lacquer or vinyl sealer and serve several purposes. Among these purposes are (1) to stiffen the wood fibers which may have been raised by the stain so that they may be cut off easily with sandpaper; (2) to seal the stain in order to prevent bleeding into successive coats; (3) to serve as a base for the filler and aid in its wiping and cleaning; (4) to improve finish clarity; (5) to prevent excessive penetration of stain or filler; and (6) to keep the finish light (Reliance Universal, 1965). Wash coats usually require a minimum drying time of approximately thirty minutes and once dry are sanded lightly prior to the application of filler.

Sealers provide a smooth surface for successive top coats and contribute to the overall buildup of the finish. The most generally used sealers are nitrocellulose (lacquer) types many of which contain a sanding oil (lubricant) that makes for easier sanding of any fibers which have been raised.

Toners, Bleaches, and Shading Stains

Because each species of wood has its own color, texture, and grain pattern, and because any given piece may exhibit a range of these characteristics, different techniques are used to achieve more uniform colors and appearance.

In order to achieve softer appearing and lighter colors in wood finishes, *toners* are often used. Toners are pigments of either an opaque or semi-opaque nature which are applied on the surface of the wood to achieve these purposes. Because of their opacity they tend to obscure or hide the grain of the wood and if applied heavily, tend to give the wood a painted appearance.

Bleach is a method employed to narrow color differences or to lighten the entire surface of a piece of wood. Often, woods are bleached and then stained to achieve otherwise unattainable effects. In the past a solution of oxalic acid and water was considered to be one of the most effective bleaching agents, but it has been largely replaced by recently developed commercial bleaches. Many commercially prepared bleaches are referred to as two-solution bleaches. Typically, these may be applied by the simple process of first spraying with one solution and immediately spraying the second solution over it. Bleaches of this type evaporate very rapidly and leave no residue behind, thereby eliminating any need to neutralize. As only small amounts of water are used, the drying time is short and successive finishing operations may be accomplished after a light sanding.

Unlike toners and bleaches, glazing and shading stains are applied to the wood only after sealers have been used. Essentially, glazing stains are made of pigments suspended in an oil or an oil and resin vehicle. They are used to impart uniformity, depth, and mellowness to the color of fine finished furniture. Shading stains are most often used in lower cost furniture to uniform or equalize the color imparted by previous staining. Most shading stains are lacquers which have been modified in color by the addition of pigments and are sprayed to achieve the selective shading desired.

Top Coats

The final clear coating or coatings which are applied to complete the finishing process are commonly termed the top coat. Top coats used in production finishing are usually selected from among lacquers, oil varnishes, or synthetic resin varnishes. Decisions on the particular type of top coat to be used are based upon the properties of the coating to provide durability and protection, the qualities which produce or enhance appearance, and the characteristics of the material as they relate to methods of application and overall production. The major volume of production top coats are accounted for by the lacquers and synthetic resin finishes. Primarily, top coats may be classified into three major categories—oil varnishes, synthetic resin varnishes, and those derived from cellulose products.

Oil varnishes. These varnishes are so named because they are made from drying oils and a resin. The oils used are primarily vegetable in origin and include linseed, castor, soya, safflower, oiticica, and chinawood (tung) oils. While not limited to this use, most oil (oleoresinous) varnishes are made with natural resins. The resin is the solid portion of the finish and imparts both hardness and luster. The natural resins are obtained from fossil gums or the gums exuded from certain trees. Among them are batu, damar, kauri, and manila. The process of producing oil varnishes requires that the resins be dissolved in the oils through a cooking process at temperatures up to 600° F. Compatible solvents, such as turpentine, and drying salts are added to the oil-resin mixture to assist in oxidation.

Synthetic resin varnishes. Produced through the combination of synthetic resins with appropriate vehicles and solvents, synthetic resin varnishes are rapidly gaining in popularity. The vehicle and solvent vary according to the resin being used but include the natural oils, coal tar hydrocarbons, petroleum hydrocarbons, and related alcohols.

Because the synthetic resins used in top coats are so diverse, table 17–1 is presented to highlight some of the more common ones.

Cellulose products. Topcoats of this type are those derived from cellulosic materials such as wood pulp or cotton. The most important of these, nitrocellulose (lacquer), came into being at the close of World War I when a faster drying finish was needed for the automobile industry. Other cellulosic finishing materials include cellulose acetate, cellulose acetate butyrate, and ethyl cellulose. Nitrocellulose is obtained from a compound formed when cotton linters are treated with certain acids. The resulting compound is soluble in esters, ethers, and ketones. The chief advantages of lacquers include their fast air drying time, brightness when polished, excellent intercoat adhesion, and ease of application (usually by spraying). Disadvantages of lacquers include their high flammability, difficulty of application by methods other than spraying, and the fact that their low solids content requires several coatings to build up a desirable film. Despite these shortcomings, lacquers are very important and widely used industrial finishes.

Penetrating oil finishes. Often referred to as top coats, penetrating oil finishes are in a category by themselves as they also serve as the stain, filler, and sealer as well. These low resin content oils are applied directly to the bare wood and a final finish is achieved after two to four applications. Because of the low resin content, these finishes are capable of penetrating the fiber structure (to a limited degree at least) and are not prone to crack or craze. The use of penetrating oil finishes has become popular when applied to some of the less porous woods such as walnut or teak and for certain furniture styles such as "Danish Modern" or "Scandinavian."

Paints

While the term "paint" is often applied to all types of coatings which are used to cover both wood and other surfaces, its usage here refers to opaque pigments suspended in a vehicle which dries to a surface film after its application. Although the primary purpose of painting is to provide some degree of protection for a surface, other purposes such as decoration, cleanliness, or light reflection may be equally important to a user. Essentially, there are two main ingredients of paint—the pigments and the vehicle. The combination of these ingredients determines the characteristics and function of the paint. Paint quality is determined by the pigment composition and its proportion in relation to the vehicle. Generally speaking the lower the pigment content, the higher the gloss. Good exterior house paint, for example, will contain 60–70 percent pigment, and 30–40 percent vehicle, while good interior paints or enamels may contain only 30–40 percent pigment and 60–70 percent vehicle.

Pigments are the finely ground solid portion of a paint and are used to (1) give the paint opacity, (2) give the paint color, and (3) serve as extenders. Seldom is any one pigment used singly. Combinations of pigments are based upon such features as their effects on hiding power, settling, workability, and stability after exposure. *Hiding pigments* (those which give opacity) are generally those which have the highest refractive index. Among those most commonly used are white lead, zinc oxide, and titanium dioxide. *Coloring pigments* are obtained from a variety of sources and include those that are found in a natural state (siennas, umbers, ochres, oxides, etc.) and those that are formulated (cadmium red, chrome green, chromic oxide green, carbon black, etc.). The *extender pigments,* or so called inert pigments, possess very little holding power. Their chief functions vary, but include

TABLE 17-1

Summary of Characteristics and Uses of Synthetic Resins Used in Finishes*

Resins	Origin	Characteristics	Uses
Acrylic	Condensation product of various substances with acrylic acid.	Exterior durability; flexibility; color and stain resistance; can be designed to range from hard, brittle to soft, rubbery; more costly than many synthetics.	Exterior wood finishes, metal coatings, electrical coatings, fabric treatments.
Alkyd	Reaction product (through heat) of vegetable oil, glycerine, and solvents to form liquid resin.	Compatability with wide range of film formers; versatile; accepts urea and melamine resins for baking; not as resistant to acids and chemicals as other resins; low cost.	Wood fillers, toners, sealers, and top coats; serves as plasticizer when co-mixed with other film formers.
Butoxy	Polymerized resin obtained by selective proportioning of butadiene and styrene.	Good thermal stability, hardness, adhesion, and chemical resistance; high moisture resistance; high gloss; requires baking for use.	Fiberboard sealers, colored enamels, undercoaters, and can linings.
Epoxy	Condensation product of which important ingredients are bisphenol and epichlorahidrin.	Good adhesion; high gloss; good water and chemical resistance; hardness and flexibility; blends well with other film formers; costly.	Adhesives, inks, variety of coatings.
Melamine	Reaction of melamine with formaldehyde and solvent—usually alcohols.	Imparts hardness when used with alkyds; chemical resistance; cures well at low temperatures; will not air dry; more costly than urea which has similar qualities.	Automotive enamels and appliance finishes, good modifier of other resins.
Phenolic	Condensation product of phenol and formaldehyde—can be hard or liquid dependent upon process technique.	Good hardening agent when blended; exterior durability; hardness; chemical resistance; tendency to yellow.	Spar varnishes, chemical resistant coatings, can and drum linings, insulating varnishes.
Polyester	Condensation product of certain acids reacted with glycols and glycerine alcohols.	Extremely hard film; good dimensional stability; rubs to high gloss; high solids content at usable stability; limited pot life; sprays rough; hard to rub.	Fiberglass binder, wood finishes, brick enamels.
Rubber-Chlorinated	Synthetic or natural rubber treated with chlorine.	Odorless and tasteless; fast drying; good resistance to gasoline, acids, and alkalies; softened by animal and vegetable oils.	Chemical resistant paints; basecoats for other finishes; compatible with other film formers.
Silicone	Result of processes that attach certain chemical groups to silicon.	High heat resistance; good moisture-proofness and high durability; tendency to crater; high cost.	Heat resistant finishes, lacquers and synthetic enamels.
Styrenated Alkyd	Reaction product resulting from reacting styrene and alkyds.	Fast drying; high gloss and gloss retention; hard; somewhat soluble in oils and grease.	Floor and gym clear finishes, fast dry enamels, primers, paper coatings.
Urea	Reaction product of urea, formaldehyde, and alcohol.	Imparts hardness, waterproofness, and clarity; upgrades most alkyd resins; must be baked unless catalyzed; reasonable cost.	Automotive and appliance finishes, clear and pigmented coatings, good modifier for other resins.
Urethane	Reaction product of diisocyanates and oils, polyesters, and polyethers.	High water and abrasion resistance; good chemical resistance and outdoor weathering; tendency to yellow.	Marine finishes, floor finishes, heavy duty coatings.
Vinyls	Chemical compounds. Includes vinyl chlorides, vinyl acetates, vinyl ether, vinyl polysilicone.	Great flexibility; good weatherability; tasteless; pale color; low solid content at usable viscosity; requires rich solvents.	Adhesives, wide variety of coatings.

*Adapted from Reliance Universal Inc., *Useful Facts and Figures,* 2d ed. (Louisville, Kentucky: Reliance Universal Inc., 1965).

the minimizing of settling, helping to adjust consistency and workability, and aiding in durability. Commonly used extenders include magnesium silicate, barium sulfate, calcium carbonate, diatomaceous silica, and others.

Vehicles are the liquid portions of pigmented paints and are so named because they serve as the carrier for the pigment. The vehicle usually contains both volatile and non-volatile constituents and is actually the film-forming part of the paint. The volatile portion—solvents and thinners—facilitates the application and contributes to the drying of the paint. The non-volatile portion (binder) of the vehicle contains oils or resins which are included to achieve adhesion of the film to the surface and are largely responsible for the protective qualities and durability of the paint. The use of synthetic resins (see table 17–1) in the vehicles of paint has grown steadily in recent years; however, oils such as linseed, chinawood, or oiticica are still widely used in the production of quality "oil" paints. The solvent used is determined by the non-volatile portion of the paint. Oil base paints may use such solvents as mineral spirits or turpentine, while the synthetic resins may require the use of hydrogenated naptha, toluol, or special solvents such as those incorporating ketones or esters. Water may be considered the solvent for various emulsion paints (the so-called latex paints) or others such as whitewash or cement paints.

Finishing Processes

Until only recently, the methods of application of the many finishing materials have evolved rather slowly. From the early days of brushing and dipping, the search for faster and more efficient methods finally led to spraying techniques, an evolutionary process which took centuries to accomplish. Since World War II, however, the quest for even greater economy and speed has led to new technological breakthroughs which have created processes now being extensively used in the finishing industry. This section will describe some of the most widely used processes which are utilized in the industry today.

Brushing

One of the oldest methods of applying finishes is that of brushing. Still widely used in the application of paints and varnishes, especially in the construction industry, brushing has declined as a method for applying the so-called industrial finishes. In recent years the acceptance of paint rollers has made further inroads on this method. In spite of all the advances made in finishing, brushing is the most widely understood process of application, and one would be hard pressed to find a home or business which had been painted without the use of a brush. Critical to the application of finishes by the brush method is the selection and care of the brush itself. Brushes are made from a variety of bristles, both natural and man-made. Since World War II, nylon bristles have gained widespread acceptance for good all-purpose brushes; however, special applications still call for the use of a variety of natural bristles in order to achieve the best results. Soderberg, in *Finishing Technology,* presents a good discussion of brushes and their care.

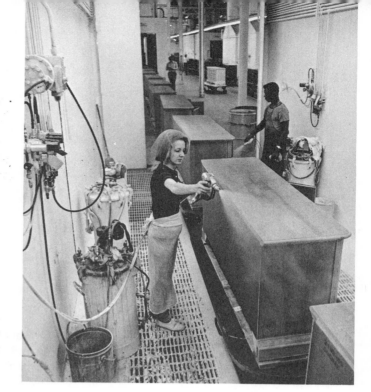

FIG. 17-1. *Atomized spraying continues to be one of the most popular and widely used methods of applying finishes. (Courtesy of Reliance Universal, Inc.)*

Atomized Spraying

Spray finishing, while one of the older and most widely used methods, has undergone considerable change in recent years and is now often a highly automated process. Essentially, spraying consists of using pressure to both atomize the finishing material and propel it onto the surface to be coated. Once deposited, the material, depending on its nature, is allowed to either air dry or be dried through the application of heat. Atomized spraying is usually accomplished through the use of either air or hydraulic pressure (a method termed "airless" spraying).

The use of air to atomize the coating material is the most familiar method and one which is widely used for a variety of coating materials. The basic components of an air system include a compressor, a regulator, an extractor, and a spray gun. The extractor serves the dual role of regulating the amount of air pressure to the gun and cleaning the air of oil and water as it passes through. If an extractor is not used, the contaminants will create many problems and not allow a fine even spray. The two major types of spray guns are called the *siphon* and *pressure* feed. The siphon feed operates by a suction which is created within the cup to draw the material upward and mix it with air. The pressure feed gun operates as the pressured air forces the finishing material to the nozzle. The nozzle, or air cap, of the gun is the point at which the finishing material is subjected to the pressurized air and atomized. Air caps are of two basic varieties, an internal mix and an external mix. Internal mix caps cause the material to mix with air within the cap and emerge as the atomized spray. The external mix cap combines the finishing material and the air immediately outside of the cap and atomization is achieved at this point. Because the siphon feed gun requires a fluid cup at the gun and its size is limited, this system is used only in smaller operations. The pressure system is the most widely used method for production work as it can be used

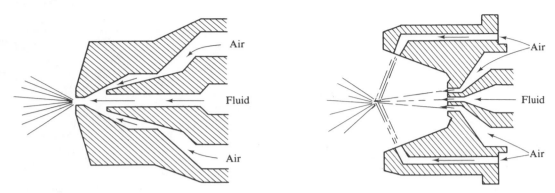

FIG. 17–2. *Internal mix (left) and external mix (right) caps. Note path of air and fluid for each type of cap. (Courtesy of DeVilbiss Company.)*

with large containers of coating material which are connected to the gun through hoses.

The use of "airless" spraying is rapidly becoming more popular in production work because it can now be used with a wide range of finishing materials and it possesses the ability to reduce the amount of overspray, a factor which can save up to 15 percent on the coating materials used. Rather than using air pressure, the airless system uses hydraulic pressure to feed the coating material to the gun. The pressure forces the liquid out of the nozzle and as it emerges it is atomized, similar to the way that water from the nozzle of a garden hose is made into a spray. Airless spray systems possess the added advantage of being able to lay down a heavier coat of material than the conventional air system. This means that fewer passes are required and that a given thickness can be achieved up to 25 percent faster.

Electrostatic Spraying

Originally developed for the field of metals coating, electrostatic spraying processes are now being used to finish products of wood. In this process the article being coated becomes one magnetic pole (usually positive) and the spraying device is made the other pole (usually negative). As a result, the paint assumes a negative charge and is attracted to the positive pole, thus coating the article. Presently there are three types of spraying devices used—a gun, a disk, and a bell. The gun operates on air pressure; the disc and bell have the fluid pumped to their surface and as they are rotated centrifugal force causes the fluid to disperse to their outer edges where it receives its negative charge and is attracted away.

Wood is a non-conductor, and it normally will not attract the paint. To overcome this characteristic the wood must be given a specially formulated conductive film coating. Once the article possesses such a conductive surface it may become the collecting electrode in the electrostatic field. Electrostatic spraying has been accomplished on raw wood in Europe. When processed at a moisture content of approximately 12 percent, the conductivity of the wood is sufficient to allow the process to be used. Wood processed in the 6–8 percent moisture content range, as most wood in the United States is, loses its conductivity and the process will not work unless the conductive undercoat is applied. Perhaps the greatest advantage of this system is in the amount of coating material used, an amount approximately 40 percent of conventional air spray systems.

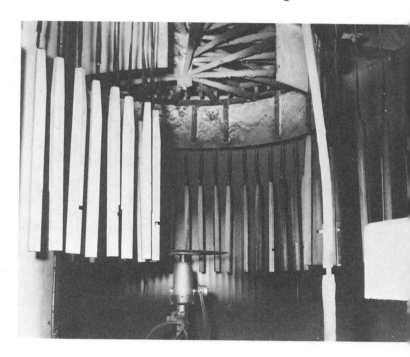

FIG. 17–3. *An electrostatic disc is used to coat a large number of duplicate parts. (Courtesy of Reliance Universal, Inc.)*

Dip and Flow Coating

Dip and flow coating are two processes used to deposit non-atomized finishing materials on the surface to be coated. Dip coating is a simple process of completely submerging the object to be coated in a tank which contains the finishing material. One of the greatest advantages of dip coating is that it is fast and economical. Whereas paint utilization in the various spray methods is approximately 50 percent, dip coating approaches a utilization of 70–80 percent. Another advantage is that surfaces which prove inaccessible to other methods of finishing are easily reached, one reason that automobile bodies are dip coated.

Flow coating is somewhat similar to dip coating in principle; the difference is that vertical streams of non-atomized finishing material are directed upon the surface to be coated. Using low pressure, the material shoots upward through special nozzles and the excess drains into a recovery tank where it is recycled. Utilization of paint in this process approximates the 90–95 percent range.

A critical factor in both dip and flow coating is the viscosity of the material being applied. Lower viscosities lead to inadequate coatings, while more viscous materials result in sags and runs. By carefully controlling the viscosity, temperature, and humidity, the most even results may be achieved.

Roller Coating

Roller coating is extensively used as an economical and high speed method of coating flat substrates such as wood, metal, plywood, hardboard, and particleboard. In essence, the roller coating process consists of passing the object to be coated between two rollers, one or both of which are covered with the finishing material. As the object moves through the rollers the finishing material is transferred from the rollers to the surface. If the article moves through the rollers in the same

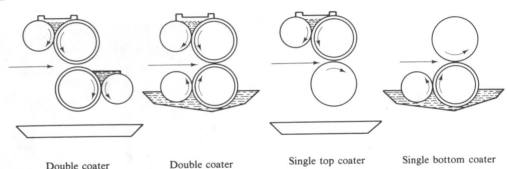

Double coater   Double coater   Single top coater   Single bottom coater

FIG. 17–4. *Schematic of different types of roller coaters. (Courtesy of Reliance Universal, Inc.)*

direction they are turning, the process is referred to as through coating.

Through coating proved to be an inadequate method for the coating of wood composition boards and other materials which possess minute openings or pore structures at their surface. In order to improve the appearance of these materials and to find a way to fill these small indentations, the reverse roller process was developed. It was found that by feeding in one direction with the roller moving in an opposite direction, the coating material would be forced into these depressions and a level, even-appearing surface would result. Today, most producers of prefinished boards utilize the reverse roller process.

A new development which is somewhat similar to the reverse process has been termed knife coating. Instead of a roller (doctor roll) which forces the coating into the pores and picks up the excess material, a fixed blade pressures the material onto the surface and then scrapes off the excess. Knife coating machines alone or in combination with reverse roll machines are most suited for filling and sealing plywood and other surfaces which possess wider areas of highs and lows.

Curtain Coating

The process of passing an object through a falling stream of coating material is referred to as curtain coating. As the object passes through the "curtain," the material which is not deposited on the surface drains off and is recycled back into the system. Basically the coating material is deposited downward through either non-pressure or pressure methods. Non-pressure methods such as a gravity feed are accomplished by the coating material being held in an overhead reservoir and merely allowed to "fall" upon the object as it passes below. While there are variations, the pressure methods are somewhat similar to a series of spray heads which are held in a vertical position and the coating material is forced downward upon the object. Curtain coating is most widely used in the finishing of flat surfaces and many wall panelings are coated in this manner.

Precision Coatings

One of the newest developments in the industrial finishing of wood is termed "precision coating." Originally a method used in coating metals, plastics, and fabrics, this method is now used on hardboard, veneers, and solid wood. The process is very similar to rotogravure printing and the machine used is almost identical to a rotogravure printing press. Basically, the process embodies the application of a uniform film thickness of finishing materials to a surface, the thickness

FIG. 17–5. *A roller coater in operation. (Courtesy of Reliance Universal, Inc.)*

being controlled by the depth and size of the impression in a milled cylinder. The applicator, or engraved screen roll, produces the exact amount of coating required to print the coating onto the substrate. The process is suitable for the application of base coatings and clear or pigmented sealers and top coats. The coating materials dry very rapidly and therefore reduce the need for long drying lines or drying equipment (Reliance Universal Inc., 1965).

Somewhat similar to this process is the gravure method itself which is used to "grain" paneling. This process uses etched copper plates which carry the image of the desired grain pattern and print the design on the substrate surface.

Electrophoresis

FIG. 17–6. *A curtain coater demonstration. Note the "curtain" of liquid near the center of the machine, and the excess pouring out to the side. (Courtesy of Reliance Universal, Inc.)*

Also known as electrodeposition, electrophoresis is a process somewhat similar to electroplating. It is accomplished by submerging the item to be coated in a vat of special paint and then connecting the item to the positive pole of a direct current supply. As the paint particles

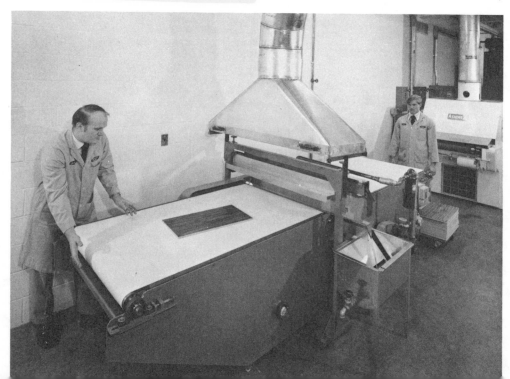

contain a negative charge, they are attracted to the anode (item being coated) where they are discharged, leaving a coating on the surface. The item is then removed and the finish is bake dried. One of the chief advantages of the process is the application of a very uniform coating. The uniform coat results because the paint particles create a resistance as the film is formed, which in turn causes the remaining particles to be attracted to the areas of least resistance. While the process as described appears to be very simple, it is in reality quite complicated. A critical factor is the formulation of the paint. All of its components must be in the proper proportions so that all are deposited together. The material in the vat must be constantly circulated and additional material added to replace that which is used. In the case of large scale production setups some cooling may be necessary to compensate for the heat created by the electrical current (Reliance Universal Inc., 1965).

Resources

Reliance Universal Inc. *Useful Facts and Figures.* 2d ed. Louisville, Kentucky: Reliance Universal Inc., 1965.

Soderberg, George A. *Finishing Technology.* Bloomington, Ill.: McKnight & McKnight Publishing Company, 1969.

United States Department of the Interior, Bureau of Reclamation. *Paint Manual.* 2d ed. Washington, D.C.: Government Printing Office, 1961.

Chapter Eighteen

Plastics and the Wood Industry

During recent years there has been an increase in the use of plastics within the various wood industries. It has been found that certain furniture components made of plastics are capable of providing better service than those primarily made from wood, and often at lower costs. In other instances certain plastic materials have come to be an accepted component in specific structural applications. Many view the introduction of plastics as a threat to the future of the various wood industries, and this may be true; however, the fact remains that their introduction and use are a reality and their continued use is a certainty. For this reason, those concerned with the wood industry must be aware of the existence and applications of various plastics.

Plastics used in the wood industry take on many forms and are used not only in specific structural and decorative applications, but in adhesives, finishes, fabrics, and synthetic surfaces as well. Among the reasons for the increased use of these materials are: the scarcity and rising cost of certain wood species; the lower relative cost of some types of plastics; their superiority in basic physical properties for specific applications; and the reduction of production costs.

Commonly used plastic materials now found in the wood industry include high pressure laminates, various film materials, and cast or molded plastics. The remaining sections of this chapter are devoted to a brief discussion of each of these types.

High Pressure Laminates

Developed prior to World War II, plastic laminates began to attain popularity during the fifties and presently constitute an industry measured in terms of hundreds of millions of dollars. Plastic laminates are probably most easily recognized by the layman through the brand

FIG. 18–1. *In this kitchen, doors, drawer fronts, and counter top are all covered with plastic laminates for colorful and maintenance-free surfaces.*

names associated with the products and include such familiar terms as "Formica," "Texolite," "Micarta," "Nevamar," or "Consoweld."

General Description

Among the chief advantages of plastic laminates are their resistance to heat and stains, their ease of maintenance, and their durability. The development of improved laminates has been paralleled by advances in adhesive and substrate technology. Adhesives often used in fastening plastic laminates to a substrate include polyvinyl resin emulsions, urea resins, and the contact cements. Of these, the urea resins and contact cements are recommended and are the most widely used. A variety of materials may be used for the substrate or core stock. Plywood and particleboard are those most commonly used; however, metal, honeycomb, foam, and lumber cores may also be used for given applications (Kosbab, 1971).

In addition to the familiar use of plastic laminates for counter tops, they are widely used in a variety of other applications. Table and vanity tops, casegoods, partitions, cabinets, furniture, and fixtures are but a few examples of such uses. Fabrication of items using plastic laminates is often done at the job site, as when custom counter tops are installed in a new construction or remodeling work. Fabrication is also done in specialty shops where items such as cabinets or counter tops are made up and then transported to the construction site for installation as a completed unit. In other instances, specialized industries, including furniture or fixture manufacturers, fabricate products within their plants for resale on the commercial markets.

Manufacture

Plastic laminates are made from three basic materials—paper, resins, and ink. Essentially, the process consists of impregnating the paper

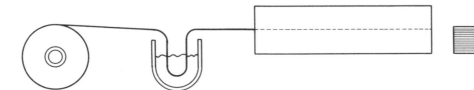

Kraft paper   Phenolic resin   Drying oven   Mat'l. cut & stacked

with the resin, stacking several layers of the paper, and binding the layers into one piece by hot pressing (Kosbab, 1971).

FIG. 18–2. *Preparation of kraft paper for plastic laminate. (Courtesy of Formica Corporation.)*

Paper used in plastic laminates is of two types—the kraft paper used for the core and a higher grade paper used to impart the decorative features. The kraft paper is impregnated with a phenolic resin, dried, cut into sheets, and stacked (fig. 18–2). The higher grade paper, used for the "pattern sheet," is first printed with a high quality ink to impart the desired woodgrain or other decorative effect. After being printed, the paper is treated with a melamine resin, dried, cut to size, and stacked (fig. 18–3).

Once the papers have been treated and cut to size the sheets are stacked in layers to produce a given thickness after pressing. This process, termed *sheet buildup* (fig. 18–4) consists of stacking the

FIG. 18–3. *Wood-grain pattern is first printed on graining paper (photo), then the paper is impregnated with melamine resin (schematic). (Courtesy of Formica Corporation.)*

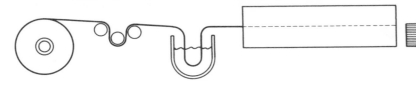

High grade
graining paper   Graining   Melamine
resin   Drying oven   Mat'l. cut & stacked

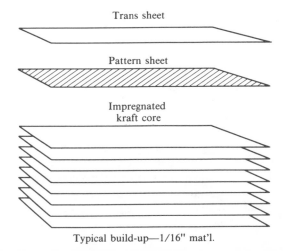

Trans sheet

Pattern sheet

Impregnated
kraft core

Typical build-up—1/16" mat'l.

FIG. 18–4. *Sheet buildup.*

sheets of kraft paper, the pattern sheet, and a transparent top (trans) sheet. The trans sheet is made from an alpha cellulose paper impregnated with a melamine resin and forms the protective outer layer. To produce the common 1/16 inch thick laminated plastic sheet it is usually necessary to use eight layers of the kraft paper and one each of the pattern and trans sheet. After build up, each stack is placed in a multiple opening press and subjected to temperatures of approximately 150° C. for one hour at 2000 pounds per square inch pressure (Kosbab, 1971).

Types of Plastic Laminate

Although there are scores of colors and patterns available in a variety of surface finishes, there are three basic types of decorative plastic laminates produced—general-purpose, vertical surface, and post-forming.

The *general-purpose* laminate is produced in the 1/16 inch thickness and is primarily intended for horizontal and certain vertical applications such as countertops, table tops, furniture and casegoods, tub and shower enclosures, doors, partitions, and elevator car wall panels. *Vertical* laminates are produced in a 1/32 inch thickness and used primarily for kitchen cabinets, casegoods, and wall panels. *Post-forming* laminates are usually made in a 0.05 inch thickness, and while their uses are similar to the general-purpose type, they are capable of being formed to a given radius whenever curved edges are required. Forming is accomplished by heating the laminate to approximately 320° F., bending it over a die of the desired shape, then holding it until cool so that the shape will be retained.

Common surface finishes available are termed polished, satin, suede, and sculptured. They range in texture from a high gloss to a deep surface treatment and, when combined with wood grain, colors, and patterns, provide effects simulating marble, slate, or expensive veneers.

Specialized types of plastic laminate are used for non-decorative purposes and are referred to as *special backing laminates.* Used to retard moisture absorption and reduce the warping of veneered panels, these types are classed as backing sheets or cabinet liners. Their production and application are essentially the same as for the decorative laminates, with the exception that a pattern sheet is not used.

FIG. 18–5. *Plastic laminates are available with a variety of surface treatments.*

Vinyl Film Lamination

Recent years have seen the acceptance of vinyl film overlays applied to wood substrates for use in a variety of applications. Rather extensive use of these films have been found in the manufacture of wood-grained radio, television, and stereo cabinets, wall panelings, and facings for drawers, doors, and cabinets.

Basic Materials

Vinyl film laminations are composed of three basic component parts —the film itself, a suitable substrate material, and an adhesive to bind the two together.

FIG. 18–6. *Cabinets such as these are typical applications of vinyl films. (Courtesy of H. J. Scheirich Company.)*

The films most often used are those derived from the polyvinyl chloride family of plastics. To produce the film sheet, the plastic resin is mixed with stabilizers, plasticizers, and other additives designed to impart specific qualities desired such as flexibility or stretchability. Typically, the mixture is then heated to a rubbery state and passed through a series of heated calendering rolls which gradually squeeze the material to a uniform thickness. Now in film form, the sheet passes between additional rollers where it is cooled, edge trimmed, and wound up on a take off roll (Baird, 1971). To produce a wood grain effect, the vinyl film is often printed with the color and grain pattern desired through the gravure process.

The substrates found in most common use are particleboard, hardboard, and certain plywoods. Plywoods frequently include the extensive use of cheaper species such as lauan. Adhesives used include vinyl emulsions and sheet resins activated by heat.

Lamination Process

Several methods are now in use to bond the overlays to the substrate; however, these may be basically classified as being either cold or hot pressing. Essentially, the cold processes are achieved by spreading the adhesive (usually the emulsion type) upon the surface of the substrate, placing the vinyl film on top of the substrate, and applying pressure to join the two materials. Because of the longer set time required of these adhesives, the panels must be stacked until proper curing has been attained. Heat processes may use either the more conventional press rolls, a vacuum application, or a pressure membrane. In the latter methods the substrate is loaded into the machine with the resin film adhesive and vinyl overlay placed on top of it. Heat to melt the adhesive is provided by coils or lamps and the vacuum or pressure is

FIG. 18-7. *Schematic and photo of press-roll laminating. (Courtesy of Black Brothers Company, Inc.)*

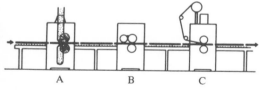

A. Panel cleaner cleans substrate. Substrate can be rigid sheets of plywood, particleboard, etc. or flexible web form such as carpet material.

B. Adhesive coater applies precise coat of adhesive to substrate.

C. Adhesive-coated substrate is fed into Rotary Press. Flexible film or paper facing is fed from unwind stand on top of Press into combining rolls where film is laminated to top of substrate.

LAMINATING OF BOTH SIDES OF SUBSTRATE

Under certain conditions, film can be simultaneously laminated to top and bottom of the substrate by feeding from unwind stand above and below combining rolls.

applied until adhesion results. After the pressure cycle the panel is removed, trimmed, and the complete part is ready for use. Often the vinyl film may be purchased with an embossed surface which simulates the texture of wood grain; in the event that this effect is desired and the vinyl sheet has not been so treated, embossing may be achieved by passing the panel through a heated and engraved roll which will impress the pattern into the surface.

Molded and Cast Plastics

The acceptance of cast and molded plastic components in the furniture and construction industry has grown steadily in the past decade and their use is expected to continue rising in the years ahead. Prime among the reasons for this are lower manufacturing costs which may be realized. Through the use of plastics, decorative components such as intricate carvings may be made quickly and cheaply. In addition, specific plastic components may be made in one operation and may be formulated so that they possess properties equal to or exceeding those of similar components made of wood. The furniture industry alone now uses several hundred million pounds of plastics annually.

Components made of cast or molded plastics range from glide buttons to completely finished tables and chairs. Other applications include decorative strips and carvings, frames for mirrors and pictures, cabinet doors, decorative grill work, lamps, bases and legs for chairs or tables, drawer fronts, and novelty items. Coupled with the use of these plastic components are the advances in finishing technology which have permitted acceptable wood simulations in terms of color and grain.

FIG. 18–8. *This chair is made of injection-molded, high-impact polystyrene. (Courtesy of Plastic Industries, Inc.)*

Plastic Materials

To this date, almost all of the plastic resins used in connection with the furniture industry are of the thermoplastic variety. Thermoplastics are those resins that soften when heated and harden when cooled. They may be heated and cooled repeatedly and are capable of being formed into a variety of shapes. This feature has helped them to become acceptable to the wood furniture industry.

Chief among the plastic resins now widely utilized are polystyrene, polyurethane, polyvinyl chloride (PVC), and polyester. The polyesters are the most widely used resin at this time. They are not thermoplastic and are used primarily in the casting of simulated wood grain decorative components. The other commonly used resins are capable of being formed through a variety of molding processes and their range of application within the industry is quite varied.

Forming Methods

Several processes are available whereby the various plastic resins may be formed to the desired shape. The processes most extensively used in the production of component parts for the furniture industry are injection molding, rotational molding, extrusion, and casting.

Injection molding processes are being used to form the polystyrenes, polyurethanes, and PVC. Essentially the injection process consists of heating the resin to a point where it becomes soft enough to flow and then forcing it through a nozzle into a mold which possesses the desired form. After cooling, which allows the plastic to set, the mold is opened and the formed article is removed, ready for use.

FIG. 18–9. *Elaborate and finely detailed furniture parts are formed by injection molding. (Courtesy of Plastic Industries, Inc.)*

Rotational molding has been most widely utilized in the forming of PVC to produce large hollow parts such as chair legs, chair backs, pedestals, and other similar products. These components are formed by placing a carefully measured amount of the resin into a split mold which is then sealed. The charged mold is mounted on a movable table

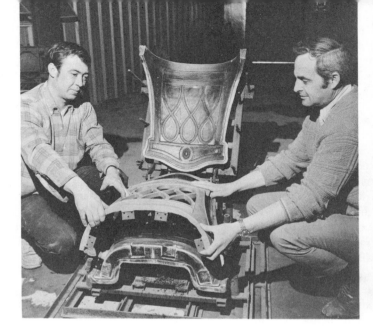

which rotates the mold in two directions at the same time. Heat is applied and the softened resin flows throughout the mold as it is rotated. Once even distribution is achieved, the mold is cooled, opened, and the completed part is withdrawn.

Extrusion is used to form almost any of the thermoplastic resins into long continuous shapes through a process similar to that of toothpaste being squeezed from the tube. In this process the heated and softened resin is forced through a die bearing the exact shape desired. As the formed plastic emerges from the die it is immediately cooled so it will retain its shape and is then cut into appropriate lengths. To this date most of the extrusions produced have been in the form of moldings used to achieve decorative effects.

Casting is another method used for forming polyester and polyurethane resins used in conjunction with the furniture industry. Most applications to date have been those used to attain the intricate shapes of simulated carvings or moldings and to produce detailed one-piece

FIG. 18–10. *Rotational molded chair back being lifted from the mold (left) and the finished product (right). [Reprinted from* Woodworking and Furniture Digest *(October, 1971), by permission of Hitchcock Publishing Company, Wheaton, Illinois.]*

FIG. 18–11. *Furniture part of cast urethane being removed from mold. The mold itself is made of silicone rubber. (Courtesy of Dow Corning.)*

products such as picture or mirror frames. Most casting processes are achieved by pouring a liquid resin into an open mold and allowing it to cure into the shape within the mold. Once cured, the cast item is removed from the mold in one piece, trimmed if necessary, and is then ready for use.

One restriction on the use of plastic components within the furniture industry has been the costs involved in the construction of molds and the specialized equipment required in the production of these parts. Molds used for injection processes are the most expensive and may cost thousands of dollars each. While casting molds made from silicones are relatively inexpensive, most mold design and construction is a specialized process. This, coupled with the high cost of machine investments, has caused the majority of furniture plants to sub-contract with specialized plastic manufacturers who produce the components for them.

Resources

Baird, Ronald. *Industrial Plastics.* South Holland, Illinois: The Goodheart-Willcox Co. Inc., 1971.

Kosbab, George, Theodore J. Berlin, and Robert E. Flannery. *Plastic Laminate Instruction Manual, Volume I.* Cincinnati, Ohio: The Formica Corporation, 1971.

Appendix

Activity 2-1

OBSERVING WOOD STRUCTURE

To provide a means for relating illustrations of wood structure to the structure of an actual block of wood.

A 10X hand lens; a stereo microscope; wood samples (3/4" cubes) as shown below, 1 each of a ring porous hardwood, a diffuse porous hardwood, a resinous softwood, and a non-resinous softwood; sandpaper ranging from No. 80 grit to No. 220 grit.

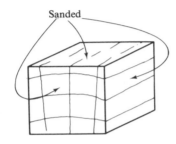

Sanded

1. Sand three surfaces of each block (transverse, radial, and tangential), starting with 80 or 100 grit paper, and using successively finer grades down to 220 or even 280 grit paper. Sand *thoroughly* with each grade. If blocks are identical in size, clamping and sanding all four at once speeds up sanding.

2. When sanding is completed, blow sanding particles from the blocks with compressed air.

   Note: When blowing off such small pieces, it is better to hold them with tongs or pliers. Compressed air too near the skin can be dangerous.

3. Observe the three sanded surfaces of each block and list the features which are visible to the naked eye. Do not list any which cannot be seen, even if it is known that they are there. Label this group "gross features."

4. Examine each block with the 10X hand lens and list the features which are now visible. Label this group "macroscopic features."

5. Place the samples under the stereo microscope and observe the structure at the highest level of magnification possible with the microscope (usually 30X to 45X). List the features visible as "microscopic features."

1. Are there any differences between the lists of features for hardwoods and softwoods? If so, at which levels? Why?

2. At the low magnifications used here, which have more features visible, hardwoods or softwoods? Would this make woods of either of these groups easier to identify? Which group?

3. Are some features listed at more than one level of magnification? Why?

Activity 4-1

MEASURING MOISTURE CONTENT—
Oven Dry Method

Objective

To gain an insight into the concept of moisture content and the procedure for determining the M.C. of any given piece of wood.

Materials and Equipment

A laboratory oven or a regular kitchen oven; an accurate balance capable of weighing to at least tenths of a gram; a thermometer (Farenheit or Centigrade); wood samples.

Procedure

1. Cut a sample the full width of a board, and not more than 1" along the grain, as shown. Avoid cutting samples too near the end, because moisture leaves the end of a board more rapidly, and that portion is drier than the rest of the board.

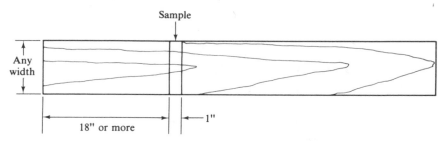

2. Weigh the sample quickly, before it has time to lose moisture, and record the weight as "W.W." or "wet weight." If the sample cannot be weighed immediately, wrap it in foil.

3. Prepare the oven by pre-heating it to a temperature of 212° F (100°C). Check the temperature with a thermometer; do not rely on calibrations of oven controls. Temperatures can vary as much as five or six degrees around the figure given without causing problems, but it is better to keep the temperature constant.

4. Place the sample in the oven. Make a note of the time.

5. At two-hour intervals, remove the sample from the oven, weigh it quickly, and return it to the oven. Record the weights as "I.W." or "intermediate weights." When two successive weighings produce the same weight, the sample is free of moisture. Record this weight as "O.D." or "oven-dry weight."

   Note: If the board from which the sample was taken was green or very wet, it may require as much as 24 hours to reach a moisture-free condition. However, air-dry or kiln-dry wood will take less time, and can often be oven-dried in 6-8 hours. Also, for wet samples, actual oven time can be reduced by predrying the sample for a day or two at room temperature (or over a radiator) after the initial "wet weight" reading has been made.

6. Calculate the moisture content of the sample according to the formula:

$$\text{M.C. (\%)} = \frac{\text{W.W.} - \text{O.D.}}{\text{O.D.}} \times 100$$

Activity 4-2

MEASURING MOISTURE CONTENT—
Moisture Meters

Objective

To gain insight into the concept of moisture content and the principles and operation of moisture meters.

Materials and Equipment

Moisture meter; wood sample.

Note: Some interesting comparisons can be made if the same board used for oven-dry tests is used for this test.

Procedure

1. Read instruction manual for the moisture meter being used. Be sure that the meter batteries are strong and that it is adjusted accurately.
2. Take three readings at different locations on the board. Do not make readings too near the end of the board, and avoid large knots, bark pockets, or other defects which would cause concentrations of moisture. Record all three readings.
3. Convert meter readings to moisture content figures by consulting the table provided in the instruction manual. Calculate the final moisture content for the board by averaging the three obtained at different locations.

Questions

1. How nearly the same were the moisture content figures obtained by the oven-dry method and by measuring with a meter?
2. Why were the two figures different?
3. What are the advantages and disadvantages of moisture meters?

Activity 4-3

DETERMINING EQUILIBRIUM MOISTURE CONTENT

Objective

To demonstrate the principle that the moisture content of wood reaches a stable condition at a certain level, according to the surrounding atmospheric conditions.

Materials and Equipment

A reliable moisture meter; at least three boards which have been stored in the same room for over two weeks; a hygrometer or a sling psychrometer.

Procedure

1. Measure the relative humidity in the lumber storage room with the hygrometer. Record both the "wet-bulb" and "dry-bulb" temperatures.
2. Using tables such as those provided in the *Wood Handbook* and the *Dry Kiln Operators Manual,* predict the equilibrium moisture content for the wet-bulb and dry-bulb temperatures obtained. Record this as "Predicted E.M.C."
3. Measure the moisture content of at least three boards with the moisture meter. Record the values for each.
4. Average the three figures to determine the actual E.M.C. of the wood in the storage room and compare this to the predicted E.M.C.

Questions

1. Did the actual E.M.C. differ from the predicted figure? Why?
2. What two atmospheric conditions affect the moisture content of wood?
3. If the relative humidity remains constant, but the temperature changes, will the E.M.C. change?

Activity 4-4

SHRINKAGE AND SWELLING OF WOOD

To determine the amount of shrinkage wood undergoes as it dries from a green condition.

Wood samples 1/2" X 2" X 2" cut as illustrated below; a container in which to soak the samples; an oven; a steel rule or other measuring instrument capable of measuring in 64ths; a balance for weighing samples.

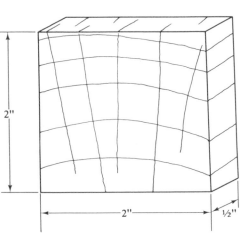

Note: It is important that the growth rings are oriented as shown, in order to obtain true radial and tangential measurements.

1. Cut wood samples. Students may choose different species of wood and compare results between species.
2. If relatively dry wood is being used, soak the samples for approximately 8 hours to simulate a green condition.
3. Remove samples from soaking container and lay them on paper towels briefly to absorb surface water.
4. Make initial measurements in the radial and tangential directions. Record the dimensions as "wet dimension R" and "wet dimension T."
5. Oven dry the samples until two successive weighings (at two-hour intervals) yield the same weight.
6. Remove the samples from the oven and quickly make both radial and tangential measurements. Record these dimensions as "dry dimension R" and "dry dimension T."
7. Calculate radial shrinkage by the following formula:

$$\text{Shrinkage } (\%) = \frac{\text{Wet dimension R} - \text{dry dimension R}}{\text{wet dimension R}} \times 100$$

or:

$$\text{Shr.} = \frac{\text{WDR} - \text{DDR}}{\text{WDR}} \times 100$$

8. Calculate tangential shrinkage by the same formula, substituting tangential measurements for radial.

Questions

1. Which is greater, radial or tangential shrinkage?
2. How do the shrinkage values obtained compare with the averages for that particular species given in the *Wood Handbook?*
3. Longitudinal shrinkage was not measured because it is usually so small that it is insignificant. Why doesn't wood shrink very much longitudinally?

Activity 4-5

COMPRESSIVE STRENGTH OF WOOD

To test and compare the compressive strength of three types of wood.

Samples of white pine, southern yellow pine, and basswood approximately 1" X 1" X 6" (if these particular species are not available, woods of similar properties may be substituted—for instance, cottonwood or willow could replace basswood); a testing machine equipped with a gauge to read the total force exerted in pounds; a steel rule or other measuring instrument to measure in 32nds of an inch.

1. Prepare samples, cut as shown below. Samples should be straight-grained and free of defects such as knots, pitch pockets, etc. Label the samples A, B, and C.

2. Measure the exact thickness and width of each sample and calculate the area of cross-section in square inches. (Area = thickness X width). Record areas for use later as "area A, area B, and area C."

3. Place sample A on end in the testing machine and apply force slowly. When the sample fails, the gauge reading will drop or fail to rise with each advance of the platform. When this happens, release the pressure and remove the sample from the machine. Record the highest reading achieved during the test as "total force A."

4. Repeat the tests for samples B and C.

   Note: When using a testing machine, be sure to consult the instruction manual for the proper procedure and precautions necessary for that machine.

5. Calculate the unit compressive stress by dividing total force required to cause failure of each sample by the cross sectional area.

1. From the results of your tests, which kind of wood would be best suited for use as a load-bearing post?

2. Why are some woods stronger than others?

3. Do you think the compressive strength of wood parallel to the grain is greater than its strength perpendicular to the grain? Why?

Index